WESTERN
EUROPEAN
INTEGRATION

Harper's Comparative Government Series

MICHAEL CURTIS, EDITOR

WESTERN
EUROPEAN
INTEGRATION

MICHAEL CURTIS

RUTGERS, THE STATE UNIVERSITY

HARPER & ROW

Publishers

NEW YORK

Library of Congress Catalog Card Number: 65-16487

To Joyce and Al, Sue and Léon,
who have formed
a successful Atlantic partnership
of their own.

CONTENTS

vii

A SHORT GUIDE FOR THE PERPLEXED

Benelux	Customs Union of Belgium, the Netherlands, and Luxembourg
BTO	Brussels Treaty Organization
CERN	European Center for Nuclear Research
CET	Common External Tariff of the EEC
COCOM	Coordinating Committee of NATO
COCOR	Coordinating Committee of the ECSC
DAC	Development Assistance Committee of OECD
ECMT	European Conference of Ministers of Transport
ECSC	European Coal and Steel Community
EDC	European Defense Community
EEC	European Economic Community
EFTA	European Free Trade Association
ELDO	European Launching Development Organization
EMA	European Monetary Agreement
ENEA	European Nuclear Energy Agency
EPA	European Productivity Agency
EPC	European Political Community
EPU	European Payments Union
ESRO	European Space Research Organization
GATT	General Agreement on Trade and Tariffs
High Authority	Executive body of the ECSC
IADB	Inter-American Development Bank
IBRD	International Bank for Reconstruction and Development
IMF	International Monetary Fund
MLF	Multilateral Nuclear Force
NATO	North Atlantic Treaty Organization
OAS	Organization of American States
OECD	Organization for Economic Cooperation and Development
OEEC	Organization for European Economic Cooperation
SAC	Strategic Air Command of the U.S.
SACEUR	Supreme Allied Commander, Europe
SACLANT	Supreme Allied Commander, Atlantic
SHAPE	Supreme Headquarters Allied Power, Europe
WEU	Western European Union

PREFACE

THE CURRENT ATTEMPT of the nations of Western Europe to form
a closer political association or entity is one of the most exciting
political developments of the century. This book is presented as
an introduction for those interested in the history and politics of
post-war Europe, in the European Community struggling to be
born, and an Atlantic organization still in the process of conception. The European integration movement has challenged our
acceptance of the nation-state as the proper or inevitable mechanism through which public problems can be examined and solutions found. I have tried to analyse and to assess the significance of
eight major European and international organizations—the Council of Europe, OECD, NATO, WEU, ECSC, EEC, EURATOM,
and EFTA—from the perspective of their control over the making of decisions formerly made by states, and to evaluate the success of these organizations as contributors to European unity and
Atlantic cooperation.

Even Macaulay would acknowledge that it is difficult today to
march through the intricacies of things in a blaze of certainty.
The speed of development of the organizations and the unusual
fluidity and complexity of political, economic, and military factors
involved in the integration movement have hampered agreement
on the ultimate nature of the new Western Europe and on the
relationship between it and the United States. It is hazardous to
predict the direction in which further progress will be made.

Like all students of the current European political scene, I am
heavily indebted to the officials of the European organizations for
their help and advice. I found them a remarkably gifted, dedi-
cated, and articulate group of people, and I am grateful to those
who paused long enough to answer questions and help clarify the

complex issues with which they were concerned. I also wish to
thank the Rutgers University Research Council for a grant which
allowed me to visit the European organizations.

MICHAEL CURTIS

WESTERN
EUROPEAN
INTEGRATION

CHAPTER ONE

The New Europe Is Planned

THE DIVERSITY of the postwar proposals for some kind of unification of European countries reflects the complexity and ambiguity of the European situation. Europe is not a given entity with a single past or tradition. Its boundaries remain in dispute, its inheritance a tangle of contradictions, its essence intangible, though familiar. If many regard Europe as the heartland of the world, others, like Paul Valéry, see it as a peninsula of Asia. Some, like Arnold Toynbee, look on Russia as the instrument of a Eurasian attack on Europe; others, from William Penn and the Abbé de Saint-Pierre to General de Gaulle, have seen Russia, intermittently, as an essential part of the European whole, or have stressed the significance of Byzantium in its history.

Though the modern integration movement has concentrated on part of Western Europe, it is salutary to remember that, while making sense as a political and cultural entity, Western Europe is not the whole of Europe. Eastern Europe, as well as the West, has been heir to Roman and Christian traditions. The activity of Byzantium, Orthodoxy, the Mongols, and the Arabs has made Europe more than a predominantly Romanic and Germanic group of people. The empire of Charlemagne excluded Great Britain, Spain, and Scandinavia, as well as Eastern Europe. But only the most extreme modern Carolingian refers pejoratively to Britain as an Anglo-Saxon maritime power which automatically must be excluded from a Continental unit.

After the fourteenth century, the word "Europe," until then rarely used, tended to be identified with "Christendom." But, though there is frequently nostalgia at the loss of a European-Christian unity, in fact there was never a single political organization for the whole of Christendom, nor a medieval international order, nor was medieval Latin a universal language. From the sixteenth century the influence of the humanists and of the new cartography, which emphasized political authority in territorial areas rather than ecclesiastical rule, began to challenge the equation of Christendom with Europe.

European culture cannot be simply defined or described by a single formula. Rationalism, individualism, the devotion to economic activity, the prominence of industrialism, the preoccupation with ideals of democracy and socialism, have all contributed to the pattern of European behavior. Political concepts like the rule of law and constitutional government, social concerns like care for the handicapped and the distressed, personal qualities like tolerance and a reliance on persuasion rather than coercion, cultural values shared in common, exemplify those characteristics still confined largely to European nations or their direct descendants. Europe is more than "the geographical expression" it was for Metternich.

The movement for European integration has a long and, on the whole, respectable lineage, going back, as do so many aspects of European civilization, to the Greeks, and continuing in differing ways throughout history until the present. The motives for integration have always been complex, though the essential reasons have remained the preservation of peace, the need for a common defense, the ambition to act as a stronger power bloc, the conservation of a common European culture, the wish to create greater material well-being, and the freeing of restrictions on trade. Conquerors have attempted unification by force, though their empires always excluded part of North Europe, and included parts of Africa and Asia. Writers from Dante to Coudenhove-Kalergi in the twentieth century have argued for institutional arrangements for safeguarding the peace and creating unity. Others, from Voltaire to Ortega y Gasset, have heralded Europe as the standard-bearer of cultural progress. On a more prosaic level, merchants from the thirteenth-century Hanseatic League on have argued the benefits of greater trade and collaboration and the removal of trade barriers.

The motives of the contemporary proponents of European integration have been as complex as in the past, and their objectives similarly diverse. But the present movement toward integration is in contrast to the past not only by the beginning and the speed of practical implementation and the feeling of urgency, but also by the awareness of two significant external factors: the recognition of the United States as a common friend, as material provider in the first postwar years and defensive protector still, and the obligation to take account of the rising revolution of expectations in the underdeveloped countries of the world, especially those formerly connected with Europe as colonies. The first factor widens the area of speculation from a purely European to an Atlantic horizon. The second involves concessions in favor of the more backward areas including preferential treatment and financial aid.

The new Europe is being created for both positive and negative reasons. Positively, there are the social and economic motives of the past, and negatively, there is response to the now historic pessimism following World War II and the bad economic conditions, the rise of the Soviet bloc, the loss of political gravity by Europe, and finally, a desire for a means of controlling Germany, provoker of two world wars.

The end of the war witnessed a period of pessimism subjectively reflected in the writings of historians who argued that the dominance of the world by Europe had ended, and that the European era, which succeeded the Mediterranean era, had in turn been replaced by an Atlantic age in which non-European powers were predominant. Foreign states had regularly helped to redress the balance of the Old World; now they were the dominant force in global affairs.

There was sufficient cause for pessimism. The material and economic resources of European countries had been depleted in the fight against Hitler. With the myth of the invincibility of the European white man dispelled and the flames of nationalism fanned, the colonial powers were liquidating their empires. The European countries, with small, separate markets, compared unfavorably with the United States and the Soviet Union who were developing their economics on a continental scale. Nature unkindly provided two poor harvests. Conditions were aggravated by farmers, short of implements, grazing their cattle on the grain instead of harvesting it. The division of labor, which Adam Smith had shown to be the basis of productivity, seemed momentarily to have broken down.

Political factors have spurred the movement to a united Europe. The German problem seemed incapable of solution except within the framework of a larger community. The economic and military dependence of Western Europe on the United States paradoxically created a desire for protection against a possible American recession as well as awe of United States strength. Europe recognized it was no longer the political center of the world, that it stood naked in the face of the possession of nuclear weapons by others, and that it would be difficult for it to play an independent political role or act as a third force. A strong fear was of the expanding Soviet imperialism which physically had reached to Berlin and to Prague, and which, ideologically, had substantial support in the West where one-third of the Italian electorate and one-quarter of the French had voted Communist.

Problems of economic collaboration and defense cannot be kept separate from those of general political policy, and the interrelation of political, economic, and military factors explains the large spectrum of alternative proposals, and the various institutions that have been set up. Politically the spectrum runs from regular meetings of heads of governments, through regional and functional conferences on specific problems, to a confederal and finally federal structure. Economic alternatives run from a tariff community, through a customs community or union, to a full economic union. Militarily, possibilities exist from alliances based on the national forces of individual sovereign states, through collective alliances with common leadership, to integrated forces and defense.

Underlying all the proposals is the place of Europe in the new complicated world picture, and in particular, its relationship with the United States and the Soviet bloc. Here the spectrum of possibility lies not only between commitment to the Atlantic cause, neutralism or general European disengagement, but between the various degrees of commitment. On one side exists the the possibility of a Europe, economically sound and militarily strong, acting as a completely independent force, if not as a third force between the two giants. On the other are the possibilities of an Atlantic alliance, Atlantic partnership, or finally Atlantic community.

At the core of the different views is the attitude taken toward the nation-state. Nationalism in Europe may have been a liberating and liberal force in the nineteenth century, it is proving the major factor in the creation of popular communities in Asia and Africa and leading to the restoration of humane ideals in Eastern Europe today. Yet although the nation-state has been a constructive force in the creation of political unity, cultural homogeneity, and patriotic feeling, the destructive and bitter wars produced by heightened nationalism have led Europeans to question whether the sovereignity of the nation-state can provide the basis of a peaceful society. The contrast is clear, in theory if not always in practice, between two alternative positions. Some argue that only the nation-state can be responsible for its own protection and welfare, and that nations can really collaborate only at intergovernmental level with unanimity as the method of agreement. Others hold that cooperation among nations of this kind, although useful, is inadequate to solve the problems of peace, order, and economic well being in the face of modern conditions, and that the nation-state can no longer adequately perform the function for which it originally existed. For them the solution is European integration. In a wider sense, these two points of view reflect the differences between those interested in creating a larger European nationalism on the old Carolingian lines, and those holding that the whole concept of nationalism is irrelevant.

Sceptics of integration, such as Raymond Aron, argue that "the European idea [of unity] is empty: it has neither the transcendence of Messianic ideologies nor the immanence of concrete patriotism." It must be admitted that the movement toward European integration was created by intellectuals and political elites rather than by mass demand. The postwar attempt to influence the citizen body and make European integration a popular movement, in fact, hardly lasted after 1949 and the institution of the Council of Europe. All the other European organizations were formulated and organized by elite political groups. The same key figures keep running through the European account, men whose dedication to Europe is strong and whose idealism has been tempered by political reality. Yet, if the integration idea does not enflame millions as communism or nationalism have done, it has attracted increasing support by the success of movements in that direction. The standardization of European beer bottles is hardly a revolutionary cause, but in a consumption-conscious economy, tangible results may have a greater impact than ideological convictions.

The European Setting

Western Europe makes up about 3 percent of the land surface of the world, and contains about 10 percent of its population. The population of the six Common Market countries is 175 million, that of the seven European Free Trade Association (EFTA) countries, 90 million. It is a largely urban society—the density of population in the Common Market is fourteen times greater than that of the world as a whole—at a high and increasing level of economic development, production and consumption, and dependence on international trade.

In 1964, Western Europe is a healthy and prospering society. Its gross product is nearly 70 percent greater than in 1950, in Germany the increase has been over 100 percent. Between 1958 and 1963 the gross national product of the European Economic Community (EEC) grew 26 percent, and the industrial production by 41 percent compared with 33.5 percent in the United States. Western Europe as a whole has overtaken the United States in steel and coal production, and is catching up in the production of machinery, chemicals, and automobiles. It is characterized not simply by full employment, but also by a shortage of labor made up by importing three million foreign workers. Other aspects of the production scene in the last decade have been the heightened increase in investment, the growth of the multinational company, and the rise of a new occupational group, the international business executive.

Increasing prosperity has been marked by a rise in agricultural productivity, a shift in resources from agriculture to industry and commerce, and a movement of population from the country to the city. In France between 1954 and 1962 over 1,300,000 people left the land, and the percentage of the population employed in agriculture dropped from 27 percent to 20 percent: in the Common Market as a whole, the agricultural population dropped from 19 million to 13.5 million between 1950 and 1962.

In industry there has been a shift from the older trades such as mining, textiles, and clothing to the newer ones such as electrical engineering and chemicals. The percentage of those employed in services, such as trade, banking, insurance, and in skilled work has increased as has the number of women at work.

The rise in production and increase in productivity has been matched by an increase in consumption and an unparalleled rise in the standard of labor. This has led to major changes in ways of life and consumer habits, and to changes in the pattern of demand and production. The demand for new or better housing has resulted in spectacular increases in urban land values, as well as in building construction. Greater opportunity for leisure, as well as higher wages, has led to a very large increase in car ownership, to the building of roads, and to other public expenditure. Consumption has become both more sophisticated and more international. The obverse of all this is that all the countries have, in differing degrees, been plagued by the rise of labor costs as a result of higher wages, a shorter working week, longer holidays with pay, and the general shortage of labor. In 1962 the wages of Italian workers rose 17 percent, compared with a wage rise in the United States of 3 percent. In France, as in Italy, the rise in wage costs in recent years has been greater than the increases in productivity.

There has been an equally remarkable increase in trade. The world trade of Western Europe is now double that of the United States, and accounts for over half of the world's total. Between 1958 and 1963, intra-EEC trade rose 130 percent, and trade with the rest of the world 44 percent, imports rising 53 percent, and exports 35 percent. The industrialized countries of Western Europe have received great benefits from, and become increasingly sensitive about, the improved terms of trade against the producers of primary commodities. The consequence of this, added to the limited increase in demand for the goods of the underdeveloped countries, the growing European self-sufficiency in meat and cereals, and the shift from many primary commodities, is that the income gap between the industrialized countries of the West and the underdeveloped areas has been widening at an alarming rate.

Western European countries have, in varying degrees, restored equilibrium in their balance-of-payments and accumulated surpluses. In 1963 the gold and hard currency reserves of the West was over $26 billion compared with $8 billion in 1945; in the same period the U.S. reserves declined from $20 billion to $16. In 1960 the monetary reserves of the EEC were $15.1 billion compared with $3.1 billion in 1950.

The First Steps to Integration

This Europe of 1964 is remarkably different in terms of prosperity and self-confidence from the immediate postwar Europe, interested in economic recovery, expansion of trade, strengthening of world liquidity, and the maintenance of peace. The impetus to European integration began simultaneously in the political, economic, and military fields, since it is impossible to separate them. One spark came from Winston Churchill, then the leader of the Opposition in Britain, at the University of

Zurich on September 19, 1946. Remembering his audience, he proposed making Europe as free and as happy as Switzerland by "recreating the European family, or as much of it as we can" through building "a kind of United States of Europe." A number of organizations were founded to form the United States of Europe, or some political unit. Coming together in December, 1947, they set up the Congress of Europe at the Hague in May, 1948, attended by 713 delegates from sixteen countries. An important gathering of influential politicians, the Congress agreed on the institution of an assembly of representatives of European parliaments, a European charter of human rights, a European court, an economic union, and the inclusion of Germany into a European community. An unofficial organization, with a suitably international group of presidents of honor—Blum, Churchill, Gasperi, and Spaak—it was created to support those working for a European union. But before any political organ was created, both economic and military bodies were set up.

Economically, Europe was suffering from its physical destruction, dislocation, lack of productivity, and reduction in trade. Before the War, trade had been hampered by currency devaluations, bilateral trade agreements, and autarky. The first postwar attempt to reduce barriers to world trade failed with the collapse of the proposed International Trade Organization which would have been an elaborate organization concerned with employment, restrictive business practices, and intergovernmental commodity agreements, as well as with trade. A less ambitious arrangement, the General Agreement on Trade and Tariffs (GATT), concerned with the reduction of tariffs and quantitative restrictions, and establishing a common set of trade rules, was signed by 23 nations in October, 1947. This global approach by GATT to problems of multilateral trade has always been an alternative to some of the economic arrangements made by the European organizations.

Meanwhile, the United States was obliged, after canceling lend-lease shipments, and after the end of UNRRA relief in 1947, to come to the aid of Europe again. A combination of factors produced a historic initiative by the United States. The British

Chancellor of the Exchequer, Hugh Dalton, pressing for economy, had caused Britain to end its economic aid to Greece, who was threatened with civil war and famine. William Clayton reported to the Department of State on the appalling economic conditions in Europe, the industrial stagnation, severe unemployment, and widespread food shortage caused by the exceptionally bad weather. The Russian refusal to treat Germany as an economic unit led to the combination of the zones of occupation of the three allies, Britain, France, and the United States. Secretary of State Marshall returned from Moscow in April, 1947, with the belief that the Soviet Union would not participate in a joint program to solve European problems. In June, 1947, Marshall's speech at Harvard proposed American aid for Europe, and "a joint recovery program based on self-help and mutual cooperation." The European response was immediate, but there could be no reconciliation between the British, French, and Russian views on an international body intervening in the economic life of nations. None of the Eastern bloc countries accepted the Anglo-French invitation in July, 1947, to join an organization of European economic recovery, since Moscow forced Poland and Czechoslovakia to withdraw their request to be included among the Marshall Plan recipients. The Iron Curtain had effectively divided Europe.

The sixteen countries who did accept the invitation set up a Committee for European Economic Cooperation under Sir Oliver Franks; they appointed a number of technical committees and by September, 1947, had sent a list of needs to the United States. Some in the American Administration, like Paul Hoffman and Averell Harriman, had hoped for the integration of the Western European economy through the formation of a single large market in which quantitative restrictions on the movement of goods, monetary barriers to the flow of trade, and, eventually, all tariffs would be ended. But since the British Foreign Secretary, Ernest Bevin, was opposed to a strong organization of this kind with broad powers, the United States did not insist on this as essential for United States aid. In April, 1948, after the sixteen governments had agreed that the organization would continue even after Marshall Plan aid had ended, a much looser body, the Organization for European Economic Cooperation, was set up, and a series of bilateral agreements concluded between the OEEC countries and the United States.

Simultaneously, Western Europe was concerning itself with its military defense. In March, 1947, the Treaty of Dunkirk was signed by France and Great Britain for mutual protection against any renewed aggression by Germany. But a number of factors—the failure of the Moscow conference on demilitarization, the refusal of the Soviet bloc to participate in the Marshall Plan, and the widespread fear of Soviet expansion—changed the orientation of military planning. In January, 1948, Ernest Bevin suggested a wider Western union which "must primarily be a fusion derived from the basic freedoms and ethical principles for which we all stand." Delegates from Belgium, France, Great Britain, the Netherlands, and Luxembourg, meeting in Brussels, quickly reached agreement on March 17, 1948, to the Brussels Treaty Organization. The BTO was set up under Article 51 of the United Nations Charter as a regional organization able to undertake individual or collective self-defense if an armed attack occured. The Organization was primarily a fifty-year alliance based on the principle of collective defense, to take steps in the event of a renewal by Germany of a policy of aggression, and pledged to automatic mutual military assistance. But it also became the prototype for later military treaties in establishing machinery for economic, social, and cultural cooperation.

The BTO was not intended to be a supranational organization, but an intergovernmental one in which the chief policy organ was the Consultative Council of the five foreign ministers. At a lower level, policy was decided by the permanent commission, composed of the four ambassadors to Great Britain, and a British Foreign Office official, meeting in London, aided by a secretariat. Of the permanent committees, the Defense Committee, assisted by the joint chiefs of staff, was the most significant. It created a military planning division, leading to a unified defense force, UNIFORCE. The Commanders in Chiefs of the allies formed a standing committee under General Montgomery, with headquarters at Fontainebleau. A peacetime international and inter-service staff, working together, was created, and to the military structure was added an appendage of economic, social, and cultural committees.

The Communist capture of power in Prague, and the suicide or murder of Jan Mazaryk on March 13, 1948, was a particularly powerful shock to the West, and raised the frightening possibility of the whole of Western Europe being at the mercy of the Russian forces. The Berlin blockade began in April, 1948; it rapidly became apparent that the BTO was not sufficiently strong to resist the threat of Communism. Already in March, 1946, Winston Churchill, in a speech at Fulton, Missouri, had called for a military alliance between the United States and the Commonwealth. In April, 1948, the Canadian Foreign Minister, Louis St. Laurent, suggested an Atlantic defense system. After the Vandenberg Resolution in the U.S. Senate in June, 1948, approving the end of the historic policy of no entangling alliances, the U.S. Administration went ahead with negotiations throughout the summer of 1948. On April 4, 1949, the North Atlantic Treaty Organization, with twelve members—Belgium, Britain, Canada, Denmark, France, Iceland, Italy, Luxembourg, the Netherlands, Norway, Portugal, and the United States—came into existence.

Discussion ranged between the "federalist" and the "functionalist" point of view about the nature of a European political institution. The federalists believed that the only way to get collaboration among the European nations and to deal with the problem of sovereignty was to set up a constitutional convention and a European constitution. The functionalists argued that vested interests, multilingual nations, diverse customs and traditions prevented such a radical step, and that any new organization must be based on the power of the states, though at the same time they recognized the need to subordinate the separate national interests to the common welfare.

In July, 1948, the French Foreign Minister, Georges Bidault, submitted proposals for a European federal parliament to the Consultative Council of the BTO. In the committee set up to study these proposals, a clear division was at once established between the French and Belgian view of a European parliament on federal lines, and the British idea of an intergovernmental Council of Ministers meeting periodically. Compromise was reached in January, 1949, with the decision to establish a Council of Europe consisting of a Ministerial Committee meeting in private and a consultative body meeting in public. The Statute of the Council of Europe was signed in London in May, 1949, and came into force in August of that year.

The debate on the composition and nature of the Council of Europe was a crucial one in which the federalist point of view was rejected. The federalists had urged an elective bicameral legislature and an executive federal council, responsible to the lower chamber of the legislature. The British, supported by the Scandinavians, pressed, more pragmatically, for a practical organization in Europe. Two features of the British attitude distinguished and separated it from the Continentals. One was the dislike of becoming involved in institutional arrangements stronger than intergovernmental consultations. The other was Britain's clear preference for association with the Commonwealth and the United States to a closer arrangement with Continental Europe.

The Emergence of the European Community

The idealism of the supporters of European unity had been sadly tempered by the inadequacy of the organizations created. Europe, it was clear, would only be born as a result of long and patient effort. Meanwhile, there was the perennial problem of Germany, its possible integration into the Western camp, and the attendant problems of the Ruhr and the Saar. For the United States the outbreak of the Korean War had made the contribution of Germany to Western defense more necessary, and Germany's rearmament inevitable. In 1948, France had given up the hope for the political detachment of the Ruhr from Germany, as well as the internationalization of its industries, and contented itself with the International Authority of the Ruhr, although recognizing that this gave it inadequate control over German production. In addition, France faced a number of problems: the need to control the rapidly recovering heavy industry of Germany, to settle the Saar problem, to reduce international tension caused by German rearmament and to avoid a rekindling of German nationalism, and to keep going the impetus toward integration. Above all, both German and French statesmen were hoping for Franco-German reconciliation so that war between them would be unthinkable.

The historic contribution of the plan for a common market for coal and steel proposed on May 9, 1950, by Robert Schuman, the French Foreign Minister, was that it offered a solution to all these problems. It could lead to joint Franco-German control over the Ruhr, and assure French coke supply. The struggle over the Saar's coal and steel would then become irrelevant. It would increase the internal market needed for economic expansion. It could control any revival of the prewar cartel, the International Steel Agreement. But above all, the motivations were political. National antagonisms could be transcended, and the reconciliation of the two old enemies could lead to a closer European political association, and be the first concrete step toward the goal of a European unity. For Germany, the plan meant the removal of Allied controls over the German economy; for Konrad Adenauer, the Rhinelander, it meant the realization of an idea of friendship he had proposed thirty years previously.

The single most important figure in the struggle for the New Europe has been Jean Monnet, the former champagne salesman whose international experience has included work with the Inter-Allied Maritime Commission in World War I, acting as Assistant Secretary-General of the League of Nations, services to a number of individual nations, supervision of the French munitions program, and the American war management program. Monnet has quoted Amiel that "it is institutions which control the relations between men, it is they which are the true support of civilization."

Monnet, with a devoted band of assistants, formulated the Schuman Plan from his key position as head of the French Planning Commission. Coal and steel were chosen partly because they were industries which symbolized the struggle between the two countries and were the foundation of armaments and military power, and partly because they formed an economic base which could be enlarged to include other industries.

Robert Schuman, who had been born in Luxembourg, fought for Germany in World War I, and did not become French until after that war, agreed to introduce the plan and capture the public imagination. For Schuman, solidarity and interdependence would replace political nationalism, autarkic protectionism, cultural isolation, and hegemony in Europe. The plan was greeted enthusiastically, but Britain refused to participate. After ten months of negotiations between the six governments of France, Germany, Italy, Belgium, the Netherlands, and Luxembourg, agreement was reached in March, 1951. Again the role of Monnet was crucial. Although nominally the head of the French delegation, in fact he introduced what has come to be familiar as the community method; the technique of acting on behalf of the general interest and getting maximum consensus. Reluctantly, Monnet decided to go ahead without Britain. On April 18, 1951, the Treaty of Paris was signed by the six countries, and on July 25, 1952, the European Coal and Steel Community came into existence, the first European supranational body.

The ECSC was regarded by both Monnet and Schuman as the first of a number of concrete achievements which would provide a practical basis for solidarity. Even before the ECSC was in existence another organization was being planned. In the Council of Europe in August, 1950, both Churchill and André Philip proposed a European army. In spite of the Korean War, the European nations were reluctant to agree to United States pressure for the admission of Germany to NATO. To prevent the development of a strong, individual German force, France proposed a European army, controlled by a European defense minister, into which the German contingents would be integrated. The original idea of "combat teams" of from five to six thousand men was rejected in favor of integration at the divisional level with divisions of different nationalities being brought together as an army corps. The revised plan was acceptable to Germany since it implied the restoration of its sovereignty, the ending of Allied occupation of the country, and the removal of conditions on its right to rearm. In May, 1952, the Treaty for a European Defense Community was signed by the six nations. The EDC would be supranational in character, with common institutions, common armed forces, and a common budget. Twelve German divisions were to be integrated into a European force under the NATO Supreme Commander. Some concessions were made to France to allow it to switch troops to its overseas army.

Confident that EDC would be ratified the Six began to discuss proposals for a European Political Community. The logic of the process of integration was operating: a defense community would lead to institutions dealing with foreign affairs and politics. In September, 1952, an ad hoc assembly, made up of the Consultative Assembly of the Council of Europe plus 87 co-opted members, was asked to draft proposals. A working constitutional committee reported to the Assembly in March, 1953, proposing a treaty for a European Executive Council, a council of ministers, a court, a bicameral assembly, and an economic and social council. Adopted unanimously by the Assembly, in spite of some opposition, the draft was sent to the six governments. The dream of a supranational European Community, founded on a union of peoples and states, seemed near realization.

These hopes were shattered by the refusal of the French parliament to ratify the EDC treaty on August 30, 1954, despite ominous threats by John Foster Dulles. Pragmatic Albion rose to the rescue of the military organization. Britain had refused to participate in EDC, to place its forces under supranational control, or to give assurances to France that it would keep troops on the Continent. Churchill, who in 1950 while leader of the Opposition, had called for a European army, said in 1953 as Prime Minister, "We are with them, but not of them. We have our own Commonwealth and Empire." Anthony Eden, British Foreign Secretary, thought of an alternative to EDC. After a rapid consultation of European capitals, the new organization was elaborated. The BTO, enlarged to include the two defeated enemies of World War II, Germany and Italy, became the Western European Union. The core of agreement was the British commitment to keep its forces—four divisions and the second Tactical Air Force—on the Continent. Germany would be admitted to NATO and supply troops to it. At the same time WEU was given functions of arms control, and, in particular, the duty of preventing German production of atomic, biological, and chemical weapons. In addition, the new organization was not only given powers over military affairs, but also could concern itself with economic, social, and cultural matters.

But nothing could disguise the fact that the integration process had been checked. Defense policy would remain essentially a national, not a communal responsibility, and the integration of military units would take place at army group level. The defeat of EDC and the EPC was doubly disappointing since other proposals for integration in various sectors—in agriculture, in transport, and in health—had all failed or been defeated.

Europe of the Six

Paul-Henri Spaak has said that those working for European unity are fated to be constantly on the verge of either triumph or disaster. Within a year the mood of pessimism produced by the defeat of the EDC was shaken off, and the move forward had restarted. The proposed EPC had included provisions for progressively establishing a Common Market based on the free movement of goods, capital, and persons. Already in 1944, Belgium, the Netherlands, and Luxembourg had signed a customs union agreement creating Benelux. Though Luxembourg was already obliged by a treaty of 1921 to accept Belgian decisions on duties and quotas, it entered Benelux as an equal partner. The customs union, coming into operation in 1948, abolished tariff barriers among the three countries—though not all of them immediately—and imposed a common tariff on imports from non-member countries which was the approximate average of the Belgium-Luxembourg duties and the prewar Dutch tariffs.

In May, 1955, the Benelux countries, discreetly aided by Jean Monnet who had just formed the Action Committee for the United States of Europe, and by Pierre Uri, presented a memorandum calling for further integration, and proposing a common market in which restriction and discriminations would be ended, suggesting the progressive harmonization of social legislation in the different countries, and specifically asking for organizations to be set up to deal with sectors of transport, power, and atomic energy for peaceful purposes. The memorandum tried to compromise between the French proposals for integration by sectors and the German support of a common market.

At the June, 1955, meeting of the six foreign ministers at Messina, it was agreed to study a possible organization to deal with a customs union and common market, and with atomic energy. An intergovernmental committee, assisted by the staff of the High Authority of the ECSC, was formed under Paul-Henri Spaak, and a number of groups set up to study possibilities for a common market, conventional energy, nuclear energy, transport, and general works. As on previous occasions, Britain refused to participate in the negotiations, but sent a delegation headed by a subordinate official as an observer. Kept in almost constant motion by the enthusiastic Spaak who acted as a spur in the same way Monnet had done during the creation of the ECSC, the committee presented a 150 page report to the six governments in March, 1956. The governments made some 150 amendments to the draft which were incorporated in the revised report presented to the Common Assembly of the ECSC, which by near unanimity approved the creation of a common market, and to the foreign ministers in April, 1956. At their May meeting, the six ministers accepted the report as a basis for drafting the treaties for the organizations: a European Economic Community, and Euratom. The Spaak report had not dealt with the question of British participation, but had argued that a common market on a global basis could not be expected, and that a community with common rules, a common policy and a system of supervisory institutions was only possible if limited to a small number of countries. The foreign ministers accepted the view that the treaties would be limited to the six countries, though provision would be made for other countries either to join the Six or be associated with them.

Most of the negotiations were concerned with the complicated problems of a common market and little progress was made on Euratom until the nationalization of the Suez Canal, and the abortive invasion of October, 1956, made the Six aware of a possible threat by Colonel Nasser to their supplies of oil in the Middle East. On March 25, 1957, with the bell on the Capitoline Hill tolling symbolically, the Treaties of Rome were signed: on January 1, 1958, the European Economic Community and Euratom came into existence. No formal agreement was reached on the location of the institutions of the new organizations, and, after some discreet bargaining, Brussels became their home by default, much as Luxembourg had done in the case of the ECSC. But no final decision was made and the institutions of the three communities remain geographically dispersed among Brussels, Luxembourg, and Strasbourg.

The Treaties attempted to compromise between the different positions taken by the Six during the negotiations. France had wanted integration in a number of sectors rather than the general community which was produced, but obtained a number of concessions: (1) the harmonization of social costs, especially equal wages for women; (2) agreements for the marketing of agricultural products; (3) financial support and an association arrangement for her former colonies in Africa; (4) escape clauses that would allow her to continue subsidizing exports for a time; (5) a higher rate of the common external tariff; (6) and agreement that progress from one state to the next would depend on objectives being reached during the transitory period. Moreover, much of the limitation of the formal powers of the executive organ, and the corresponding increase in those of the Council of Ministers as compared with the balance in the Treaty of Paris, was due to the desire to avoid a rejection of the Treaty by France as in the case of the EDC. The challenging words "supranational" and "High Authority" were deliberately avoided, and the more neutral "Commission" substituted. Contrary to the French, and to a lesser degree the Italian desire for a high common tariff, the Dutch were the principal advocates of low external tariffs and of strong Community institutions. The Belgians supported the latter view, although in general were more flexible. For Germany the two communities were another major step to political respectability, and for Chancellor Adenauer a further link in the rapprochement with France. Germany agreed that its nuclear industry would be organized within the European framework, although France would maintain its own nuclear program.

The British Response

In spite of ambiguous statements by Winston Churchill while in opposition, both major political parties in Britain have been reluctant to enter into any binding relationship with the Continental countries. As a country which survives by its commerce, Britain has continually proposed, as an alternative to the plans of the Six, a free trading area in Europe, based on the removal of trade barriers to industrial goods, tariffs and quantitative import restrictions, and the extension of trade concessions to other OEEC countries on a reciprocal basis. To prevent the import of goods into high tariff countries via those with low tariffs in such a free trade area, the "rule of origin" was proposed by which a product would be considered to have originated in an area if the value of the material of non-area origin did not exceed a given percentage of the final value of the product.

While the negotiations for the EEC and Euratom were under way, a working party of OEEC under the Belgian Baron Snoy studied the possibilities of association between a customs union of the Six and other OEEC members. In January, 1957, it reported that a free trade area in Europe, including the Six, was technically possible, and further working parties began exploring the form such an area could take. The OEEC Council of Ministers set up an intergovernmental committee, with the British Paymaster-General Reginald Maudling as chairman, which, throughout 1957 and 1958, discussed problems ranging about the reduction of tariffs, rules of competition, agriculture and fisheries, coordination of economic policy, and harmonization of legislation.

Differences between Britain and France became increasingly

marked, gradually changing from ideological conflicts into a struggle for power. Allies by necessity, the two countries have more usually been rivals, either in foreign conquest or the hegemony of Europe. The leadership of Europe was again fought over on the improbable battlefield of technical trade problems. The French demanded negotiation of agreements on an industry-by-industry basis, the "sector" approach which meant that conditions of competition would be studied in sectors in which any country foresaw difficulties, and that trade would be liberalized at different rates in different industries. Against this the Maudling Committee had agreed that no commitment on individual points would be made until a final agreement had been reached. The French position was partly based on fear of British competition; France also asked for the preferential arrangements made with the Commonwealth to be extended to European goods. But France, supported by those favoring European integration, also argued that acceptance of the British position would weaken the political objectives of integration, and that a Free Trade Area was incompatible with the EEC.

Although Britain moved from her original position and agreed that any sector in which difficulties were anticipated should be examined, she still wanted a Free Trade Area with no common external tariff, no common anti-trust policy, no free movement of capital and labor, the exclusion of agriculture, and no objective for economic or political unification. In November, 1958, an impasse was reached with the French rejection of the British "rule of origin" concept as inadequate and difficult to administer, and insistence on a common external tariff. Britain regarded such a tariff as a restrictionist trade policy as well as inconsistent with its preferential treatment of Commonwealth goods. In December, Mr. Maudling confessed that his committee could not "secure the establishment of a European Free Trade Area to take effect parallel with the Treaty of Rome."

Though the London *Times* called France "the wrecker," the differences were irreconcilable between a Britain, surprised at the rapidity of the moves to unity by the Six in 1955–1956, refusing to surrender any sovereign power, wanting a minimum of centralized machinery, seeing the Free Trade Area in economic terms only, opposed to an economic union, and wanting negotiations limited to industrial goods only, and France, opposed to British economic and political competition, supporting the move to integration, and seeking a closer political rapport with Germany. Indeed the British, hoping for support from Germany for their proposals for multilateral trade, had inadequately appreciated the significance for Chancellor Adenauer of such a rapprochement with France. The French position, a mixture of economic protectionism and political realism, was supported for tactical reasons by the proponents of integration, afraid that the impetus to political and economic unity might be halted and wanting delay until the new Communities had forged stronger links. In reply, supporters of the Free Trade Area suggested that it would have ended trade discrimination while preserving the EEC and that the absence of a common external tariff would allow the preservation of the low tariffs of countries such as Scandinavia and Switzerland and the Commonwealth preferences.

But the free trade idea was not dead. The OEEC nations excluded from the EEC wanted to increase trade with one another, to strengthen their individual and collective position in relation to the EEC, and to prevent the EEC from acting in a nonliberalizing fashion towards them. Spurred by proposals by Switzerland and then Sweden, representatives of seven nations—Austria, Denmark, Great Britain, Norway, Portugal, Sweden and Switzerland—met in the summer of 1959 near Stockholm, and decided to form an organization concerned exclusively with the liberalization of industrial trade and with no political objectives. Agreement was rapidly reached in eight weeks, and in November, 1959, the Stockholm Convention created the European Free Trade Association. In Western Europe, the Seven now confronted the Six.

Britain Crosses the Rubicon

In explaining the EFTA agreement to the House of Commons in November 23, 1959 the British Chancellor of the Exchequer, Heathcoat Amory, said that the EFTA countries wished to enter into "discussions with the Governments of the EEC countries as soon as the latter are ready to do so, with a view to some form of economic association between the two areas." Before long they were preparing to go even further, and, as British Prime Minister Harold Macmillan said, to take "the biggest and most forward-looking decision in our peacetime history."

The Labour and Conservative Governments in Britain had both been wary of anything closer than intergovernmental arrangements with the continental countries. Britain had emerged from the war triumphant and unoccupied, if financially weakened. It was the center of the largest empire in the world, of a Commonwealth increasing in number and diversity, and of a sterling area responsible for a considerable part of the world's trade. The basic similarity of language, culture, and political behavior with the United States led to the belief in a special relationship between them.

But the failure of Macmillan's hopes for a successful summit conference in Paris in 1960, the relative stagnation of the British economy while the Six were booming, the realization that trade with the Commonwealth was becoming a less significant part of British commerce and that the preferential arrangements were not altogether to Britain's advantage, the reduction in status as a Great Power with the increasingly rapid liquidation of the British Empire, the change in British defense policy with the cancellation of the Blue Streak rocket and the evaporation of hopes for an independent deterrent, the increasing intellectual and industrial support for union with the Six, and the report of a group of top level civil servants under Sir Frank Lee at the beginning of 1960 in favor of British entry on political grounds, led to Macmillan's announcement in July, 1961, that Britain would enter into official negotiations with the EEC with a view to membership. Ireland and Denmark followed the British example.

The Macmillan pronouncement was not greeted with unanimous approval in Britain. Support came from those arguing the economic necessity of British entry to strengthen its markets and productivity, and the political desirability of influencing European political development. Opposition came from those arguing that

British agriculture would be harmed, that food prices would rise, that the Commonwealth was being abandoned, that the EEC was a group of nations essentially Catholic and that the Treaty of Rome might be seen as a Roman treaty, the triumph of the Counter-Reformation. Foreign reaction was generally favorable. The conference of EFTA ministers in the summer of 1961 approved the British application for membership, as did the U.S. Administration and most of the Six. The main opponents seemed to be French agriculturalists afraid of the traditional cheap-goods policy in Britain, and of Commonwealth preferences. Of the EFTA countries, Denmark had followed Britain because of concern over possible EEC discrimination against her agriculture, Norway was hesitant, and the three neutrals, Austria, Sweden, and Switzerland, and Finland, an EFTA associate, were cautious for political reasons but were interested in protecting their economic and trading positions in Europe. The members of the Commonwealth remained concerned over possible removal of their preferences.

A strong British team worked on the negotiations with the EEC: four Cabinet Ministers, five senior Civil servants, and almost the whole of the Foreign Office, under the leadership of Edward Heath, President of the Board of Trade. Differences arose immediately on the conduct of the negotiations: whether by the Community as a whole, or by the six governments as France held; in the EEC headquarters or in Paris; on who should provide the facilities. France gained a formal victory in that the negotiations were held as an ad hoc intergovernmental conference in Brussels, in which the Six might speak collectively but the states could also speak individually. The organization of the conference was worked out pragmatically, the chairman being the current chairman of the Council of Ministers of the Six. Although the Commission of the EEC was not a participant in the same way as the six states, in fact, it played an important role by preparation of material, formulation of solutions, and constant optimism. The negotiations were conducted by ministerial meetings once a month, meetings of the permanent representatives once a week, and by working parties, including representatives of the states and of the Commission.

Paul-Henri Spaak has complained that during the negotiations, Britain should have been treated as a future partner, rather than as an adversary confronting the Six, and that the French insistence on a strict interpretation of the Treaty of Rome and on the prior settling of EEC agricultural policy and relations with the Associated African states, prevented accommodations from being reached. Part of the problems arose from the fact that the Community was formulating its own position on many issues which were under negotiation, and was thus compelled to deal with them sooner than it would have expected. Not unnaturally, Heath said he sometimes felt that negotiating was "like dealing with a moving staircase" since the problems were continually changing. The Belgians and the Dutch, wanting Britain as a balance against a possible Franco-German bloc, argued that negotiations on British entry must have priority over other Community business. The other four countries, with differing degrees of emphasis, held that the first task of the Community was to preserve its own identity.

Negotiations began on October, 1961, were suspended in August 1962, were resumed in September 1962 but were abruptly terminated in January 1963. In a carefully staged press conference on January 14, 1963 General de Gaulle stated that "the structure, the economy peculiar to England differ profoundly from those of the Continentals," and that England would only be acceptable if she transformed herself to participate in a European Community without restriction, without reservation and without preference. His opposition to Britain and his contempt for the negotiations that had been going on for 14 months was shown a week later when he unilaterally offered membership of the EEC to Denmark, and on January 22, when the Franco-German treaty of cooperation and friendship was signed.

With the action of de Gaulle has come the danger of a revival of European nationalism which may prove contagious. The immediate effects of the veto on the British economy have not

been disastrous; in fact, the reverse has been true and British—
EEC trade has expanded. But the action was a sad blow at the
whole concept of Community behavior and multilateral decision-
making from which the Community has not yet fully recovered.
In the following chapters the European story is traced in terms
of the organizations balancing in their different ways the national
and the communal interests.

CHAPTER TWO

European Political Cooperation:
The Council of Europe

THE COUNCIL OF EUROPE set up in Strasbourg in August, 1949, was an unhappy compromise. On one side the French and Belgian governments and federalists in general, like André Philip, had pressed for a strong political organization of a supranational character as the only way in which European problems could be solved and unity attained. Arguing against this, Britain considered the federal approach as unrealistic and inopportune, and at most would accept instead the cooperation of governments and their citizens in specific projects linking their activities in their common interest. The compromise produced a parliamentary Consultative Assembly meeting in public with powers of recommendation only and a semipermanent Committee of Ministers on which Britain, Ireland, and the Scandinavians had insisted.

The Consultative Assembly is a body of representatives, in rough but not exact proportion to national population, chosen in a manner decided at first by the national governments, and, since 1951, by the national parliaments. In most countries the parliament itself makes the choice, although in Britain members are appointed by the government after agreement between the party leaders. Since seven countries—Germany, Turkey, Greece, Austria, Switzerland, Sweden, and Cyprus—have joined the original ten in the Council—Britain, France, Belgium, Denmark, Ireland, Italy, Luxembourg, the Netherlands, Norway, and Sweden, the number of representatives has risen to 144. Of this total Britain, France, Germany, and Italy have the largest number with 18 each.

The membership of the Assembly has never been fully representative of national views, since communists and those overtly opposed to the concept of Europe have been excluded. Moreover, the members are representatives of themselves only in their speeches and votes: perhaps like the House of Lords they have the full confidence of their constituents. Although the Assembly uses the traditionally continental semicircle chamber in the Maison de l'Europe in Strasbourg, specially built for the Council of Europe, the members sit in alphabetical not party order. In 1954, the Assembly organized itself into three political groupings, Christian Democrat, Liberal, and Socialist, and a number of other members consisting of British Conservatives and a few others which get financial aid and whose chairmen attended meetings of the Bureau. But, as with the Western European Union Assembly, the groups largely solidify around official positions rather than programs or substantive policy. The national parties act together more than do the party groups, and a small number of individuals are more influential than either. The Assembly meets in spring, autumn, and winter for four or five days each time, and has a joint session with the European Parliament once a year. Only one extraordinary session has been held so far: in 1953 it discussed the proposed European Political Community. The official positions—the president and seven vice-presidents who make up the Bureau, responsible for the agenda and timetable and for authorizing Committee meetings outside of Strasbourg— are normally shared on national lines, with the 4 large powers always being represented. There are eleven permanent committees, which meet between sessions and prepare reports which form the basis of discussion in the Assembly, and a standing committee which coordinates the work of the committees and facilitates the work of the Assembly which it represents between sessions. In this last capacity it can adopt recommendations which have the same status as those of the Assembly. There are also a number of permanent and temporary working parties on specific subjects. The most notable of these is the working party concerned with establishing close links between the Assembly and the national parliaments.

The Assembly is a deliberative organ debating matters within its jurisdiction—and in the case of defense exceeding its jurisdiction —and presenting its conclusions in the form of recommendations, resolutions, opinions, or orders. Of these, recommendations which require a two-third majority and call for action are the most significant. Of the 350 recommendations made by the Assembly since 1949, about half have been accepted by the ministers either fully or partially. There is often no adequate formal explanation for the nonacceptance of recommendation by the ministers. The Assembly has suggested that the ministers themselves rather than their deputies should express their opinion on the proposals sent to them.

Any real power in the Council of Europe belongs to the Committee of Ministers which disposes while the Assembly proposes. It is an intergovernmental body meeting twice a year at irregular intervals and deciding all important issues and making recommendations to governments by unanimity, although most decisions are taken by a two-thirds majority. In practice most of the work is now done by deputies who are senior officials, meeting about once a month and, since 1955, making decisions by majority vote although still seeking for agreement by all. But the deputies have not become a corporate group or collective entity though they form something more than a diplomatic conference. Some of them are permanent representatives of their country at Strasbourg, but half of them come from their national capitals to attend meetings; the deputies largely remain exponents of an official national viewpoint. The deputies in turn base their activity on the work done by committees of experts—governmental, private, and international civil servants—in various fields.

The Council of Europe is staffed by a secretariat of about 450, headed by a secretary-general and a deputy appointed by the Assembly on the recommendation of the ministers, and with some balance attained between nationals of different countries. But only since 1957 have the ministers recommended more than one candidate and given the Assembly a choice. The secretariat serves both the Committee of Ministers and the Assembly: the secretary-general is responsible to the ministers. The secretary-general attends meetings of the Committee of Ministers and has the right to place questions on the agenda though it is not always easy for him to do so. In the spring session of the Assembly, he presents an annual report on the progress of European cooperation. He interprets the recommendations of the Assembly to the national governments, especially through papers called "observations" in which the value of the recommendation and the anticipated problems are pointed out. The office of the secretary-general and the degree of its influence has varied with the incumbent. Under the first two occupants, Jacques-Camille Paris and Léon Marchal, it was considerably more significant then under Lodovico Benvenuti, a former Italian deputy. The appointment in January, 1964, of a British politician, Peter Smithers, has again made it a position of some importance. The first actions taken by Mr. Smithers on his appointment in arguing that the Council of Europe might play a role in the solution of the Cyprus problem, and that the Council may play a role in the settlement of regional disputes within the jurisdiction of the United Nations Charter suggest that the role of the secretary-general is likely to be more pronounced in the working of the organization and in facilitating cooperation with other organizations.

The first years of the organization saw a struggle between the Assembly and the Committee of Ministers, with the former pressing for greater independence and control. The Assembly wanted to fix its own agenda, broaden its jurisdiction to discuss any matter within the competence of the Council, set up a liaison committee between itself and the ministers, and have its recommendations sent directly to governments. The Committee conceded these except the last. It also granted the right of the Assembly to consider the part of the budget that affected it, and the Assembly's proposals have generally been accepted. In 1954 the ministers agreed to submit the budget to the Assembly after adoption so that the Assembly could make suggestions for the next budget. The Assembly was given the concurrent right to call for a special session if it felt it to be necessary. It was to be consulted on the admission and expulsion of members of the Council, though decision still remain with the governments. Selection of members of the Assembly by governments was replaced by parliamentary decision. Since 1950, when Churchill at Strasbourg suggested the creation of a European army, debates on defense have been tacitly allowed, though theoretically the discussion of national defense is forbidden. But since the creation of WEU, the Consultative Assembly has been content to leave detailed technical discussion of defense matters to the WEU Assembly.

The Committee of Ministers agreed to refer matters to the Assembly for its opinion, but this has largely been an endorsement of international agreements arrived at by the ministers. Ministers appear before the Assembly both in an individual capacity and as the spokesmen of the Committee, and since 1955 have been participating in debates on both the report of the Committee presented to the Assembly and other matters. Moreover, the chairman of the Committee of Ministers answers questions orally at one sitting in each Assembly session as well as providing written answers to written questions. But this provided neither supervision nor control over the work of the ministers. In 1951, a joint committee of the ministers and eight representatives of the Assembly was set up to coordinate the activities of the Council of Europe. Again the Assembly expected that this liaison committee would allow it more influence over the ministers. This has been a pious hope. The Assembly was dissatisfied with the fact that the deputies, rather than the ministers themselves, attended after the first few meetings, and ended them. In 1960 they were revived, but this has not proved to be a significant instrument of coordination. Other joint meetings have taken place on specific subjects, such as population, cultural, and legal matters, with the Assembly being actually represented on the Council for Cultural Cooperation and the European Committee for Legal Cooperation. More important then the joint meeting has been the annual colloquy held each December in Paris since 1961, between almost all the foreign ministers and a group of the Assembly in which there has been very frank and free discussion on political issues.

The Limitations of the Council

The work and functions of the Council of Europe has hardly fulfilled the hope of the Hague Congress for the full unification of Europe or the expectation in the statute that "like minded European countries" should "create an organization which will bring the European states into closer association." The discussions of "questions of common concern" and "agreements and common action" mentioned in Article I, although embracing a wide diversity of subjects—economic, social, cultural, scientific, and legal matters and human rights—have not been politically meaningful after the first few years. There has never been more than a minority of the members interested in the realization of a political union. Wide differences divide the foreign policies of the states. Strasbourg has not been the clearing house of family political affairs. As early as 1951, the Assembly, itself realizing that the unanimity rule prevented all real political progress, recommended that the Council of Europe should concern itself with less contentious matters.

The Council is an organization with little effective political power, partly for political, partly for organizational, and partly for procedural reasons, inspite of a request by the Consultative Assembly that it do so. The Council does not possess organs whose sole function is to represent common interests, though a strong secretary-general could act in that capacity. The inclusion of the neutrals has meant a certain unwillingness to discuss disputed political affairs, particularly where military action is involved. In theory it might have formed an admirable place for the formulation of a solution to the explosive Cyprus problem in 1964 since all four nations directly concerned were members of the Council; the Committee of Ministers did not concern itself with the problem. In May, 1963, the Committee of Ministers resolved to make full use of each of its sessions to hold comprehensive discussions on the major political problems of European unification, and to instruct the deputies to prepare in detail for the political discussions. But it seems unlikely that this will provide a mechanism for strengthening the political will necessary for European integration.

Procedurally, the Council operates through a double process of recommendations: the Assembly recommending action to the Committee of Ministers, and the ministers in turn recommending action to the member governments which are free to accept or reject these recommendations. Though the Committee of Ministers consists of foreign ministers or their alternates, it has no authority to make binding decisions. As most meetings are, in fact, of deputies, eventual government agreement remains uncertain. Since 1950 the governments have assented to 43 conventions and agreements on subjects as diverse as human rights, patents, social security, extradition, and university qualifications, and have adopted common action on other matters such as the standardization of passports and cultural exchanges. But these, useful and important though they are, do not include topics of political magnitude.

Paul-Henri Spaak, who had come to Strasbourg "convinced of the necessity of a United States of Europe," and who became the first President of the Consultative Assembly in 1949, resigned in December, 1951, disillusioned at the lack of progress towards this objective. In January, 1964, he delivered an epitaph of a kind at Strasbourg when he doubted whether the Council of Europe could ever play a decisive part in bringing about a unified Europe since it was composed of three groups of countries, each having particular and divergent views on important issues: the Six, those nations committed to NATO, and the neutrals. Another disillusioned federalist, Paul Reynaud, complained that the Council had two bodies, one for Europe, the other against it.

The pressure of the federalists for European political machinery of a supranational character quickly evaporated. Less ambitious proposals, that the functionalists had originally suggested as an alternative, for institutions that would deal with particular areas such as currency, commerce, transport, investment, and production, were blocked by Britain. In 1948, Britain refused to accept the idea of a federal parliament. In 1950, Hugh Dalton, on behalf of the Labour Government, had resisted the proposal that all Assembly delegates at Strasbourg should pledge themselves to vote in their national parliaments in favor of any decision reached by the Assembly. To the surprise of many, Winston Churchill, as head of the Conservative Government after 1951, was no more eager to expand the power of the Council. Both the Labour and Conservative Governments, arguing that Britain was a participant in three interlocking circles, the Commonwealth, Anglo-American partnership, and the European Community, refused to be drawn into any closer political arrangement with the last.

The Contributions of the Council

If the Council of Europe has not been the avenue to European integration, it has performed five valuable functions. It has served as a European platform for political utterances. It has tried to act as a connecting link between the rapidly proliferating European organizations. It has been an instrument for reaching agreements and common action. It has performed useful functions in the social, cultural and legal realm. It has founded the European Court and Commission of Human Rights.

In its early years the Council provided the most important single platform for discussion of European integration and collaboration. Not until the formation of the European Communities did it lose this preeminence. As a unique political body, the Assembly was the place for Schuman to call for Franco-German reconciliation, for Churchill to introduce a resolution for a European army, for debates on the future of the Saar and the reunification of Germany, the Pleven Plan, the EDC and WEU, the Hungarian and Suez crisis of 1956, and general problems of European security. Though the discussion of defense had been specifically excluded from its province, a debate took place in the Assembly in August, 1950, on the political aspects of European defense. The Committee of Ministers gave tacit approval to this extension of jurisdiction provided no recommendations were made on the subjects. In the few later discussions the Assembly kept within this limit by occasionally passing resolutions expressing its opinions on defense problems. In the realm of economics, the Assembly has discussed a European economic union, control over cartels, creation of a patents office, economic affairs in general and tariff problems in particular, especially the problem of avoiding the division of Europe into rival trading blocs. In 1952 the discussions led to the Strasbourg Plan for the more intensive development of African territories, and later to the institution of a study group for the development of Africa.

There are a multitude of international and essentially European organizations. Among the latter are the eight major organizations dealt with in this book and others like Benelux, the Customs Cooperation Council, the European Organization for Nuclear Research, the Rhine Commission, and so on through the alphabet. The Council has tried to act as a link between the different organizations. In 1950 the Assembly proposed closer cooperation between the existing European organizations and more effective control over intergovernmental organizations. The secretariat also suggested that specialized authorities with competence in political, economic, social, legal, and cultural fields be created within the framework of the Council, rather than outside of it, and that each member be free to join whichever organization it wished. Thus within the umbrella provided by the Council, the integration movement could develop.

But although the Council had hoped it would be consulted on the plans for new European organizations, it took no direct part in the framing of the European Coal and Steel Community, or subsequent organizations of the Six. Its role was limited to a sympathetic debating of the proposals for the new organizations, and the sending of observers when the EPC treaty was being drafted. The hopes that some kind of organic link would be set up between the Council of Europe and the institutions of the Six were doomed to disappointment, partly because of the strong objections of Monnet who felt the Council might hold back the development of future organizations, and was loath even to make use of the physical facilities of the Assembly at Strasbourg. However, a number of ties were established. Reports and information are transmitted by the European Parliament to the Consultative Assembly, and by the executives of the European communities to the Council. One joint session of the Consultative Assembly and the Common Assembly of ECSC has taken place each year since 1955. But the proposals that the joint sessions should vote after their debate and that joint meetings of committees should take place were refused by the European Parliament. Joint meetings occasionally take place between the European executives and the Committee of Ministers. Since 1955 there has been a Consultative Committee of the secretary-generals of the different organizations who exchange information about the different bodies and try to avoid possible duplication of activity, but a unified European point of view has been hard to attain.

With the institution of the European communities and the growing split between the Six and the rest, other suggestions were made for reconciliation. In 1956, Selwyn Lloyd, then British Foreign Minister, proposed a grand design in which a single European Assembly be set up with separate commissions for political, economic, social and cultural, legal and administrative affairs, and for defense. The Italians, members of the Six but not unsympathetic to the British predicament, proposed instead that the existing assemblies, the Consultative Assembly, Western European Union Assembly, and the Common Assembly be kept, but that there be an identical membership. The plan appealed to the Consultative Assembly more than to the British.

The Council had been disappointed that in 1954 the new WEU decided to set up its own assembly consisting of the representatives of the seven countries to the Consultative Assembly instead of operating within the Strasbourg framework. The Consultative Assembly proposed a common secretariat for both bodies, but the WEU Assembly framed its own rules and organized itself in Paris with its own secretariat. Not until 1960 did some rationalization take place when the social and cultural activities, rather inappropriately attached to WEU, were transferred to the Council.

In 1957 the Assembly recommended the amalgamation of the Council of Europe and the OEEC, as earlier it had suggested a single Council of Ministers for both organizations, with the Assembly also becoming the representative body of OEEC. But neither this, nor the hope of the Assembly that the British Commonwealth be closely associated with the economic development of Western Europe, were fulfilled.

In 1961 and 1962 when the negotiations between the Six and Britain dominated intra-European politics, the Assembly again provided a useful platform for the discussion of outstanding problems, and enthusiastically urged a successful outcome. After the failure of the negotiations in January, 1963, many regarded the Council of Europe as the most appropriate framework in which the process of European integration could be continued. With the exception of Portugal, all the members of the EEC and EFTA belong to the Council, and it, therefore, remained the meeting place for them all. Though the Six and Britain decided to use the machinery of WEU rather than the Council for a rapprochement, the latter remains as a possible bridge between the divided nations.

For the purpose of information and advice the Council is linked not only to other European bodies, but also to a large number of global organizations, and to nongovernmental groups such as trade unions and social bodies, and to nonmember European states. Some 64 nongovernmental international organizations now have consultative status with the Council of Europe. Since 1957, Spain, still politically anathema to some members of the Council, has taken part in its cultural work. And Switzerland, before it became a member in 1963, and Israel which sends observers, participated in the economic debates of the Assembly. All this interaction has meant that representatives can be well informed on the work and functions of a wide number of other organizations, but it has not given them any greater control over or responsibility for that work.

A less dramatic but effective role of the Council has been that of proposing a number of conventions and agreements, not all of which have been ratified and to which not all members adhere. In addition the Council has set up bodies or has stimulated other international organizations to reach agreement on a wide variety of topics such as registration of personal matters, maintenance allowances, recognition of foreign judgments and national refugees, overpopulation, and statelessness. The conventions are playing a valuable part in harmonizing certain aspects of the laws of the members, in giving citizens of other member countries the same rights as the citizens of any one member, and in laying the foundation of a European legal community. In some cases the texts have been incorporated into the national courts.

Both the organs of the Council cooperate in drawing up the conventions. The greater part of the work of negotiating and drafting conventions is performed by committees of governmental experts, but the Assembly proposes most of them. In general, though there are variations to the procedure, the Assembly proposes a convention, the Committee of Ministers examines it and redrafts it, the Assembly amends this draft, the ministers again review it, and when the two are in agreement, the ministers adopt and sign the convention. It becomes ratified when a certain number of countries have signed, and only those states which ratify the convention are bound by it.

In legal, social, and cultural affairs, the Council has been playing an increasing role in facilitating intergovernmental cooperation. It drew up an agreement in 1964 making illegal the establishment or operation of unauthorized radio stations. It has helped establish minimum standards for old age pensions, family allowances and benefits for sickness, maternity, and unemployment. It has been active in the field of health, especially since 1960 when the functions of the Committee of Experts on Public Health were transferred to it.

After seven years of preparatory work the European Social Charter was signed in Turin in October, 1961. Its ambitious objective is to improve the standard of living and promote the social welfare of the peoples of Europe. The Charter covers wide areas of general social policy, including the acceptance of certain fundamental rights such as the right to work, to form trade unions, to social security, and to social and medical assistance, and it lays down minimum standards which are to be implemented gradually. It also allows all countries to make inquiries into the social policy of the others. The Charter has not yet gone into operation.

Since 1949 the Council has been interested in cultural affairs. It has promoted the mutual recognition of university degrees, impartial books on European history, university courses on European problems, a series of outstanding European art exhibitions, scholarships, university exchanges and European conferences. In 1960 it acquired the cultural functions, largely concerning youth problems, education, and the media of entertainment, attached to the Western European Union.

The Council has been responsible for a number of projects involving cultural cooperation. On January 1, 1962, the Council for Cultural Cooperation was created which absorbed the other groups in the Council concerned with cultural matters, and became the chief intergovernmental executive body for European cultural cooperation. Its activities were based largely on the work of three permanent committees, each concerned with a sector of eduction and groups of experts assisting in other cultural fields. The main stress of the new Council, reinforcing a growing concern of both the OECD and EEC, is on European cooperation in the field of education. Cultural affairs have, in the main, ceased to be an appendage of foreign policy and have become the concern of officials specializing in particular technical fields. In addition, the governments have been made aware of the need to safeguard the cultural heritage of Europe in an era of prosperity and increasing leisure.

A Legal Innovation

The fifth major contribution of the Council of Europe and possibly its most lasting achievement, is the European Convention for the Protection of Human Rights and Fundamental Freedoms. Disappointed by the deficiencies in the United Nations Universal Declaration of Human Rights, the 1948 Hague Congress recommended a European Declaration of Human Rights and a Court of Justice to adjudicate alleged transgressions. The Consultative Assembly, at its first meeting in September, 1949, recommended to the ministers a convention limited to political and civil rights, excluding economic and social rights that socialists wanted included, and allowing governments to take measures for the protection of a democratic society. The British view of a detailed definition of rights was accepted rather than the statement of principles that the Continentals wanted. In November, 1950, the European Convention was signed in Rome; it came into operation in September, 1953, after ten countries had ratified it. Today, seventeen countries have signed the Convention, but France and Switzerland have not yet ratified it. Ten countries have accepted the right of individual application for all persons under their jurisdiction, and eight countries have recognized the compulsory jurisdiction of the Court.

The Council set up organs with the powers of control and binding decisions lacking in the United Nations to decide on infringements of rights, even though their jurisdiction is limited to the rights enumerated and the jurisdiction of the Court to those states accepting it; the states have an obligation to see that their domestic legislation is compatible with the Convention. In a number of countries judgments in the national courts have been made referring to the Convention, and eight states, including Germany, have incorporated the Convention into their national law.

The functions of the Convention are divided among three institutions: the Committee of Ministers, the European Commission of Human Rights, and the Court. The European Commission of 17 members contains one member from each ratifying nation and is composed of judges, former judges, law professors, and practicing lawyers sitting for a term of six years as individuals, not as representatives of their states. Its president is a distinguished Swedish lawyer, Sture Petren. In theory the members are chosen by the Consultative Assembly; in practice the governments submit a list of three candidates from whom the parliamentary delegation of the country concerned makes a choice.

The Commission has a double function, partly judicial and partly as conciliator. In its judicial capacity it examines complaints by one state against another, and, since 1955, receives petitions from individuals if their states have agreed to allow them. Since 1953 there have been only three applications by states, two by Greece in 1956 and 1957 on the treatment of Cypriots, and one in 1960 by the Austrian Government on the conviction by Italian courts of men in South Tyrol. The Greek complaints were withdrawn by mutual agreement, Both the Committee of Ministers and the Commission felt that the Italian action had not been a violation of the Convention. Of the 2,400 individual applications, only 30 have been declared admissable and another 70 referred to the government concerned for comment, on the grounds that all domestic remedies have not been exhausted, or the petition is manifestly ill-founded, or because they concerned events before the establishment of the Convention.

A working group of three decides the merits of admissability, and the Commission has held very considerable proceedings involving long, written pleadings and oral hearings. If it accepts an application, the Commission, through a sub-Commission of seven members, attempts to reconcile the parties. If it fails, the Sub-Commission reports to the Commission which in turn reports to the ministers and the states concerned on the facts and legal issues, states its opinion, and may make proposals. It has no power other than that of moral suasion. The ministers, after an interval of three months during which a case may be brought before the Court, can decide by a two-thirds majority whether there has been a violation of rights, and in what period action is to be taken. Up till now they have dealt with eight cases.

In 1955 the Consultative Assembly by secret ballot elected for nine years the 15 judges of the Court who chose their own President and Vice-President and who decided that Strasbourg would be its seat. The President is Lord McNair, a former President of the International Court of Justice. Though nominated by their governments, the judges are independent and include men with a high judicial reputation. Individuals cannot bring a case directly before the Court which can function only when a case is referred to it by the states concerned or the Commission if the latter believes a matter of general importance is involved. Proceedings in Court are public, but they are secret before the Commission. Procedurally, the Commission acts as an adviser to the Court, not as a party to the case.

Of the two cases so far brought before the Court, only one was heard. In 1961 the Court acquitted Ireland of having unjustly arrested Gerald Lawless, a member of the Irish Republican Army. In 1962 the de Becker case was ended before the Court could act since Belgium modified the law of which he complained, forbidding people sentenced to prison for treason from later expressing themselves in public. It is unlikely that many disputes between the states will reach the Court since it is preferable for states to settle such disputes in the Committee of Ministers rather than before a public tribunal. The Court, also, is a less authoritative body than the Court of the EEC; it is the states that put the judgment into effect and the Committee of Ministers which decides whether this has been done. There is no sanction other than public opinion to make a state comply with a decision of the Court, though in both these cases the governments bound themselves in advance to accept their decisions.

The present tripartite sharing of jurisdiction between three organs is a rather unfortunate qualification of the original proposal to set up a Court. In practice, the Commission has become the only organ of conciliation. It has been criticized for having expanded its function beyond that of a screening body or committee of inquiry to that of making a detailed judicial examination of a question. The proceedings have generally been too lengthy. The Committee of Ministers has necessarily had to exercise a judicial function since the Court has not been accepted by all the members. Though it is not altogether desirable that an executive body perform such a function, the fact that most cases arise out of inadvertance rather than deliberate flouting of the law, that no prosecution is involved, and that the Committee is essentially concerned with collaboration and settlement rather than with purely judicial actions, lessen the inappropriateness of such procedure.

The impact of the Convention has been considerably reduced by the fact that France has not ratified it nor have Britain and Italy accepted the right of petition or the jurisdiction of the Court. A suggestion that three governments collectively could sponsor the application of an individual if his own state had not accepted the right of individual petition was turned down. Neither the Commission nor the Court has been allowed to give advisory opinions on the interpretation of the Convention. Yet in spite of these limitations the Convention remains as an important innovation allowing the right of individual appeal to an international body in an effective and increasingly important way. Neither the Court nor the Committee of Ministers has yet held there has been a violation of the Convention, but the Convention allows a balancing of the right of the individual against the duty of the state to take action in areas like public safety, morals, or the protection of the rights and freedoms of others. Not unexpectedly the Ministers have not been courageous enough to extend the example provided by the Convention and accept the proposal of the Assembly that a European supreme court be set up to interpret the numerous European conventions formulated under the auspices of the Council of Europe.

A Federal Europe is Checked

As a major political force the Council of Europe has not been a success. Instead of leading to a "political authority with limited functions but real powers" as was hoped, it has been an organization with limited powers, but exercising a variety of nonpolitical functions. It has been called the "Cinderella of European organizations," but there is no Prince Charming on the horizon to wed her, except an Atlantic Assembly if the fathers in the U.S. Congress would agree to such a marriage.

British distaste for a strong European body reduced the Committee of Ministers to insignificance, and ended all hopes for the emergence of a federal structure. The constitutional provisions for political unity had deliberately been left vague. The unanimity rule which applies in the Committee of Ministers for all important decisions reduces its effectiveness as a political body. It is rendered even more ineffective because of the rule preventing states from taking decisions applying to a group of states only. Unlike the deputies or permanent representatives of the European Communities, the deputies of the Committee of Ministers have not played a dynamic or communal role in the organization. Moreover, the fact that they are representatives of their foreign offices but deal to a large extent with matters affecting the internal policies of their countries means that there is normally an inter-

mediary between them and the national official responsible for
policy in social or economic affairs. Yet the Committee is the
dominant body in the Council since powers remain with the governments.

The Consultative Assembly has been the moving spirit, the
source of ideas and the reflection of public opinion in the Council, originating most of the proposals and stimulating the Ministers
to action. It provided the best postwar forum for the discussion
of European political affairs, but its effectiveness has been reduced
by the presence of neutral or nonaligned nations which has tempered the political and military proposals it might have made.
Politically its main importance has been that leading European
figures have used it as a sounding board, that it has generally
supported the formation of supranational institutions, and that
it has been a laboratory of ideas and the initiator of a large number
of successful organizations and conventions. With the setting up
of the European communities its role has been reduced. The
availability of the WEU Assembly has meant an alternative and
more restricted platform for discussions between the Six and
Britain, as happened during the 1962 negotiations.

In its early days the Consultative Assembly included the leading
members of the European opposition parties and some influential
representatives of the majority parties: its personnel in recent
years has hardly been of comparable weight. In 1963 the Assembly
criticized itself and its working methods. Instead of allowing itself
to be submerged in a mass of recommendations and reports, it
suggested it concentrate on a few major issues, and that its
recommendations should reflect a clear political purpose. The
Assembly realized that the Council needs a general program of
work with precise targets, and that greater progress can be made
toward integration in some fields, especially where deadlines have
been introduced.

The Council has not given up the hope for a role of major
significance or for becoming the arena in which the framework
of European collaboration can be laid. The current President of
the Consultative Assembly, Pierre Pflimlin, also, fortuitously,
Mayor of Strasbourg, energetically urges such a role. Yet the

hope that it might be used by Ministers for comprehensive discussions on the major political problems of European unification in 1964 has been disappointed.

The Council has played an honorable role in the development of Europe and has provided a kind of perpetual conscience. It has been the pioneer organization attempting to promote unity among the member states. Today it largely concentrates on specialized functions which are marginal rather than central to the interests of governments. It would be too unkind to say that it has been swept into the dustbin of history, but it exists in a state of penumbra and unnatural quiescence. It is disheartening for those who looked to the Council so enthusiastically fifteen years ago to feel that it might, like old soldiers, never die, but only fade away.

CHAPTER THREE

Economic Collaboration Across the Atlantic: The Organization for Economic Cooperation and Development

THE Organization for European Economic Cooperation came into existence in April, 1948, with a membership of 16 countries. Essentially it began as a body for the distribution of American economic aid on a joint basis, but it became concerned in a broader way with the economic problems and recovery of Western Europe. Each country pledged to increase its production, stabilize its currency, make full use of its manpower, remove restrictions on European trade and payments, achieve a multilateral system of payments and study the possibilities of a customs union.

OEEC was an intergovernmental organization headed by a council representing all the governments and making formal decisions by unanimity. It normally met at the level of the permanent officials in Paris rather than at ministerial level. Much of the operating work was done by an annually elected seven member executive committee, composed of heads of delegations, on which the most important nations were always represented and which supervised the working of the organization in detail. OEEC contained a large variety of bodies ranging from those composed of senior officials concerned with financial and commercial policy such as the governing board of the European Productivity Agency and the managing board of the European Payments Union, which were given some permanently delegated powers, to working parties of the Council and special restricted committees composed of senior national officials to decide certain types of dispute.

Below this level were some 20 technical committees on which all countries were represented. The so-called "vertical" committees dealt with specific commodities or services. The "horizontal" committees dealt with general aspects of economic activities such as trade, payments, or general economic questions. The first type was composed of experts; the second, which met more frequently, was made up of civil servants. Besides these two types of committee, there were also boards composed of national experts, who were not governmental representatives but were appointed in their personal capacity to advise on payments, trade, and general energy problems. Usually they were senior officials from the more specialized departments or from central banks.

In principle, decisions in OEEC were made by unanimous approval. However, the governing board of the European Productivity Agency (EPA) could approve a project by majority vote, and the managing board of the European Payments Union (EPU) could, by majority vote, make decisions which were binding on all parties. But in practice there was considerable qualification of this principle since reports and proposals were prepared in committees of experts, votes rarely taken, and every attempt made to reach maximum agreement. The permanent Council itself attempted to reach compromise rather than insist on unanimity, and preferred to make recommendations rather than decisions when unanimity appeared to difficult.

In spite of the fact that Robert Marjolin, the brilliant and dynamic French economist, was appointed Secretary-General of OEEC, the International Secretariat in Paris was a weak body compared with the authority of the national delegations, and had limited powers of initiative.

The Activity of the OEEC

OEEC was responsible for six major functions. It set up the institutions necessary for distributing United States aid for the recovery of Europe. It brought about the reduction and almost the elimination of quotas which had been restricting trade. It set up a payments mechanism which provided for mutual credits, greater transferability of currencies, removal of exchange controls, and aid for the European countries short of dollars. It issued a series of useful technical studies, and published annual reports which were a general economic and financial analysis of individual countries. It created autonomous bodies such as the European Nuclear Energy Agency and the European Productivity Agency, and helped others such as the European Conference of Ministers of Transport. And it became the central forum for the harmonization of economic policies and for economic consultation to the mutual enlightenment of civil servants, economists, and businessmen.

The first task of OEEC in 1948 was to recommend the division of United States aid. This was entrusted to a group of "4 Wise Men" who also reduced the requests for Marshall aid from $5 billion to $4,875 million. In 1949 a special body under Baron Snoy of Belgium and Robert Marjolin was created to recommend the division since OEEC could not produce unanimous agreement. The distribution of aid continued on the lines recommended and was not subjected to annual renegotiation. The collapse of Europe was prevented, but the more ambitious idea of a coordinated recovery program on a long-term basis failed because of differences of outlook.

However, in 1949 OEEC began dealing with two subjects helpful to recovery, trade liberalization and currency transferability, in an attempt to stimulate the flow of international trade. The OEEC objective was to replace bilateral trade quotas by over-all quotas for members and then proceed to the total abolition of quotas between members. Through a Code of Liberalization the members agreed to remove quantitative restrictions on a minimum percentage of their imports from each other. Nations might temporarily suspend liberalization if they suffered from an adverse balance-of-payments problem and were free to select the commodities involved. Despite temporary defaults by Britain and France, the degree of liberalization was successively raised to 60 percent, 75 percent, 90 percent, and to 95 percent in 1961, implying an almost total disappearance of quotas in the industrial sector. The main restrictions were in the agricultural sector, primarily for the maintenance of agricultural income and employment and of food production. Though liberalization was highly successful, there still remained administrative rules, technical regulations, and restricted business practices which formed barriers to trade.

Trade was also checked by the shortages of reserves and foreign currencies, especially of dollars, possessed by the European countries. The OEEC attempted to remove exchange controls through the introduction of currency clearing arrangements. The European Payments Union was set up in 1950 to introduce a system of multilateral payments which would avoid discrimination, all intra-European payments being settled monthly within the EPU rather than bilaterally between the individual countries. Each country's net balance with the other OEEC countries as a whole was settled partly by payment in gold, and partly by the granting of credit. Those countries which incurred persistent balance of payments problems were granted special credits.

Several advantages accrued through multilateral transactions. The states settled their accounts by drawing minimally on their scarce gold and foreign exchange reserves. With a small initial capital, EPU enabled settlement to take place by compensation alone of 70 percent of the $46 billion involved. Trade was freed on a nondiscriminatory basis. Debtor countries, while being assisted to redress their balance-of-payments difficulties, obtained automatic credit facilities to help over emergency periods. Since sterling was one of the EPU currencies, the whole sterling area was included in this easing of exchange controls; about half of international transactions came within the scope of the agreement. There was less discrimination against imports from the United States for currency reasons. The ending of bilateral settlements increased competition among all OEEC members in the European export market. The procedure provided a valuable opportunity for intergovermental consultation and mutual assistance, and for mutual influence on the domestic economic policies of the members through the managing board of seven, although Great Britain had opposed granting it strong powers.

Through British initiative, the EPU was extended to 1955; agreement was reached on a European Monetary Agreement to replace it when a specified number of EPU members had made their currencies convertible. Since 1952 OEEC had been preparing a collective approach to the convertibility of currencies. By 1958 general convertibility had been restored, and the EMA was established. The system by which intra-European balances were automatically settled on the basis of 75 percent in gold or dollars and 25 percent in credit was ended, as well as the centralized monthly clearing of intercountry balances and automatic credits to and from the Union. Western European payments were put on a hard currency basis: each member was now concerned with its over-all balance of payments rather than with a regional balance or with other OEEC members. Among other things this meant that there was now no financial basis for trade discrimination against the United States or the dollar currency. The EMA itself was to provide short-term credits and make suggestions for stabilizing a country's economic situation, as well as acting to settle intercountry payments balances through a system of multilateral settlements. In fact little use was made of it.

Towards the end of its existence OEEC became increasingly interested in the freeing of "invisible transactions": freight payments, insurance premiums, tourist allowances, interest, and even in the difficult problem of movements of capital.

Productivity and Energy

Europeans were also concerned to improve their productivity. To gain knowledge of American methods, a number of European missions were sent to the United States to study the operations of different industries. In 1952 a permanent committee composed of government representatives and technical experts was set up to promote coordinated action in the area of productivity. It recommended that National Productivity Centers be established to stimulate interest in the subject. With American pressure and technical assistance the European Productivity Agency was set up in 1953 to act as a central coordinating body for these centers, and to help promote the most effective methods for increasing productivity in individual enterprises. The EPA was headed by a governing board whose members were chosen annually by the governments because of their knowledge of productivity. They were assisted by an advisory board nominated by professional groups in industry, agriculture, and labor. The governing board began developing close links with the national agencies; its assistance was generally given through the national productivity organizations and professional bodies, not directly to the firms themselves. The EPA gradually extended its interests to include applied research and technical assistance for a number of European countries facing special economic development problems, especially the more underdeveloped areas such as Sardinia. It therefore became an "operational" agency and came in direct contact with businessmen, trade unionists, farmers, and universities, as well as government officials. The EPA was an example of successful international cooperation in research, the promotion of technical and management training, the improving of techniques of merchandising and distribution, aiding of planning for economic development, and a general exchange of ideas. Towards the end of its existence it changed its pattern of behavior and became more interested in direct action.

An interest of OEEC, related to that of productivity, was in the field of energy. In 1957 the European Nuclear Energy Agency was set up to foster the development of nuclear energy for peaceful purposes. It functions to promote cooperation among the national research organizations, and prepares joint periodic reviews of work performed. It helps in the development of uniform European nuclear laws; it has studied the problems of radioactivity and obtained agreement for common national measures for health protection against ionizing radiations. It helped work out international regulations concerning the transport of nuclear fuels and radioactive materials, and has held conferences on nuclear safety. The Convention on Security Control prevents the use of

jointly developed nuclear facilities for military purposes. The
Agency studies the future of nuclear power in the over-all energy
balance of Europe.

The most significant objective of ENEA in its first years has
been the establishment of international joint undertakings, each
participating country contributing money to the budget, scientists
and technicians to the staff, and sharing in the research, construction, and experimental work. Each undertaking is controlled by
an international management committee which approves the
research and development, and which is assisted by an international technical and administrative staff including specialists
from all countries. ENEA is represented on both the management and technical committees, and each undertaking reports
annually to the ENEA Steering Committee.

Three international undertakings have been started. In 1957
the Eurochemic Company was set up for reprocessing irradiated
nuclear fuels at a plant in Mol, Belgium. It is probable that the
plant will also be capable of processing highly enriched uranium.
In 1958 a three year joint project to exploit the Norwegian experimental reactor was begun at Halden, Norway. It began work on
the world's first boiling heavy-water reactor in 1960, and has
continued since then. In 1959 the Dragon high-temperature reactor project was begun at Winfrith Heath, England, and an experimental gas-cooled, graphite-moderated reactor built. The participants in Dragon are Austria, Britain, Denmark, Norway, Sweden,
Switzerland, and the Euratom Commission. The project became
"critical" in August, 1964, when a self-sustaining chain reaction
was achieved.

In the last two years, since the breakdown of the EEC-Euratom
negotiations with Britain in January, 1963, the ENEA has reinforced its position as an instrument of cooperation between the
Six and the other European members of the new organization,
OECD, and has changed the direction of its interest. It has concerned itself less with the type of cooperative research that it
previously sponsored, and is now concentrating to a greater degree
on providing common facilities and services that its members need
and for which they will pay. It has planned three projects in

particular. Italy has differed from other members of ENEA on a type of commonly owned nuclear fuel treatment plant to be developed. A second project, a nuclear ship to provide experience to guide countries when they come to build their own commercial nuclear ships, has been opposed by Britain which has been building its own atomic ship. A third project, a high powered research reactor, has been under study since November, 1962.

OEEC and European Cooperation

Parkinson's Law has shown that functions expand to occupy the numbers of those available to perform them. OEEC is an example of an organization that expanded its activities and its methods to deal with logically interrelated problems through intergovernmental consultation and with effective links between the member governments and the organization. Generally, cooperation and mutual help led to the formulation of joint general plans and the reduction of obstacles to the expansion of trade and productivity, and to the fostering of other European regional arrangements. But OEEC was also a valuable forum in which national officials discussed not only common trade and general European fiscal and material problems, but also national monetary policies, taxation systems, banking policies and foreign exchange practices.

OEEC helped re-establish internal financial stability by dealing with the problem of rising prices, especially in nonferrous metals, after the Korean War had created a shortage. It helped bring into existence the International Materials Conference which aided the stabilization of prices and regulation of trade. It examined the constant balance-of-payments deficits of the members —in 1950 Germany, in 1951 Britain and France, in 1956 France, and in 1957 Britain—and the almost equally perplexing problem of the persistent German surplus after the early 50s. It made recommendations on the kind of private and public investment that was likely to promote economic development as well as on an international payments equilibrium. It exerted influence on the broad economic policies of its members, and helped those countries such as Austria and Greece who were economically weakest. It was successful in obtaining the modification of governmental policies in the interests of greater economic cooperation as in 1952 when Britain and France withdrew their severe quota restrictions because of OEEC pressure, and between 1953 and 1955 when EPU was extended and later replaced by EMA in 1958 to facilitate convertibility. Above all it was important because governments came to take for granted the constant discussions and criticism of the affairs of their country by the other members, and even to profit by the interchange. The cooperative procedure has continued.

OEEC benefited from the caliber of the men associated with it. The national delegations were, in general, composed of highly competent individuals who had influence in their national capitals; the special representative of the United States was Averell Harriman who had resigned a cabinet position to take the post. The organization was fortunate to have as its Secretary-General until 1955, Robert Marjolin who established close relations with both the chairman of the Ministerial Council and with Sir Edmund Hall-Patch, the chairman of the Executive Committee, and who, in collaboration frequently presented an "OEEC point of view." The members of the permanent missions representing their governments came to experience what has now become increasingly familiar in the European organizations: they performed the dual role of defending the particular interests of their countries while at the same time developing some kind of corporate personality and trying to secure from their governments the greatest cooperation and compliance with the wishes of other members. Even without the presence of a supranational organ, this behavior made proceedings more than merely intergovernmental negotiation.

For all this, OEEC was not the strong organization that some had originally envisaged. The U.S. Economic Cooperation Act had anticipated the establishment of "a large domestic market with no international trade barriers" in Europe. The French pressed for a supranational body, and the United States for a strong organization with more important powers given to the Secretary-General. But Britain, supported by the Benelux countries, opposed an economic union, and would agree only to an organization for mutual aid. A number of attempts at closer economic union within OEEC failed, including coordinated recovery planning, investment coordination, and the rationalization of new investments. The Franco-Italian proposal for a European investment bank was rejected. In 1950 the idea of harmonizing all economic policies was not accepted on the grounds that the states must be free to deal with the problems of full employment, growth, and finance. Three of the main projects of economic integration—the Stikker, Pella, and Petsche plans proposing some kind of customs union—were studied in OEEC but not accepted. Throughout 1958 the Intergovernmental Committee was concerned with the attempts to set up a European Free Trade Area which absorbed much of the time of the OEEC. Much of the obstruction was due to the unwillingness of Britain to limit its interests to European economic matters since it thought in terms of global trade and of the General Agreement on Trade and Tariffs (GATT) which extended tariff reductions to all trading nations. A complex situation was thus created. The problem of trade liberalization—the removal of exchange controls and import quotas—was necessarily linked with that of the reduction of tariffs and other barriers to trade. But OEEC as an organization was not willing to grant tariff reductions without reciprocal advantages which GATT was already doing; at the same time Britain had vetoed the possibility of a customs union which would end all internal tariffs.

The Extension of Economic Cooperation

At the time the Marshall Plan was proposed, all of Europe caught influenza when the United States sneezed. By the end of the 1950s it was clear that Europe had not only recovered its economic health but was capable of acting as doctor to others. The return to convertibility in 1958, and the successful liberalization of trade demonstrated European economic strength. The institution of the EEC and EFTA caused some anxiety, especially on the part of the United States, that these larger trading blocs might become protectionist and exclusive. With the economies of the United States and Western Europe so interdependent, the European countries were as concerned as the United States about its persistent balance-of-payments deficit. Also, there was a growing realization of the urgent need to aid the underdeveloped nations, many of which had only recently come into existence, and about 35 of which had been former colonies of OEEC countries.

In 1960, largely on the initiative of the United States, ministers from 20 countries examined the need for a new organization to take account of changed conditions. A group of four experts, Randolph Burgess, Bernard Clappier, Paul Gore-Booth, and Xenophon Zolotas, was set up in Paris to report on the problems of reconstituting OEEC. It worked rapidly and in May, 1960, it recommended that OEEC be transformed into a remodeled economic organization, with Canada and the United States as full members. In December, 1960, the convention for an Organization for Economic Cooperation and Development (OECD) was drawn up and signed in Paris by the 18 members of OEEC, the United States, and Canada. Yugoslavia and Finland were to cooperate in certain activities of the Organization: Japan, a member of the existing Development Assistance Group, became a member of OECD in 1964.

The new organization—strictly speaking no longer a European or even an Atlantic organization with the admission of Japan in 1964—is a body with some 50 committees and 100 subcommittees and working parties, together with experts from the secretariat, concerned with a variety of studies of economic and social problems. As with its predecessor, OECD is directed by a governing council on which all members are represented. Decisions are reached by unanimity but a country is not bound if it abstains. A formal decision by the Council has the force of an international treaty and is binding on members, but the Council can also adopt a nonbinding recommendation for consideration by individual governments. Between ministerial meetings the Council is composed of permanent representatives, mostly high-level civil servants, who meet weekly in Paris and operate on instructions given them by their national capitals.

The secretary-general, who takes the chair at these weekly meetings, but not at the ministerial meeting, can put forward proposals and exercise his influence as he and his senior officials think desirable. After some opposition by the United States, an executive committee of ten heads of delegations was set up. The members are elected annually, but the five from the most important countries are always chosen. Meeting weekly under the chairmanship of M. Ockrent, the Belgian permanent representative, it prepares the agenda and work of the Council, discusses the same kind of problems as the Council, with a different nuance, isolates delicate policy issues, executes the decisions of the Council, and itself makes decisions on certain matters. Outside the formal mechanism there are other deliberative bodies such as the informal meetings of heads of delegations.

Such bodies as the EMA, the ENEA, and the European Conference of Ministers of Transport, continue relations with the new organization. Others, such as the European Productivity Agency and the Office for Technical and Scientific Personnel, have been dissolved.

OECD is a more outward looking organization than its predecessor and is more concerned with the free world as a whole. It has three basic objectives: the promotion of economic growth, employment and a rising standard of living with financial stability, the expansion of trade on a multilateral, nondiscriminatory basis, and the encouragement of the economic expansion of the underdeveloped countries through financial and technical assistance.

The most important single committee in the new organization, and the main body on economic matters, is the Economic Policy Committee, composed of the chief economic advisers and policy making officials of governments, aided by the directors of central banks; it meets three or four times a year. The chief difference from the old OEEC Committee lies in the impact of the entrance of the United States. Although a formal group, it provides a forum for a frank interchange by senior officials on existing or contemplated policies.

In 1961, OECD set an ambitious targent for economic growth of 50 percent in the gross national product of the 20 member countries taken together between 1960 and 1970; the joint target was itself recognition of the increasing interdependence of the separate economies. The EPC is concerned with this problem of growth and employment, and analyzes the factors leading to economic expansion. The Committee not only makes an annual appraisal of the economic situation and examines the financial policies of the members, but also assesses the probable international effects of their individual policies. Interrelated with this interest in economic growth is interest in the maintenance of equilibrium in international payments, the external balance-of-payment accounts of members, the maintenance of internal price stability, and the existence of an incomes policy for members which should take account of equity, efficiency, and incentive. A particular aspect of this concern has been the problem of farm incomes, which have lagged in relation to those in industry, the transfer of surplus farm workers to other sectors of the economy, and a general concern for healthier conditions for trade in agricultural products.

The Economic Policy Committee relies heavily on two working parties composed of high-level civil servants at about Under-Secretary of Treasury rank, and representatives of central banks. Working Party 2 contains specialists on economic growth dealing with problems of expansion. More successful and important is Working Party 3, restricted to those countries influencing international payments, which analyzes the effect of monetary, fiscal, and other policy measures on international payments, and consults on policy measures influencing the equilibrium of international payments. The frank discussion among high-level policy makers has been valuable partly because of the account taken of the criticism of others in national decision-making, and partly in leading to genuine understanding and common approaches without the need for formal decisions. The work of Working Party 3 has been helpful in preventing sharp runs on sterling or the dollar, in dealing with short-term flows of capital, in facilitating intercentral bank cooperation and in reducing the differences between interest rates. Working Party 3 includes the same nations as does the Group of 10, which is concerned with the problems of international finance, the adequacy of current monetary mechanism, and the threat of a shortage of liquidity; in this way OECD overlaps the work of the International Monetary Fund.

OECD does not possess broad trade functions nor does it have responsibility for cutting tariffs. But, through its Trade Committee, it fosters trade by the mutual confrontation of general trade policies and practices, the examination of specific trade problems of interest to members and their overseas territories, and consideration of any important trade problems. As in OEEC, there is an annual review of the economic development of each country, and consultation on business trend policies. The OEEC code of trade liberalization for commodities was not taken over since quotas had been largely ended and convertibility attained, but the code of liberalization of capital movements and current invisible operations remained. With the reduction of import duties and quantitative restrictions, the restrictive effects of existing administrative and technical regulations, imposed either for trade or health protection reasons, have become more apparent. OECD is concerning itself with the elimination of unnecessary technical and administrative regulations which may hamper trade, and with the simplification of procedures and standardization of rules from country to country, acting either at the request of exporters or on its own initiative. In addition, OECD undertakes systematic country-by-country surveys of the regulations in force in a particular field. It is, therefore, primarily interested in regulations made for reasons of security, public health, quality control, or prevention of fraud rather than in those directly related to trade. Its interest in harmonizing health regulations overlaps with that of the EEC. A Committee of Experts on Restrictive Business Practices carries on the work of the old OEEC Group of Experts in studying the problems raised by restrictive practices and recommending policies and procedures for removing their harmful effects. Its most impressive and weighty achievement is a large, four-volume *Guide to Legislation on Restrictive Business Practices.*

Agriculture, as always, presents special problems. While trade in general has become freer and balance-of-payments difficulties have been reduced, state intervention in trade in agricultural products has often been maintained as the consequence of national policies concerned with farm prices and income-support programs. Moreover, the gap between agricultural income and the rest of the economy has widened in a period of excess supply of agricultural products. The role of OECD in these circumstances has been to persuade nations to adapt their agriculture by structural adjustments and greater efficiency, to promote the improvement of trade in agricultural products, and to encourage coordinated programs of food aid as a contribution to economic development.

Aid to Underdeveloped Countries

The third and newest function of OECD is that of assistance to the underdeveloped countries to ensure their growth and development. In 1960 the Development Assistance Committee, was set up; its members are: Belgium, Canada, France, Germany, Italy, Japan, Denmark, the Netherlands, Norway, Portugal, Great Britain, the United States, and the EEC Commission, often assisted by representatives of the International Bank for Reconstruction and Development (IBRD), the International Monetary Fund (IMF), the Inter-American Development Bank (IADB), and the Organization of American States (OAS). Its task is to make national resources available to help the underdeveloped countries, to widen the geographical area of the recipients, to stimulate the flow of long-term capital, and to coordinate the efforts of the different countries. The DAC has no funds of its own, but provides a meeting place for the major industrialized and capital-exporting countries to discuss their aid efforts, which are reviewed and assessed each year. The DAC formed coordinating teams to discuss problems relating to the development plans of a country in which several members are interested. Most of these teams meet in Paris, although some meet elsewhere as, for instance, the East African group which meets in London. The Committee has a special working party which examines over-all technical assistance policies of its members. A technical cooperation committee helps supply experts, training facilities, organizes conferences, and sets up various pilot schemes for the benefit of those areas of member countries in the process of development. A development center, set up in 1962, trains people from the developing areas and those from the industrialized countries working with them, conducts research on development problems and provides information and documentation. But the main reliance of the DAC is not on a large secretariat or a multitude of working groups to deal with problems of coordinating aid, but on the information and judgment of members helped by periodic reviews and consultations between them. The DAC often meets at a high official level and tailors its composition to the subject discussed.

Aid has been given to the underdeveloped countries in a number of forms: financial, technical assistance, and food.

Financial aid is of four main kinds: bilateral public grants in cash or kind, bilateral public loans, private lending, and contributions to multilateral agencies. Public grants are given to cover the costs of capital facilities and the services of officials. Public loans are for public development projects such as transport, power, or water resources, or for commercial undertakings or export credits. Some objections have been raised by the recipients to the fact that part of these loans have been "tied" to the goods of the donor countries.

In 1962 the amount of public grants and loans from DAC member countries to less developed countries and multilateral agencies was $6 billion, of which the United States supplied $3,606 million, and France the second largest amount with $996 million. Surprisingly enough Portugal with 2.44 percent ranked highest in terms of a percentage of its gross national product, compared with 2.34 percent for France and .86 percent for the United States. Private loans have largely been made for investment in manufacturing or mining industries or have been a reinvestment of the money earned in those countries. In 1962 they amounted to $2,443 million. The loans have been given either directly through individual countries or indirectly through the International Bank for Reconstruction and Development, and are affected not only by the willingness of the lenders, but also by official regulations on the export of capital, tax regulations, and the access of foreigners to capital markets. The DAC countries have doubled their public aid since 1956, but private investment has remained roughly constant at $2.5 billion. But the trebling of the volume of loans has placed a growing burden on the underdeveloped countries, who have sometimes complained about the hard financial terms of aid, and who have also been arguing for a greater increase in trade and outlets for their exports.

Technical assistance and educational aid have been largely confined to the Mediterranean states and to Iceland. The most important programs have been those for Regional Development Aid in Sardinia, Epirus, Turkey, and Portugal. In these a special area is studied and analyzed by economic specialists of the OECD, who draw up proposed action programs. Since OECD is also concerned with manpower problems, special training centers have been set up, scholarship programs train graduate students in planning and related matters, and a third program trains people in public administration and marketing. In most of the Mediterranean countries, national research teams composed of economists, sociologists, statisticians, and others have been established with OECD financial and expert assistance.

Several countries, but predominantly the United States, have made food available to the developing nations either free or on very favorable terms. The total value of food aid currently represents about a quarter of the total of public aid being given to underdeveloped countries. But coordination of effort is difficult, since programs of food aid have generally been on a bilateral basis.

The DAC has carried out the first systematic reviews at an international level of the aid programs of its members. It has stressed the need for close coordination of assistance efforts because of the great variety of sources of financing and aid, and because of the greater number of developing countries in which several donors are simultaneously providing such aid.

The DAC has stressed that some kind of coordination is necessary, not only in general aid programs, but also in individual country programs. It has tried to obtain some harmonization of aid and policies through its Annual Aid Review, and by dealing with various issues common to a number of donor countries. In addition, the DAC has begun organizing meetings concerned with "regional" problems for countries in Latin America and the Far East, bringing together experts on the various bilateral programs in those countries. But coordination of aid remains at only a formative stage, and the DAC is still far from being a policy making body determining the amounts and conditions of aid.

Since 1955 exports from the less developed areas have been expanding at only half the rate of total world trade; there has also been a significant deterioration in terms of trade against them. Parallel with this is a more rapid growth in trade among the Western nations than in imports from the primary producers. This trend has been reinforced by two factors. One is that the industries currently expanding, such as chemicals and durable consumer goods, have a lower proportion of imported materials than trades such as textiles and clothing, which are growing more slowly. The other is the increase in the use of synthetic substitute products, and the growing European self-sufficiency in meat and cereals. The problem now facing the West is not only to increase the flow of capital, but also to provide increased export opportunities for the underdeveloped areas.

This problem has become even more serious because of the widening income gap between the industrialized and the underdeveloped countries. In 1962 the per capita Gross National Product for the 470 million people of the more-developed OECD countries averaged about $1900 as against $130 per capita for the 104 billion inhabitants of the noncommunist less-developed world. In addition, average increase in per capita incomes for the industrialized countries is about $60 a year, while it is only $3 a year for the underdeveloped. Moreover, since about half the growth in the real product of the underdeveloped countries was offset by increases in population, the projected increase of about 300 million population in these areas between 1962 and 1970 will exacerbate the situation.

The Diverse Interests of OECD

The interdependence of economies and the outward-looking attitude of OECD explain the large variety and scope of activities with which it concerns itself: the removal of obstacles to trade such as national administrative regulations, restrictive commercial practices, the movement of labor and capital, hot money and capital exports, double taxation, the coordination of energy, inflation, balance-of-payments deficits, increased scientific education, and mundane, undramatic activities such as research on scraping barnacles off the hulls of ships and setting international standards for classifying animal carcasses.

Transport had been one of the many subjects in which the OEEC countries were interested, and in 1953 the European Conference of Ministers of Transport was created. The Ministers of Transport of the now 18 ECMT countries—the European members of OECD plus Yugoslavia and minus Iceland—meet twice a year in Paris at OECD headquarters, where its secretariat is attached to that of OECD, or in a national capital. The major concerns of the Conference are the decline in rail transport, the increase in road transport, the improvement of European transport links, road safety, and the framing of a European highway code, the "Eurofima" scheme for financing modern railway equipment, the development of the European oil pipeline network, and the standardization of waterways and barges.

Currently the OECD has special interest in scientific education, research, and training as an instrument of economic activity, leading to better machinery, methods, and use of manpower, and thus to increased economic growth. Higher rates of economic growth need an increase in qualified manpower and development of skills, and is dependent on research, the new technologies, education, and training. In 1958 a working party suggested collecting information and plans to help increase the number and quality of scientists and engineers trained in member countries. The Governing Committee for Scientific and Technical Personnel has been compiling such information through a series of international surveys on the demand and supply of personnel. The Committee has also tried to stimulate new academic thinking on the contribution of education to the development of the economic system, and has encouraged members to establish policies for educational expansion.

In recent years the growth in international scientific research, has been rapid, and a large number of international scientific organizations have been set up. Some, like the European Center for Nuclear Research (CERN) and the two space organizations, the European Space Research Organization (ESRO) and the European Launching Development Organization (ELDO), are intergovernmental organizations with a specific purpose. Some, like the three OECD projects, are scientific undertakings maintaining a useful contact with the parent body for financial and legal reasons. In others, like the functional collaboration promoted by OECD for individual topics of technological research, groups of existing laboratories formulate a common program, each being responsible for a particular aspect.

In October, 1963, the Ministers of Science of the OECD countries, recognizing the growing importance of science and technology in the economic and social development of their countries, met to study national and international science policies. The ministers decided to set up a science committee of high level scientific officials to help rationalize scientific research on an international scale, to foster the exchange of information in certain fields, and to examine the relationship between research and productivity.

Some of the multifarious activities of OECD inevitably overlap with, or duplicate, those performed by other organizations, as in the widespread interest in scientific research. Awareness of this possible waste of effort led, in 1964, to an agreement between OECD and UNESCO by which the two organizations will determine those sectors of their activities of common interest and exchange information and documents.

Though the OECD is not itself an operational organ, some of

its activities, such as the Development Center, the scientific program, the European Monetary Agreement (EMA), and statistics department are geared to the rendition of services, and many OECD committees carry out important operational functions in the fields of manpower, agriculture, and financial and technical cooperation with a view to assisting member countries.

Cooperation and Confrontation

From the point of view of international cooperation, the most important aspect of both OECD and OEEC has been its method of procedure by "confrontation." To determine the distribution of Marshall aid in 1948, each country submitted to the OEEC an economic program setting out its economic aims, the resources available, and the external aid thought necessary to fill the gap. Each national program was fully and critically examined, in the different committees of the organization by representatives from all other countries. After the Marshall aid had been ended, the periodic confrontation continued for the discussion of balance-of-payments problems, the persistent dollar shortage and later surplus, and the economic recessions of 1953 and 1958.

Within OECD, confrontation has taken place on a number of subjects. The most important occasion is the annual review of each country's general economic situation and problems in the Economic and Development Review Committee, on which all 21 countries sit. Each country submits a memorandum on its economic situation and aims, which is examined by economists of the OECD secretariat, who prepare a report. Representatives of two examining countries, aided by the secretariat, put questions to the country being examined. Senior civil servants from the country answer questions at the meeting of the full committee which discusses the whole matter. The draft report of the secretariat is then reviewed, and a final version approved and published, containing both factual analysis and recommendations for economic policy. The committee, on the proposal of its members or the secretariat, may also undertake ad hoc surveys either of a particular country or of special economic problems. It may then report to the Council on the need for concerted action by the Organization. For economic matters, there is also confrontation, two or three times a year, in the Economic Policy Committee, which keeps current international economic trends under review.

A similar procedure exists for other subjects, such as science and manpower. OECD conducts reviews of national policies for science and education to assess their bearing on economic growth. A small group of experts visits the country under review for discussions with government officials, members of the academic and scientific communities, representatives of industry, and other institutions. The report of the group becomes the basis for a "confrontation" meeting at OECD headquarters in Paris in which the examining team, a special delegation from the country under review, and delegates from each of the other countries participate. This particular confrontation is not so much a cross-examination as a discussion for the mutual benefit of all participants. As a result of the Country Review Program of the Committee for Scientific and Technical Personnel, pilot teams of scientists and economists have been operating to strengthen education in those areas of the Mediterranean having special problems of scientific development.

Government manpower policies and practices have also been subjected to systematic and comprehensive country-by-country examination. Experts in the field of manpower policy visit the country under examination and draw up a report on their study of the situation, which serves as a basis for discussion in the OECD Committee for Manpower and Social Affairs. At the same time the government of the country provides a background report. After discussion in the Committee, a third report is drawn up cooperatively by the Secretariat, experts and officials of the country concerned, and is published. The intended object of these studies is both to permit a country to examine and improve its own practices, and for these practices and policies to serve as an example or warning to other nations.

Confrontation is not coordination, and no country is bound to apply recommendations or decisions with which it disagrees. National sovereignty has not been curtailed by this procedure. But confrontation not only allows countries to be aware of the policies of others, but also provides for mutual influence as a result of exhaustive and friendly interchange. It is said of Charlie Murphy, the artful boss of Tammany Hall, that having chosen a candidate for Mayor of New York City, he would say to his associates, "Now shove him down my throat." It has not been unknown for national governments to make use of OECD opinions in similar fashion and thus be "forced" to implement economic policies which they might otherwise have been reluctant to do for fear of internal criticism.

Very few decisions are made by OECD itself. The value of the organization is less to make formal decisions than to be a forum for key officials to meet together on fiscal, economic, and development policies, and to obtain the assistance of experts and those international nongovernmental organizations, such as the Trade Union Advisory Committee, which are granted special consultative status. The major advance over normal intergovernmental organizations is that in OECD it is the policy-making officials who are brought into touch with each other, reach understandings, and develop a working camaraderie. Sometimes overt cooperation has resulted from the work of OECD, as with most of the bilateral conventions on double taxation concluded since 1958, which have followed the articles drafted by the fiscal committee of OECD, the measures taken by Germany to stop inflation, the French stabilization program, and the agreement among 16 nations in December, 1964, to end a dispute over shipping by supplying information in bulk form through OECD. But in general it is difficult to measure the impact of OECD discussions on national decisions, or even the influence of the meetings on the individual representatives. Yet it is not coincidental that, after a series of discussions on the level of money incomes, a number of countries have set up mechanisms for the examination of wage claims, and have become interested in the evolution of some form of national incomes policy. It is also clear that in particular cases such as the French decision to increase interest rates in December, 1963, some account was taken of the views of other OECD members, even if it did not alter the decision.

CHAPTER FOUR

The Defense of the West: The North Atlantic Treaty Organization

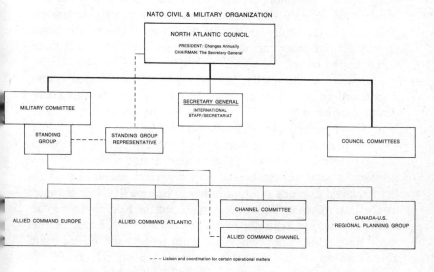

NATO CIVIL & MILITARY ORGANIZATION

SOURCE: *NATO Handbook*, Chart 1, p. 89. Reprinted by permission.

"In POLITICS," said Tocqueville, "a community of hatred is almost always the foundation of friendships." If the aphorism is not universally true, the existence of the North Atlantic Treaty Organization is a good example of it. The real unacknowledged creator of NATO was Joseph Stalin, for its essential *raison d'etre* was, and remains, common protection as a deterrent against the threat of Soviet expansion and control in Europe. Fear of Soviet power is the tie that binds the now 15 nations who could be brought into a military alliance. In April, 1949, the North Atlantic Treaty was signed in Washington by Belgium, Canada, Denmark, France, Iceland, Italy, Luxembourg, the Netherlands, Norway, Portugal, the United Kingdom, and the United States. In February, 1952, Greece and Turkey were admitted, and in May, 1955, Germany joined. The alliance thus includes non-European and non-Christian Turkey, while excluding the three neutral members of the Council of Europe, Sweden, Austria and Switzerland. It includes nondemocratic Portugal while excluding nondemocratic Spain. It includes Iceland which has no armed forces but which until recently had several communists in its government. It is not geographically contiguous, for three of the members are separated from other members by nonmember states, and three others by the ocean.

The western allies today are strong, and the United States disposes of an enormous armoury. In 1964 it had 760 intercontinental missiles as compared with 180 for the Soviet Union. The U.S. Air Force had 540 jet bombers constantly on the alert, half its force of over 1,000 bombers against 120 Soviet heavy bombers and 150 medium bombers. The United States had 192 Polaris missiles in submarines. Behind this powerful shield the West has remained in peace and no frontier in Europe has been changed in the last 16 years. Yet contentious issues in Europe divide the allies. Conflicting attitudes to foreign affairs in the rest of the world have resulted not only in a certain tension and mistrust but also in an apprehension that states may become reluctantly involved in hostilities against their will. Unavoidable clashes have occured between those states still possessing some colonial interests and the United States, consistently taking an anticolonialist position. The allies disagree about the nature and significance of the alliance itself, and, since the Sino-Soviet dispute, about the imminence of danger from the Soviet Union. Above all they have differed on the problem of nuclear weapons and on the paradox of a prosperous and independent Western Europe dependent on the deterrent power of the United States. The only approximate historical precedent to NATO was the coalition of the Greek states against Persia 2,500 years ago. NATO members may remember with anxiety that this ancient alliance became ineffective after its initial period of success.

The North Atlantic Treaty signed in 1949 is an international military agreement from which states can withdraw after 1969 on a year's notice. But NATO is more than a simple alliance of the classical type. It is also a complex method of Atlantic defense, a mechanism of consultation, and a means of reaching political and strategic decisions. As an alliance it provides a joint political commitment by which members will regard an attack on one as an attack on all. This essentially implies a United States commitment to defend Europe and constituted a historic end to American peacetime isolationism. Under the impact of the Korean War in 1950, the alliance developed into a more effective and integrated defense of the North Atlantic area through collective military planning and decision-making, integrated military commands and international military institutions, and political and economic consultation of an unprecedented nature in peacetime. The intrinsic interconnection of military, political and economic factors led NATO even further. Peace, as Lord Ismay, the first Secretary-General of NATO argued, is not merely the absence of war: its maintenance requires, and NATO has sought to establish, continuous cooperation by governments in the economic, social and cultural as well as the military fields.

The Civilian Organs

The North Atlantic Treaty is a remarkably brief, clear document of fourteen articles. Institutionally, it confined itself to establishing a council on which each party would be represented, and which would set up subsidiary bodies as it thought necessary. Only a defense committee was mentioned by name.

In September, 1949, the NATO Council constituted itself in Washington, and decided that normally it would be composed of foreign ministers meeting regularly once a year and more frequently if requested. It created a defense committee, composed of the defense ministers, to coordinate defense plans, a military committee, a standing group, and regional planning groups. At the end of 1949 organizations were set up to deal with problems of production and the economic and financial aspects of defense. It was soon apparent that the Council, meeting infrequently, could not effectively control and supervise the civil and military agencies of the Alliance. In May, 1950, the Council Deputies, with an American chairman, was established in London as a permanent group. In May, 1951, the structure of NATO was reorganized and the defense committee abolished. The Council became the sole ministerial body of NATO, which heads of government as well as ministers of different kinds might attend; it thus became a council of governments rather than of ministers.

In 1951 the Council set up a Temporary Council Committee of 12 to reconcile the requirements of collective security and military planning with the political and economic capabilities of the states, troubled by rising prices, unsatisfactory balance-of-payment situations, and raw material problems. The Committee delegated its detailed work to an executive board, the "Three Wise Men," Averell Harriman, Jean Monnet, and Sir Edwin Plowden. The Committee's report was the first comprehensive review of the military capacity of the allies. It suggested not only the maximum level of forces and measures for future increase, but also economic principles such as equitable sharing of the financial burden, and procedures such as the annual review as the basis of a sound alliance.

As a result of the recommendations of the committee, the civilian agencies were again reorganized in 1952. The Council remained as a council of governments, represented by ministers of foreign affairs, defense, or finance. But the deputies were replaced by the permanent representatives in charge of national delegations, who meet in Paris. The chair of the Permanent Council was to be taken by the Secretary-General, head of the International Staff and Secretariat also located in Paris.

At the ministerial level the Council meets twice or three times a year. Only once in 1957 have heads of governments attended the Council: this was the result of anxiety at the Russian demonstration of its nuclear weapons. The permanent representatives meet once or twice a week, and have held over 700 sessions. The chairman of the Council is now the Secretary-General. At both levels decisions are made by unanimity, and discussion continues until such unanimity is reached. But the Council is clearly a group of ambassadors from sovereign states, not a supranational body.

The Council is responsible for making political decisions, for the coordination of defense and logistics, and for the provision of manpower and equipment. But some have argued that the Council has little authority over military planning in the Standing Group or at Supreme Headquarters Allied Powers Europe (SHAPE). Underlying this criticism is the premise that the Pentagon in Washington has determined the military strategy of NATO, sometimes without consulting the Council in Paris. At times the military infrastructure programs of NATO have been decided by the Standing Group in isolation from any political discussion in the Permanent Council. The critics conclude that there is a need to strengthen the Council by giving cabinet status to the permanent representatives who are generally diplomats, and that the Council must become a body responsible for unified strategic planning similar to the Combined Chiefs of Staff in World War II.

Many, including former Secretary-General Dirk Stikker, have suggested that the interrelation between the civil and military sides of NATO is unsatisfactory. The physical factor of having the main responsibility for civil affairs in Paris and the main responsibility for military affairs in Washington is not only an administrative inconvenience but also emphasizes United States logistical strength. The smaller nations, at present having little impact on the process of strategic planning, hold that a genuine NATO policy can only exist if there is an integrated NATO civil and military planning staff in Paris to settle the interrelated questions of strategy, force requirements and the resources available to meet them. This would mean a NATO Chief of Staff—a senior senior military officer on the staff of the Secretary-General who at present lacks independent military advice and depends on Supreme Allied Commander in Europe (SACEUR)—the moving of the Standing Group to Paris, and in the long run a NATO defense ministry.

Besides 24 permanent intergovernmental committees which

report to the council and a large number of ad hoc committees or study groups, there are a number of other nonmilitary organizations such as the Central Europe Operating Agency created in 1957 to operate the network of pipelines, the NATO Maintenance Supply Services Agency created in 1958 to provide a common system for the supply of spare parts for the allied forces, and the Hawk Agency set up in 1959 to coordinate the European production of the Hawk engine in the five countries taking part in its production.

The Secretary-General is a partly political and partly administrative official. As administrator he is in charge of the 1400 civilian employees and is responsible for the work of the twelve subsidiary agencies, and the 185 committees and subcommittees which meet constantly at biweekly intervals. The Council committees and working groups are normally composed of members of the permanent delegations to NATO and members of the Secretariat who prepare papers and follow up action. The Secretary-General takes the chair at all Council meetings, has the right to put items on the agenda, and has the duty to see that the decisions of the Council are carried out.

But the Secretary-General is or can be a political creature. He has direct access to all NATO institutions and to all member governments. He prepares an annual report analyzing the chief political problems of the alliance, in which he assesses the extent of governmental consultation and cooperation. He can bring intra-NATO disputes to the attention of the Council. In disputes he can act as mediator, and set up machinery to investigate, as in the British-Iceland fisheries quarrel, or help formulate a compromise as in the Cyprus dispute.

The three men who have held the position of Secretary-General —Lord Ismay, 1952–1957, Paul-Henri Spaak, 1957–1961, and Dirk Stikker, 1961–1964—have held differing conceptions and emphasized different aspects of their roles. On August 1, 1964, Manlio Brosio, former Italian Ambassador in Paris, replaced Stikker. Discreet and administratively competent, heroically patient, Ismay was widely regarded as a brilliant success. The ebullient politician Spaak, not unexpectedly, resigned out of frustration. Stikker seems to have had less of the skill of Ismay and less of the vigor of Spaak, but was interested in the efficiency of the Secretariat. As a corollary to the strengthening of the Council, it has been suggested that the office of the chairman of the Council be separated from that of the Secretary-General, and that the former be a distinguished political figure while the latter be a civil servant with a strong secretariat. Whether this is desirable or not, it is doubtful that the present Secretariat is large or strong enough for evaluating long-range trends or political and economic problems. Many have urged that the Secretary-General have more power, and that he be better informed both militarily and politically, especially on the bilateral accords between NATO governments that might affect Western defense.

The Military Organization

The NATO military organization is headed by the Military Committee, its permanent representatives, the Standing Group, and the allied commanders. The Military Committee is the senior military authority in the organization. Composed of the chiefs of staff of each country plus a civilian from Iceland which has no forces, it meets about twice a year normally in Washington to make recommendations to and guide the work of subordinate organizations. Between these infrequent meetings the Committee has permanent military representatives meeting in Washington under a chairman who may hold no other position during his term of office.

The Standing Group—in a sense a transposition of the combined chiefs of staff of World War II—is composed of the permanent military representatives of the United States, Britain, and France, and meets in Washington, assisted by a staff from the three countries. It is responsible for a number of specialized military agencies such as the NATO Defense College in Paris, the Military Agency for Standardization in London, and the European Military Communications Coordination Committee. In theory the Standing Group is the executive agent of the Military Committee and was intended to be an important organ for framing military directions for the NATO Supreme Commanders, planning logistic support, and connecting political and strategic policy, especially since it could avoid the NATO rule of unanimity. But three factors seem to have reduced its significance. The Standing Group has referred more and more questions back to the Military Committee. The Standing Group cannot control the major striking forces of the allies, the Strategic Air Command and British Bomber Command. And it has not been able to dominate the group of highly gifted supreme commanders whose personal qualities and political influence have tended to obscure the activity of the Standing Group. Symptomatic of its decline in importance is the fact that the U.S. Chief of Staff generally does not attend its meetings. In the last year another problem which had arisen from the demand of Germany for inclusion either in the Standing Group itself or in its staff was met by appointing a German general as chief of staff of strategic planning.

In his last speech as Secretary-General in June, 1964, Mr. Stikker suggested that a representative of the Secretary-General should attend all meetings of the Standing Group in Washington, and complained that the Group could draw up plans which neither the Secretary-General nor NATO civilian officials could see until they were in final form.

The Standing Group is represented on the Council in Paris by an officer whose function is to ensure close cooperation between the NATO civilian and military authorities. But in practice SACEUR deals directly with defense ministers, governments, and national delegations, and Supreme Allied Commander in the Atlantic (SACLANT) has the right of direct access to the national chiefs of staff, and if necessary to the governments themselves.

In December, 1950, the Council decided to set up an integrated force in Europe under the supreme command of an American officer, and asked specifically that General Eisenhower be chosen. Early in 1951 he established headquarters outside Paris with an international staff drawn from the nations contributing to the force. In 1952 two new commands were added. The Atlantic Command was to develop defense plans for the Atlantic ocean and to organize training exercises in it. The Channel Command was to prepare plans for the control and defense of the English Channel area under a Channel Committee composed of the naval chiefs of staff of Belgium, France, the Netherlands and Britain. Besides these three major commands there is the Canada-United States Regional Planning Group.

The present command structure has grown up piecemeal since 1951 and consequently has presented some problems. This is true in the Northern European Command where a unified command for the Baltic approaches was lacking for some time since Denmark was unwilling to accept a German general as the commander in Schleswig-Holstein, and Germany was not prepared to accept a Dane. In the Mediterranean there is a division of function between the two naval commands, Allied Forces in South Europe (AFSOUTH) in Naples under United States command, and the British command based on Malta, thus allowing fleets under different commands to operate in the same area. The command problem has become even more complicated by the French decision in 1959 to withdraw her fleet from the NATO command, and by her decision in 1964 to withdraw her top ranking officials from the NATO naval commands.

At the head of the European command is the leading military figure in NATO, the Supreme Allied Commander in Europe, SACEUR. The post of SACEUR was established in 1950 to train national units assigned to his command and to organize them into an effective integrated defense force. In peacetime SACEUR commands only those units directly assigned to NATO: the U.S. 7th Army, the French 1st Army, the British Army of the Rhine, the 12 German divisions, and units of 9 other forces; in war, however, he would control all operations in the area. But the assigned forces cannot be moved or deployed without agreement of the states, and normally this is difficult to obtain. Under these conditions it is debatable that SACEUR "commands" the forces. The lack of supranational authority in NATO means that it cannot prevent troop withdrawals or even ensure consultation before withdrawal. The Council has not modified the principle of voluntary assignment of forces nor been willing to lay down minimum levels of force which could not be reduced without majority approval. The wildly unrealistic and ambitious goal of raising 96 divisions by 1954 was quickly abandoned because of the uncooperative attitude of the members. A similar difficulty exists in the area of logistics since the states have not transferred sufficient control over materials.

SACEUR has been the outstanding military personality in NATO partly because he has always been a distinguished United States general: Eisenhower was followed by Matthew Ridgway, Alfred Gruenther, Lauris Norstad, and Lyman Lemnitzer. But also his function of formulating strategic plans and submitting proposals to the Standing Group, his contact with allied General Staffs and with the defense ministers of the allies means he is in close touch with the policy and the personnel of the states who, except Iceland, have all established liaison officers known as National Military Representatives at his headquarters, Supreme Headquarters, Allied Powers Europe (SHAPE). SACEUR has become the military adviser and the real center of NATO military planning. However, SACEUR's position is an ambivalent one. He is theoretically under the control of the NATO Council for the use of conventional forces, but he is also an American officer who would take orders only from the U.S. President for the use of nuclear weapons. Occasionally this double responsibility to NATO and to the United States has led to a conflict of loyalties as in 1962 when General Norstad was obliged to resign because of his differences with the U.S. Administration over the problem of stationing medium range ballistic missiles in Europe.

The United States influence in NATO is also shown by the fact that the Supreme Allied Commander in the Atlantic (SACLANT) has always been an American Admiral, the Commander in Chief of the U.S. Navy: Admirals Lynde McCormick, Jerauld Wright, Robert Dennison, and Page Smith. The Command is situated at Norfolk, Virginia. Although SACLANT has no forces permanently attached to his command in peacetime, all eight NATO nations with deep-sea naval forces temporarily assign their forces to him and engage in training programs under his direction. Although these forces are largely naval, he also commands certain ground forces and land based air forces. In spite of criticism, the states and therefore the Council have refused to agree to the assignment of naval forces in peacetime to the allied naval commands.

The Parliamentary Conference

There is no parliamentary control or supervision over the working of NATO provided for in the Treaty. In 1955 parliamentarians from the allied countries established the Parliamentarians Conference by ad hoc agreement. It is not a formal part of the NATO organization, all parts of which have been set up by intergovernmental agreements or treaties. Since 1955 the NATO Parliamentarians Conference has met in Paris once a year for a few days. Each national legislature decides the size of its delegation, but each nation is given a number of votes. Out of a total of 175, the United States has 36 and Great Britain, France, Germany, and Italy have 18 each. The Conference has set up a number of committees, of which the political, military, and economic committees are the most significant.

The Conference is addressed by military and civilian leaders of NATO but there is little real debate in its proceedings. The meeting in November, 1963, took 20 minutes to adopt 22 recommendations, unanimously, with one exception. The Conference has provided a convenient setting for European parliamentarians to meet their North American colleagues and introduced yet another perspective into European discussions. But the Conference is well aware of its own limitations: its responsibilities are ambiguous, it does not receive an annual report, its arrangements for receiving information from NATO are unsatisfactory and it does not have the right to question ministers or the NATO Secretariat. Some of its recommendations have been successful: a Science Adviser to the Secretary-General of NATO has been appointed, an Atlantic Congress held in 1959 which proposed far-reaching political innovations including an Atlantic Community within the next decade, and an Atlantic Institute established in Paris.

In 1962 the Conference explored the possibility of a common parliamentary body for all Atlantic institutions. Some members urged the transformation of the Conference into a strong Atlantic Assembly with access to information it needed, and able to advise the executive bodies of the Atlantic organizations. By the following year these hopes were disillusioned. It found that a genuine Atlantic parliament with real powers could only exist if NATO were transformed into more than an intergovernmental organization, and that it was still inopportune for the existing European assemblies to be merged. More modest proposals were made to maintain an effective link between NATO and the national parliaments, and between the executive organs of NATO and the parliamentarians. But the main recommendations, that the Conference should meet twice a year in future, once in the United States, that there could be more continuity in the composition of the national delegations, and that a Rapporteur General be appointed to follow the work of all NATO bodies and to report to the Conference, were a sad disappointment for those who had aimed much higher. The hopes of the Conference to be an important allied forum for discussion not only of defense, but also of international political and economic problems in general, and a means of keeping public opinion in the Atlantic area informed, have not yet materialized.

Military Problems of the Alliance

The core of the Alliance is the collective security arrangement of mutual aid, and the aim is to check Russian expansion in Europe. The strategy adopted by NATO to achieve this objective and its disposition of forces has varied with the growth of Soviet nuclear strength, the temperature of relations with the Soviet Union, the rapidly changing weaponry, the improving European economic position, and political events. But the brutal fact that NATO consists of one giant and fourteen others with varying degrees of power means that inevitably the United States has dominated the adoption of strategic policies. Since the economic revival of Europe, the institution of the Common Market in 1958, and, above all, the return of General de Gaulle to power in France in 1958, this U.S. dominance has been increasingly resented by the European nations who possess a feeling of strength and self-confidence lacking in 1949.

At first the United States supplied massive aid to Europe while keeping its own military power as a deterrent to Soviet aggression. After the outbreak of the Korean War in 1950 and the first Soviet nuclear experiments, the United States committed itself to the defense of Europe, stationing five divisions and strategic air bases on European soil and increasing its military assistance. The adoption of a "forward strategy"—resistance to aggression as far east as possible—brought the need for German participation just five years after the Nazi defeat. Since then the changing NATO strategy has been characterized by picturesque metaphors. After the policy of "containment" of Russia came the dubious concept of "massive retaliation" against any aggression, formulated by John Foster Dulles as Secretary of State. When the events of 1956 showed the unreality of this concept, a strategy was adopted in which military and political flexibility might allow a response other than massive retaliation. This "trip-wire" or "sword and shield" theory was predicated on the existence of a forward line of thirty divisions supplied with conventional arms and tactical nuclear weapons which could hold up an attack until the nuclear sword, primarily the U.S. Strategic Air Command, could be used if the conventional retaliation were not sufficient. The 1957 Russian Sputnik accelerated NATO activity, and the strategy changed to one of "intermediate" response. Now that the Soviet Union has a retaliatory capacity for inflicting unacceptable damage on the United States, the latest strategy is to regard the NATO forces as a "fire-break" capable of defeating a Russian attack at every level of force. The United States has been emphasizing the need for stronger European conventional forces, partly to allow flexibility of response, but also to prevent the development of other independent nuclear deterrents and to increase the likelihood of reaching agreements with the Russians such as the ban on atmospheric testing. In this way the approximate equilibrium between East and West in both the conventional and nuclear fields can be maintained, and the economic and political difficulties of producing an antiballistic missile which might threaten to upset the strategic balance can be avoided.

As a result of divergence of outlook on the strategy and needs of the Alliance, a number of problems have arisen. The most important have been the size of conventional forces, nuclear control, the increasingly independent attitude of France, and the sharing of the defense burden.

If the allies spoke of the need for a balanced international collective force, their military goals were overly ambitious. The 1951 Council decided to create a NATO ground force of 43 divisions by 1954; the 1952 Council increased this to 96 divisions. The economic problems involved in raising such a force, together with the beginning of a thaw in East-West relations, led to a revision of the target more acceptable to the states. By 1957 NATO had agreed on a minimum of 30 divisions on condition that they could rely on tactical support by nuclear means. Even this more limited obligation has not been met and only 25 divisions have been raised. In 1964 France was contributing two undermanned divisions totaling 30,000 instead of 80,000 men. Britain was over 5,000 short of its commitment of 55,000. Germany which has raised 11 divisions and has half the first-line strength in Central Europe, has an army made up to a large degree of young conscripts. In men, as in money, the United States is carrying the largest burden with 400,000 men. Military integration involves both interdependence and coordinated specialization of national forces, but the allies have been unwilling to surrender control of their forces or make economic sacrifices to this end.

The refusal of the allies to bring their conventional forces up to the requisite strength has reinforced their dependence on the deterrent power of NATO, the Strategic Air Command, the intercontinental ballistic missiles and the Polaris submarine force, all exclusively controlled by the United States. But the greatly increased nuclear power of the Soviet Union has led some NATO members, particularly France, to question the probability of an automatic response with its deterrent force if the United States itself were not directly attacked. Moreover, there has been dissatisfaction with the United States insistence on retaining the control of the intermediate range ballistic missiles based on the territory of the allies with whom it has made bilateral agreements; only in the case of Britain did the United States agree to make a joint decision on the use of missiles.

The Problem of Nuclear Control

NATO has become increasingly divided by sharp disputes over the control of nuclear weapons. Essentially, variants of six alternatives to the present position have been suggested: greater control by the Europeans over the U.S. deterrent force, a European deterrent, a NATO deterrent, a Franco-British force, independent deterrents, and a multinational and multilateral force.

The demand by the allies that they be more closely associated with the U.S. nuclear research and development, strategy and targeting, was met in 1963 in a number of ways. NATO officers from eight countries participate in the liaison group attached to the Joint Strategic Target Planning Staff at the U.S. Strategic Air Command headquarters in Omaha. Throughout the different levels of command in Europe, there are over 1000 allied officers participating in nuclear planning and other activities. Most NATO countries take part in tactical target planning since the United States has supplied them with tactical nuclear weapons such as the Honest John and Corporal missiles and 8-inch howitzers in addition to the nuclear bombs. However, the warheads for the missiles and the bombs still remain under United States control. In 1963 a nuclear data information team representing the Joint Chiefs of Staff toured European capitals briefing civilian and military officials of NATO nations. SACEUR was given a deputy for nuclear affairs, Belgian General van Rolleghem, who would be a senior staff officer acting as a focal point for all nuclear activities in the SHAPE staff, who would act as the special adviser to SACEUR on nuclear matters, and collect information on important nuclear developments. As a further concession to the other allies the British V bombers and three United States Polaris submarines, as well as some air units from other allies, were placed under SACEUR.

During 1964 the United States has been developing highly mobile, lightweight, nuclear rockets with a 1500 mile range to boost the strength of the allies. In this way the NATO tactical air forces can be gradually replaced by missiles. But dissatisfaction at the lack of European control over the use of the weapons remains. In 1958 de Gaulle proposed that the United States, Britain, and France connect their policies in areas not covered by the Treaty, and that the employment of atomic weapons be under the joint control of the three countries, the so-called "directorate of three," but this was rejected.

Though a European deterrent is technically possible, the problem of control in the absence of a politically integrated Europe, remains difficult to solve. A variant of this proposal is for the WEU nations to have a deterrent of their own. This has several advantages: it takes account of the Western European demand for independent action, it is limited to a geographically compact area, it might spur political unification, it helps allay the fear that Germany might obtain atomic weapons, it avoids the embarrassment of a possible Franco-German nuclear arrangement, it would avoid the practical difficulties associated with a mixed-manned force, and it could take advantage of an existing assembly which can debate defense problems. Yet even the WEU Assembly which once proposed such a deterrent no longer supports the idea.

A NATO deterrent would link the United States and Europe. Such a deterrent was proposed by General Norstad in 1959, starting with medium range ballistic missiles (MRBM) and including U.S. atomic aid to France. Because the United States was concerned to remove the temptation of diffusion of nuclear weapons, Christian Herter, as Secretary of State in 1960, suggested a force of Polaris submarines and missiles under multinational control. General Norstad proposed a highly mobile multinational unit under a single commander. When in 1961 the United States, building a greater second strike through Minutemen intercontinental ballistic missiles and Polaris submarines, changed its policy and thought land based MRBMs, either liquid-fueled or solid-fueled, were no longer viable, Norstad, who was opposed to this seeming withdrawal from European bases, was retired as SACEUR. In December, 1962, the WEU Assembly called for integration of the allied nuclear forces into a single NATO nuclear deterrent within a single command structure under the control of a single political executive representing the Alliance as a whole. Only in this way could the problem of a veto by a single member be avoided. But the proposal that political control over such a deterrent be vested in a subcommittee of NATO, comprising the United States, Great Britain, France, Germany and one other NATO nation, while taking account of the realities of power, has caused misgivings among the smaller nations.

A third proposal has been for the development of a Franco-British nuclear deterrent rather than a NATO one. The argument in favor of such a weapon is that it would grow out of existing programs, it would avoid any further independent deterrents and it would draw Britain politically closer to Europe. Moreover it would be an important stimulant for the aeronautical industry and production of ballistic engines in the two countries. But if France was interested in such a project in 1958, by 1963 the possibility of a joint Anglo-French nuclear policy was remote in spite of British hints that nuclear assistance might be given to France in return for concessions by EEC on Commonwealth trade.

The main argument for the independent deterrent has come from France and, in particular, from General de Gaulle. It is based partly on the view that the U.S. nuclear umbrella of protection over Europe is a myth since the United States would not use either tactical or strategic nuclear weapons in defense of Europe. But primarily it is an assertion of French prestige and independent political action for "France cannot leave her own destiny and even her own life to the discretion of others." Since France felt it had no real voice in any decision on the use of nuclear resources located in France, it began building the *force de frappe*. It plans to have not only its own deterrent, but also its own tactical nuclear weapons. The French effort has caused political and military problems through the refusal of France to agree that coordinated action should take precedence over its unilateral effort. The comparative cost of building supersonic bombers and fighters, ballistic missiles and nuclear submarines has been a reduction in the conventional forces of France by one third. The formation of independent deterrents is dangerous for two reasons. First, it might lead to diffusion and eventually to one of the allies resorting to its use unilaterally. Secondly, the development of such deterrents can, and in 1963 did, limit the value of test ban agreements with Russia since France refused to sign the agreement. Ironically, the French effort is of dubious military value as a deterrent to Russia. Perhaps the deterrent is best symbolized by the name of the French plane which is at present its main strength, the "Mirage."

To avoid the problems of independent deterrents and to respond to the rising European demand for nuclear participation, proposals were made for a multinational or multilateral force. In 1960 Norstad proposed a mobile multinational unit with both conventional and nuclear weapons, composed initially of a brigade each from the United States, Great Britain, and France under a single commander. President Kennedy, a year later, offered to commit five Polaris atomic submarines to a NATO force. In 1963 Britain proposed a force based on national contingents of units from the U.S. strategic forces, the British Bomber command, and tactical nuclear forces already in Europe; the political control over the force would be by a NATO nuclear subcommittee, each member of which would have a veto and a right to withdraw its contribution in an emergency. But in general, the multinational solution means that while the allies influence strategic and political planning, operational decisions in a nuclear crisis are left in the hands of the nuclear powers.

As distinct from a multinational force (MNF) which is composed of national units, a multilateral force (MLF) is one whose personnel is drawn from all participating countries, mixed so that there is no identifiable national component and, therefore, with no part which can be withdrawn by, or operate under, an individual country. Strictly speaking, the MLF would not be a NATO force, but a force manned by NATO members, and therefore linked to it. After the Nassau Agreement of December, 1962, under which the United States agreed to sell Polaris missiles to Britain since it was ending the development of the Skybolt, the air launched ballistic missile promised to Britain, and its criticism by General de Gaulle who regarded it as an insidious Anglo-Saxon conspiracy, the United States proposed an MLF. The first proposal was for a force of submarines; later, it was changed to surface ships, armed with Polaris missiles, with mixed-manned crews, whose action would be decided unanimously. Enthusiasm about such an integrated force has been restrained. France regards it both as impractical, and expensive, and an ingenious way of sidetracking the French independent deterrent.

At the bottom of the MLF is the problem of West Germany. Its proponents fear that so long as Britain and France pursue independent nuclear policies, similar demands and heightened nationalism might arise in Germany which would lead to further spread of nuclear weapons. The MLF is, to some extent, the American attempt to woo Germany from her French suitor. European Socialists see the MLF as precipitated by a political problem and as a method of giving Germany a share in nuclear defense while ensuring she will not be tempted by the idea of an independent deterrent. The probability that Germany is likely to be the largest single European contributor to such a force—about 40 percent of the total—has raised misgivings that this may lead both to the reassertion of demands in Germany for greater control, and also to greater resistance by others to a German-dominated force. Others question its military necessity, and argue that it will divert money from the production of conventional weapons.

The problem remains that the United States will contribute only about 5 percent of its total nuclear strength to an MLF, and therefore 95 percent will remain outside the control of NATO, under U.S. control. Therefore, critics of the MLF have suggested that it is more desirable to have an authority within NATO capable of planning the strategy of the Alliance as a whole and for all types of weapons. In this way the allies, or some of them, would possess a degree of influence over the formulation of U.S. strategic policy and nuclear weapons. "Nuclear terror," Jean Monnet has said, "is indivisible." The logical conclusion to the modern technological developments that have made the countries of Western Europe too small to survive individually is that a common institution be established capable of taking nuclear decisions for all since there can be only one driver at the nuclear wheel. In 1964 General Norstad suggested that the nuclear problem be solved through the establishment of a small executive body of three with the Secretary-General as a nonvoting member to represent all 15; as an alternative, Germany might be given some representative status on the body, or two additional members might be elected from among NATO nations on a rotating basis.

Yet the idea behind the MLF is not only to form a military body within which Germany could act on the basis of equality with the nuclear powers, but also to form a basis for closer ties among the allies in a wide variety of ways and for the reinforcement of Western unity.

If nuclear control has been the most contentious issue in NATO, the increasingly independent attitude of France has caused most consternation. M. Couve de Murville has confessed that France is a difficult, though loyal, ally. Certainly her actions —in 1959 removing her Mediterranean fleet from NATO operational control, and in 1964 removing her naval officers from staff posts in NATO naval commands, in not appointing an officer to the post of naval deputy to SACEUR, normally held by a French admiral, her refusal to participate in a unified air-defense system for continental Western Europe, her decision in June, 1964, to use a smaller caliber ammunition than that agreed upon by NATO for light weapons, her refusal to permit stockpiling of nuclear warheads on French soil unless she were given some share of control, her argument in support of the breakup of integrated NATO commands and forces and for a return to purely national units, and her failure to contribute more than one-third of her promised number of conventional forces—have helped limit a coordinated policy for NATO. General de Gaulle has challenged the motive of U.S. strategic policy, argued that the U.S. is unlikely to risk its existence for Europe, opposed a return to large conventional forces, continued the development of the French independent deterrent, and refused to join the proposed multilateral force. In foreign affairs de Gaulle's policy on China, South East Asia, Cuba, and Latin America has been contrary to the majority of his NATO allies. His attitude to the organization of NATO has been philosophically similar to that he has adopted towards the other European organizations. He has opposed the whole concept of integrated commands, and argued instead for a planning staff which would coordinate national forces instead of commanding them.

Apart from differences on conventional and nuclear forces and problems raised by French political and military policies, a fourth source of dissension has been the disparity of effort and of sharing the burden of NATO. Total NATO expenditure increased from $21.5 billion in 1950 to $73.5 billion in 1963. Of this the Europeans contributed $18.5 billion, and the United States $55 billion. Moreover, delivering of military assistance by the United States to the NATO countries from 1949 to 1963 have amounted to almost $17 billion. The United States has as many men under arms as all the NATO countries. It spends $277 per capita and over 10 percent of its national product in defense compared with. a NATO average of $53 per capita and 6 percent. Not unnaturally the United States has raised the question of whether the European allies are carrying their fair share of NATO defense.

Political Consultation

NATO has been successful as a means of protection against the particular threat of Russian aggression. But if it has not been able to solve differences on military matters, it has been even less successful in settling political differences between the allies or pursuing common policies. The Europeans have complained that the United States did not support them in South East Asia, the Middle East, or Africa; the United States has complained that Europe did not always support its Pacific, China, or Latin America policy. In fact NATO is not a world alliance. It is still primarily a regional alliance for the defense of Europe and North America. Though some members have talked of the need for NATO co-operation in dealing with the Communist threat in Asia, Latin America, and Africa, the allies have differed in their policies to these areas. France has refused to sign the 1963 test-ban agreement. There have been differences on the question of trade and long-term credit arrangements with the Soviet Union. The individual countries have disagreed over admitting China to the United Nations, the British sale of jet planes to Peking, fishing rights around Iceland, the financing of British troops in Germany, the conscription period in Belgium, the command structure in the Baltic area, the conflict in South Tyrol, Portuguese policy in Angola and Guinea, and the Cyprus problem. The imminent threat of Soviet military aggression has receded; the myth of 175 Russian divisions prepared for action appears dispelled. But the very reduction of Russian pressure, and the idea of "building bridges" to East Europe, has meant differences between the allies on support for a rapprochement with the Soviet Union and on trade with the Communist bloc. One of the main problems in this connection is that of controls on trade in strategic goods. Exports controls on these are operated by a coordinating committee (COCOM) in which all members of NATO take part, with the exception of Iceland, together with Japan. COCOM lays down a list of strategically important goods, the export of which the member states are regarded as being bound to prohibit. But since the embargo list of goods is a minimal one of only 118 items, members can add to it at their discretion. The varying interpretations of what goods are of "strategic importance" have caused divisions in the West.

Article 4 of the NATO treaty provides for consultation when "the territorial integrity, political independence, or security of any of the Parties is threatened." NATO was not originally conceived as a policy-making body. But consultation and cooperation has taken place within NATO since May, 1950, when the

Council deputies first met and discussed political problems of common interest. Disappointment with the effectiveness and scope of political consultation during the Suez invasion in 1956 led to the setting up of the Committee on Nonmilitary Cooperation. This second group of 3 Wise Men—Gaetano Martino, Halvard Lange, and Lester Pearson—emphasized the need for political consultation. This implied not only an exchange of information and a notification of national decisions already taken, but also collective discussion of problems in the early stages of policy formation and before national positions had become fixed. Hopefully, this might lead to collective decisions on matters of common interest affecting the Alliance. But political consultation has never meant that one NATO member must get the concurrence of the others before embarking on any political or military action.

The chief forum for political consultation is still the Council itself, with the permanent representatives discussing immediate and long-term problems such as the possibility of a summit meeting in 1958, disarmament plans in 1960, the Berlin problem, the export of steel pipes to the East bloc in 1962, the Cyprus problem, and the changing nature of Soviet policy in general. Working by unanimity, its recommendations are sent to the governments, which may accept them as did Germany which stopped its steel exports to Russia in 1962, or refuse them as did Britain which continued its exports. The Council is still far from being a genuine organ of policy coordination, and procedure is slow since the representatives consult on the basis of instructions from the governments.

The specific recommendations of the 3 Wise Men led to the institution of the Committee of Political Advisers in January, 1957, and to the expansion of the role of the Secretary-General in trying to solve disputes, as in the case of Cyprus and the Icelandic fisheries, before they went to any other international agency. In practice, the Committee of Political Advisers is normally composed of the second senior person in the delegations headed by the permanent representatives with the assistant Secretary-General for Political Affairs as chairman. The committee has three main functions. It meets once a week with a flexible agenda for informal discussion of political matters of interest; every other week there is a discussion with a formal presentation of papers. It deals with the details of a problem or with a particular question which the Council has asked it to take up, and on which the chairman has made a report And it has a general supervisory function over experts from the national governments who provide information for the ministers' meetings. The committee appears to be more effective in providing an education for the smaller powers in the facts of international life than in preparing a basis for the solution of concrete issues. The Council is also assisted by groups of national experts or observers chaired by a member of the staff which discuss various political problems and issue reports which go to the ministers. There are five basic groups of this kind, the first and most important of which is the group which assesses the trends and implications of Soviet policy. There is also consultation within NATO on disarmament issues and questions of European security. Every two weeks in 1964 the NATO permanent council was briefed by a representative of one of the powers at the Geneva disarmament conference on developments. Before the United States proposed any initiative, it consulted its allies.

The Council meeting at the level of heads of government in December, 1957, decided that NATO should review economic trends and assess economic progress in the member states from time to time. The following year the Committee of Economic Advisers was created; it meets periodically under the chairmanship of the Assistant Secretary-General for Economics and Finance to deal with the political aspects of economic problems, and with questions on Soviet economy. It is assisted by experts on Soviet problems seconded from the governments for three years and paid by NATO.

Coordinated Activity

More successful than the attempts at political cooperation have been, in varying degree, three other forms of coordinated activity;

the annual or triennial review, the infrastructure program and the standardization of arms.

The annual review, replaced by the triennial review in 1962, has been a striking example of intergovernmental consultation. The report of the first group of 3 Wise Men in 1952 led to an annual review of the defense efforts of NATO members by a multilateral examination. The examination is guided by two principles. Defense programs would be reconciled with the political, economic, and financial capacities of the members. And the defense contributions of the members must be equitably distributed.

For the first time on an international basis states agreed to exchange information on the details of military, production, and fiscal programs, and to submit to the criticism of their allies. The review process extends over the whole year during which the governments are questioned on their programs. The answers are analyzed by NATO military authorities, civilian staff, and the other national delegations, after which a final report sets goals for the forces of countries, and other recommendations are forwarded to the governments. As a result of this interchange, the triennial review enables the NATO authorities to be assured of the forces each member will supply or is supposed to supply the Alliance. During the two years following the triennial review, the defense effort of members is subject to an interim review on similar lines.

Through the procedure of the annual review there has been a regular assessment of the military build-up and modernization of forces. The procedure has resulted in methods of estimating the costs of military establishments which have helped in the planning of resources and forces. And it has been useful as a way of comparing the efforts of the different allies. There is no absolute standard for measuring or comparing the defense efforts of the Alliance nor any way of establishing a precise mathematical formula to determine the limits of resources a country can spend on defense. In a general way the standard of comparison between countries is the percentage of total national resources devoted to defense expressed in monetary terms. But the problem of deciding the equity of effort and sharing of the burden has often dominated

NATO discussions. The complexities of the problems of man-power, fiscal systems, different degrees of governmental activity, dependence on foreign trade, colonial burden, and different national traditions of military service, have made it difficult to reach solutions. In spite of the valuable procedure of the triennial review the disparity between the contributions of the allies remains a source of discontent.

The most successful example of interdependence in the NATO organization is the infrastructure program, all the fixed installations necessary for the deployment and operation of the armed forces. This is the common network consisting of 220 airfields, 5,300 miles of fuel pipelines, storage tanks containing 440 million gallons, signal installations covering 27,000 miles, harbor facilities, radar installations, and special ammunition sites.

The idea of a common infrastructure paid for by all members originated with the Brussels Treaty Organization in 1950. A year later NATO took over the idea and began its program which was accelerated with the outbreak of the Korean war. Between 1950 and 1964 about $3.5 billion, about 1.5 percent of total defense expenditure, was spent on the program, the United States contributing about 35 percent of the total.

The cost is shared among NATO members, and is based partly on the ability of a country to pay, and partly on the economic benefits accruing to the host countries. At first there were annual and somewhat acrimonious disputes over sharing the cost. In 1953 Lord Ismay, then Secretary-General, got agreement in typically commonsensical fashion, to a cost-sharing formula, although each nation thought its own share was too high.

The NATO commanders submit triennial plans and estimates of costs for projects required in implementation of strategic plans. The plans are examined by the Standing Group in Washington and the Infrastructure Committee of the NATO Council on which all countries are represented. The Standing Group examines the projects from the military aspect and sends them to the Military Committee with its comments. The Infrastructure Committee inquires whether the installations are suitable for common use and qualify for common financing. The Council is responsible for final approval of the program.

The host country decides the site, draws up a plan which is submitted to SHAPE and a detailed estimate of cost which is sent to the NATO Infrastructure Payments and Progress Committee for approval before any money can be appropriated. During construction the project is supervised periodically by engineers from the NATO international staff and NATO military commands. After construction it is visited by an international team of civil and military authorities. Though criticism has been made of the delays in construction, and in particular of those projects which are less popular and useful to the local population, the infrastructure program remains as a significant example of communal endeavor.

But the infrastructure program represents a small part of the logistical needs of NATO, and logistics remain a purely national responsibility. SACEUR can only advise and coordinate, he cannot control the national stocks and depots. Some progress has been made in logistical coordination as in the area of codification, the process of classifying and numbering all items of military equipment in a uniform manner. For the first time an international uniform system has been adopted, permitting effective coordination in procurement and reducing administrative problems. However, the lack of any significant coordination has been disappointing. In the area of SACLANT and Channel Commands there is a lack of integration of the supply services of the different nations, and ships of different nationalities depend on their own supply system. Similarly, the incompatibility between the principles of assignment of national forces to integrated allied commands and retention of national responsibility for logistics has resulted in a lack of standardization in the tactical air forces. For a truly integrated force it is necessary that allied commanders have adequate authority in the logistical area and that a completely integrated logistics system be organized beginning with common stockpiles, common depots, and common transport.

Equally disappointing has been the slow progress in the standardization of armaments. Individual governments are unlikely to make cooperation arrangements if they will lead to unemployment or redirection of industry. In the economic area, as Spaak said while Secretary-General of NATO "are to be found all the egoism and the nationalist illusions." The Military Agency for Standardization in London has drawn up a number of standardization agreements, but they are generally restricted to secondary equipment like spare parts for vehicles or technical data. The armies for a long time used 14 different types of small arms ammunition, and the number of types of rifles and machine guns has increased rather than decreased as have the different types of vehicles used. Even after standard NATO ammunition for firearms had been agreed upon, some countries adopted firearms which could not fire the standard ammunition. A cutting comment has been that the only common element in the 12 types of jeeps used by NATO is the air blown into the tires.

It was soon realized that standardization can be more easily achieved for nuclear and modern weapons than for conventional. Research, development, and production of new weapons and equipment are becoming increasingly expensive; it is becoming increasingly difficult for individual countries to bear the cost alone, and wasteful in terms of time and manpower for them to do so. The most ambitious joint project NATO is undertaking is the Defense Ground Environment (NADGE), a complex electronic early-warning and air command system, to cost $300 million and to be completed by 1968. At the 1957 Council meeting at the level of heads of government, the United States suggested a coordinated program of research development and production of a selected group of modern weapons including IRBMs. This has led to a number of coordinated schemes in planning and production such as the Hawk anti-aircraft guided missile, the Bréguet maritime patrol aircraft, the Sidewinder air-to-air missile, the Mark 44 anti-submarine torpedo, the F104G fighter-bomber aircraft and the Bullpup air-to-ground missile, as well as production facilities in Europe incorporating many of the latest U.S. techniques. But apart from the Fiat G91 reconnaissance plane produced jointly by a number of European countries since 1954, the French Bréguet long range plane and the 81 mm. mortar and the future Transall transport aircraft, all joint production has been of American equipment. Of the over-all military procurement budgets of the seven WEU nations, only 9 percent goes for joint equipment.

European critics have complained that none of this production has been procured for the American forces, nor have many European projects been adopted for joint production. Interdependence through standardization implies facilitating operations and reducing costs by producing one common or standard product. But two conflicting factors are involved. The European economic recovery has meant that the European allies could now produce, and want to produce, many of their own weapons. Necessarily this has resulted in conflicts between the economic interests of the two continents where similar research, development, and pre-production tooling-up has taken place. At the same time the expense involved in technological responses to developments in the Soviet Union entails an outlay that no single country can easily afford. The critics have suggested, therefore, that the United States should rely exclusively on European production for certain items while Europeans rely on the United States for others. Yet the problem is an intra-European as well as an Atlantic one. With the medium heavy tank due for replacement in the different armies, three separate types are being developed in Great Britain, France, and Germany, with consequent waste of manpower, time, and research. In May, 1964, Belgium somewhat cavalierly disregarded the NATO recommendation on its tank replacement program.

Interdependence takes place through the NATO Armaments Committee and through bilateral or multilateral discussion between the NATO countries concerned. The Armaments Committee defines in detail the type and quantity of weapons needed for a limited number of projects which the Military Committee and the Standing Group have approved and which make up the NATO basic military requirement. The projects are examined by mixed working groups of experts, military, civilian, operational, or technical, from the allies. Besides this, the nations, bilaterally or multilaterally, discuss the possibility of joint schemes, largely through steering committees composed of representatives from the defense departments and NATO delegations. Often, the membership of the steering committee overlaps with that of the mixed working group. The material problems are dealt with by committees and groups working within national ministries, in continual contact with their counterparts in other countries. In general, agreement on the allocation of research and production has proved difficult partly because it has been difficult to get consensus on types of weapons, and partly because of differences on the actual distribution of tasks. In 1964, a NATO Committee of National Directors of Research and Development was set up to improve the coordination of research and development of military weapons and equipment in NATO. It will encourage the allies to work together on military research and development and to reduce the number of national weapon programs.

Scientific Cooperation

The nature and degree of political consultation in NATO has been disappointing, and the formulation of common political policies rare. Article 2 of the Treaty states that the members may "promote conditions of stability and wellbeing. They seek to eliminate conflict in their international economic policies and will encourage economic collaboration between any or all of them." But NATO has not proved to be the place where such collaboration can take place. On the other hand NATO has concerned itself with some matters, such as water desalination, which appear rather marginal to its function. It has also played a small role in scientific cooperation. The Council created a science committee and a full time adviser to the Secretary-General who advises on scientific matters effecting the alliance. Scientific cooperation has resulted in a science fellowship program, an advanced study institutes program in which scientists are brought together to discuss their work, and a research grants program concentrating on oceanography and meterology. The most ambitious proposal, an International Institute of Science and Technology, has been approved in principle, but no measures have yet been taken to establish it.

There is considerable intergovernmental cooperation in technical matters with which NATO is concerned. In 1954 the SHAPE

Air Defense Technical Center was set up; the costs were borne by the United States until 1960 and have been shared by the Alliance since then. The Center, composed of 70 experts from the member countries, provides technical advice on air defense and aids SHAPE in coordinating the various contributions to the common air defense system. It also keeps in touch with research and development in the different countries through regular meetings with the national research and development institutions.

Responsibility for civil defense is still primarily in the hands of the national governments. But the national measures in their field are reviewed annually by the Council, and civil emergency planning is coordinated by the NATO Senior Civil Emergency Committee set up in 1955.

The Uncertain Future

In its early days NATO was said to be like that more popular Parisian institution the Venus de Milo, all SHAPE and no arms. In 1964 the military posture of the Western alliance is strong. The land forces of the Alliance defend a front line about 2,000 miles long, from North Norway to East Turkey. The sea forces cover the Mediterranean and the North Atlantic down to the Tropic of Cancer. Yet its forces remain understrength, its strategy debatable and its common policy uncertain. The natural condition of NATO seems to be a state of "crisis" or "disarray"; its future remains in doubt, for General de Gaulle, who talks in terms of its "reorganization" is possibly using a euphemism for "abolition." Though NATO is strong, many of the allies have not fulfilled their obligations either in raising the agreed number of troops or in maintaining the agreed period of military service. After the United States, it is Germany, who has placed all her armed forces under NATO command, who most favors a strong organization. At times strategic and tactical policies in NATO seem to be the result of a happy coincidence of American and German interests as in the advocacy of a forward strategy. This coincidence of interest may have replaced the "special relationship" between the United States and Britain, so beloved by Harold Macmillan, which seems to have come to an end with the harsh realization that Britain is no longer an equal partner and cannot economically afford to continue its independent deterrent after the obsolescence of its V bombers. National differences have been shown by the differing views on nuclear control and diffusion.

NATO is an alliance with integrated commands and coordinated technical and research groups. But it remains an intergovernmental organization to which the states have surrendered none of their sovereign power, not an integrated entity. An inextricable contradiction exists between the institution of a joint supreme command and the independence of individual armies. It is the individual countries who provide military information and the military advisers to SACEUR. The unanimity rule has been a handicap to integrated planning. Yet if NATO is unlikely to be transformed into more than an effective working alliance, its great achievement remains that it has provided the protection and security through which Western Europe has been able to recover economically and proceed with its progress toward integration.

CHAPTER FIVE

Western European Union

IN 1947 Great Britain and France signed the Treaty of Dunkirk, a pact of mutual military assistance, essentially against any future German aggression. In Brussels a year later in March, 1948, the Treaty was extended to include Belgium, Holland, and Luxembourg and altered in scope to provide for automatic military assistance in case of attack. The Brussels Treaty Organization was a 50-year collective defense arrangement and alliance in which each member retained full control over its armed forces. But the Treaty was also the prototype of future organizations or plans like the European Defense Community (EDC), the Western European Union (WEU), and even NATO, in that cooperation in economic, social, and cultural matters was linked with a military pact, and agencies set up to deal with a number of functions. Though the machinery of the BTO was largely consultative, with a consultative council of foreign ministers and a permanent committee of ambassadors, there was also provision for a Western Union Supply Board made up of persons from the government services, and an infrastructure program, both of which were later taken over by NATO. Its major military organs were the Western European Defense Organization, the Western Union Chiefs of Staff Committee, the Western Europe Commanders-in-Chief Committee, and a coordinated military headquarters under Field Marshal Lord Montgomery at Fontainebleau which was to be absorbed into NATO. Alas, the Commanders had no troops to command.

After the failure of EDC in 1954, Great Britain proposed, as an alternative, an intergovernmental rather than a supranational or federal organization. Ironically, the proposals for a Western

European Union by the British Foreign Minister, Anthony Eden, virtually conceded in substance what Britain had been reluctant to promise to the proposed supranational organization. The London conference to discuss the proposals led to a series of agreements signed in Paris in October, 1954. The Western European Union was to last until 1998. The Brussels Treaty was extended to include the two former enemies, Germany and Italy, but at the same time the level of forces would be determined by the council of ministers, and an agency for the control of armaments was set up. A common military policy was agreed upon. Great Britain gave a statutory promise to keep troops on the Continent. Germany would contribute 12 divisions under the command of SACEUR. German entry into NATO was allowed, but safeguards were established over the rearmament and weapons of Germany, since it was not allowed to manufacture atomic, biological, or chemical weapons, and all its military arrangements would be made within the NATO framework.

Great Britain gave to the Continental countries, and France in particular, the pledge for which they had been asking in vain in the framework of EDC. It would continue to maintain four divisions and the Second Tactical Air Force assigned to SACEUR on the Continent, with the reservation that it might withdraw them if there were an important overseas emergency. France was satisfied with this assurance and with the fact that Germany would not be able to exercise its military power in isolation. Germany, although restricted militarily, was happy to regain its sovereignty and to become formally an independent power again, with the agreement to end the allied occupation.

The Brussels Treaty was to be expanded for use as a political instrument. The purpose of WEU was not only to strengthen peace and security, but also to promote unity and encourage the progressive integration of Europe and closer cooperation between the seven members and with other European organizations. But, unlike the defeated EDC, there was no provision in Western European Union for fusion of national forces, and no supranational organs to exercise administrative and budgetary authority over common defense.

Like NATO, WEU is an organization whose parts are separated by the sea. The WEU Council in permanent session meets in London, while the subsidiary agencies, the Standing Armaments Committee and the Agency for the Control of Armaments, and the WEU Assembly have their headquarters in Paris.

The Executive Organization

The WEU Council, replacing the old Consultative Council, is composed of the seven foreign ministers, meeting occasionally at no fixed intervals until the last year when it has been meeting every three months. At a lower and permanent level, it is the ambassadors of the six countries to London and a British Foreign Office official meeting under the chairmanship of the Secretary-General who is responsible for preparing all meetings. The location of the Permanent Council in London was intended to symbolize the step taken by Britain towards common European activity and cooperation, if not integration.

The Council acts by unanimity to approve an increase in the level of forces, but it can also decide questions concerning types of armaments not to be manufactured by Germany by a two-thirds majority, and questions concerning infractions of agreements on the production or level of stocks of armaments by a simple majority. With this qualification of the unanimity principle, it should have been possible for the Council to be a useful and efficient decision-making body. Yet in the face of irregular behavior such as the British withdrawal of promised troops, the Council, which could have taken action by a majority, acquiesced in approval. Though the Council provides a convenient meeting place for the foreign ministers of the Six and Great Britain, in fact its contribution to the solution of European problems has so far been almost nonexistent. The Council of Foreign Ministers did not meet for 18 months while negotiations for British entry into the European Economic Community were taking place in Brussels in 1962. France vetoed a meeting after the January, 1963, breakdown, and it was not until July, 1963, that the foreign ministers finally met.

The Permanent Council has an almost equally unimpressive

record. Membership on the Council is only one of the activities of the six ambassadors to London, whose primary function is to represent their governments in London. In practice, meetings at the permanent level tend to be of first secretaries rather than of the ambassadors themselves. Suggestions have, therefore, been made to transfer the WEU Council and its secretariat to Paris and to have it composed of the seven ambassadors to NATO. But since this would probably lead to the ambassadors regarding their WEU role as subordinate to that of NATO, perhaps a preferable solution might be for the states to be represented on the Council by permanent representatives, specially appointed for this task on lines similar to those appointed to the Council of Europe, OECD, NATO, and the European communities.

A secretariat to the Council headed by a secretary-general was set up in London. The office, if not the policies, was internationalized, and the secretary-general, his three assistants, and the director of the Agency for Control of Armaments are all of different nationalities. The work of the secretariat has been largely invisible, and though suggestions have frequently been made to appoint a secretary-general with political and administrative experience, the office has not been strengthened in personnel or function. Moreover, it is difficult to see what functions are performed by the deputy and the assistant secretary-generals in London (the third assistant and the director of the Agency for Control of Armaments are in Paris), since the specific functions they were called upon to perform—responsibility for Saar questions and the supervision of the social and cultural activities of WEU—no longer exist.

There are two subsidiary agencies of the Council in Paris, the Agency for the Control of Armaments and the Standing Armaments Committee.

The Agency for Control of Armaments inspects and reports on the level of stocks of certain types of armaments on the mainland of Europe, sees that prohibited weapons are not being made, and determines how many atomic weapons are being produced on the mainland. The Agency obtains its information partly from documentary sources supplied by the states on their production and on their stocks of armaments subject to control, and partly by a series of about 65 field control operations a year. The latter include combined Agency-SHAPE inspections at military depots, inspections at units under national command covering both land and air forces, and investigations at factories and naval shipyards.

The paradox is that, while WEU is given the function of seeing that the level of forces laid down in the treaty is not exceeded, the problem has in the main been one of keeping up the forces at the agreed level. In theory the consent of the Council is necessary to allow the withdrawal of British troops from the Continent. But WEU has had little control over the actions of the national governments. Britain obtained reluctant permission for the withdrawal of troops from Germany in 1957 and the reduction in their number from 77,000 to 55,000 after threatening to act unilaterally. Even this last commitment has not been kept, for the British garrison has been several thousand short since 1959. The British White Paper of 1957 that changed British defense policy and abolished conscription was published without previously informing the Council.

On the continent, France has consistently broken its obligations without WEU taking any action. France at first took advantage of a legal loophole and claimed its atomic bombs were being made for experimental purposes, not for the "production" mentioned in the Treaty. France has never notified WEU of its atomic production. After its experimental efforts in the nuclear field, France has decided upon its level of stocks itself, and has refused to allow the Council to fix its level of nuclear weapons.

The only real application of the treaty provisions is against Germany, which is forbidden to make atomic, bacteriological, and chemical weapons, heavy warships, large submarines, and strategic bombers. Even here there has been some relaxation of restrictions. Although submarine construction in Germany was limited under the treaty to vessels of up to 350 tons, in October, 1962, the limit was raised to 450 tons, to meet the NATO requirement for large coastal submarines, and in October, 1963, the Council gave permission to build six submarines up to 1,000 tons, following the recommendations of SACEUR.

With the limited means at its disposal, it is impossible for the Agency to check on the armed forces of the Seven. Nor can it exercise any real control in the factories of the states. Part of its difficulty has been that it has no specialists in the field of nuclear weapons, and thus WEU has no real control, qualitative or quantitative, in this field. For even greater protection against Germany, France had suggested in 1954 that the production of the permitted categories of weapons be linked among the seven nations.

The Standing Armaments Committee exists to increase the common production of weapons and their standardization, but its work has been negligible compared with that of NATO in the same area. The United States has urged that the Committee be brought directly into NATO since it does not welcome negotiations on the common production of armaments being conducted outside NATO, but Britain did not want it abolished while it was itself trying to join EEC.

The Assembly has continually stressed the need to standardize armaments, both to lower the costs of production and to achieve better interchangeability of arms and supplies. Since it is difficult to standardize arms already in existence, the Assembly called for the standardization of future armaments, both conventional and missiles, and in 1957 for a pooling of resources and the setting up of concerted research, design, and production in ballistic missiles. Although the Committee was given full responsibility for cooperation in arms production, and although the British proposed an ambitious plan for a joint program of research, development, and production in some 20 different spheres of weapon manufacture, little action has been taken. Most of the standardization plans for armaments, vehicles, and equipment have failed, partly because agreement is difficult to reach, and partly because of economic differences and national financial pressures. Of the standardization proposals accepted, most, in fact, have been the result of bilateral or multilateral negotiations.

The Assembly

In the treaty there is only a casual reference to an assembly, which would be composed of the parliamentary representatives of the seven nations to the Consultative Assembly of the Council of Europe and which would receive an annual report from the WEU Council, especially on the control of armaments. It is probable that the ministers envisaged the assembly as a group coming together to talk about this control. But the Assembly has been the only active part of WEU and has provided a useful, if not overly influential, meeting place for discussions among the parliamentarians of the seven countries.

Meeting for the first time in Strasbourg in July, 1955, the Assembly asserted its right to discuss all the responsibilities of the Council as defined in the treaty. It became a constituent assembly and began organizing its own functions and procedure by unilateral action. It obtained full control over its own agenda and staff but not as much budget antonomy as it wanted.

The Assembly, composed of 89 representatives who are also members of the Consultative Assembly, generally meets three times a year in Paris, where its secretariat is located, though in 1961 it met in London and in 1964 in Rome. It set up four committees, of which the Committee on Defense Questions and Armaments, and the General Affairs Committee are the most significant. A working party for liaison with the national parliaments is responsible for seeing that the texts adopted by the Assembly are followed up. The Assembly can also set up ad hoc committees of inquiry as it pleases. The WEU Assembly, therefore, though overlapping in membership, is a different body from the Consultative Assembly. It has its own secretariat, its own clerk, its own financial means, and its own locale.

The representatives, who sit in alphabetical order, are divided into three party groups in the same way as in the Council of Europe. The French Gaullists of the Union pour la Nouvelle République, who once belonged to the Liberal group, and the British Conservatives are unaffiliated. As in the Consultative Assembly, the Christian Democrat is the largest and the Liberal the smallest group. The divisions are of little substantive effect. The groups caucus before the meetings and on amendments, will occasionally unify on policy matters, and cohere in voting on recommendations. An outstanding example of this was the unity of the Socialists, always the most homogeneous group, in opposing successfully a proposal to support the multilateral nuclear force in December, 1963. The groups share the official positions. In 1964 the Bureau of the Assembly was made up of a Socialist President, and two Christian Democrats, two Liberals, one Socialist, and one UNR member as vice-presidents. The chairmen of the four committees included two Christian Democrats, one Socialist and one British Conservative. National delegations also normally meet to consider the question of appointments, although where an important national problem such as Berlin arises, they may also meet for policy discussions. The Bureau of Seven contains one person from each country; of four chairmen, two are Germans, one is Belgian, and one is British.

The WEU Assembly is a consultative body which can make recommendations to the Council, send resolutions to governments and national parliaments, gives its opinions on documents sent to it by the Council on both military and political matters, and can move a "motion to disagree" with a report from the Council. Its formal competence, unlike that of the Consultative Assembly, extends to defense matters, which are theoretically its main responsibility. The WEU Assembly is the only official international assembly having this competence.

The impact of the Assembly has been limited by two factors. The first is that the defense of the seven powers cannot be isolated from that of the NATO nations as a whole. Since 1955 the WEU Assembly has in fact debated NATO affairs, and justified this on the grounds that the WEU Council is still responsible for the mutual defense obligations of the treaty. The Assembly passes recommendations which have been communicated to NATO. But the NATO Council is in no way responsible to it. This dilemma has led the Assembly to recommend that the WEU and NATO Councils be harmonized. Since the harmonization already exists at the ministerial level, because the members of both are the foreign ministers of their states, the recommendation in effect is for harmonization at the level of deputies. Such harmonization would remove the obstacle that, while the Assembly can discuss defense, the WEU Council cannot, except for limited matters such as the control and standardization of armaments.

The second limiting factor is that the Assembly, like the Consultative Assembly, has the functions of discussion and supervision but not of control in the Anglo-American sense. The Council is required to submit an annual report on its activities to the Assembly which can debate, approve, or criticize it. The one time that the Assembly moved the "motion to disagree" with the report was in 1957, in protest against the British decision to withdraw substantial forces from the Continent. But the result of this activity is at best informal pressure, through national parliaments and public opinion, not formal control. In addition, a considerable part of the time of Assembly meetings is taken up by speeches of ministers or other invited individuals—including two members of the Harvard faculty in December, 1963—leaving little time for debate on substantive issues.

In general the Assembly has always been dissatisfied with the amount of information given it. It has been especially handicapped by the so-called NATO ruling; in 1958 the NATO Council decided that only unclassified information could be communicated to parliamentarians. This has led the defense committee to complain that its briefings are more limited than they should be.

On defense matters the Assembly obtains information in a variety of ways: by joint meetings with the Council, by a liaison subcommittee, by visits of inspection to military establishments, by written questions to the Council, and by statements of ministers before the defense committee.

Since 1956 joint meetings have taken place once or twice a year between the defense committee, the Secretary-General, and the Council at ambassadorial level. From 1958 the foreign minister who is the current chairman of the Council has attended the meetings and supplied the representatives with information, though rarely confidential information. Though the Assembly suggested that defense ministers and the NATO permanent representatives also attend, they have not done so. Nor have the NATO representatives kept the defense committee informed in sectors with which it was concerned. Instead, the WEU Council agreed it would answer questions which came within its jurisdiction. For matters outside the scope of WEU it would ask the

NATO Council, which in turn would ask the military authorities to prepare a reply. In addition, representatives of NATO civilian and military agencies have also attended the joint meetings as technical advisers to the chairman. Today the purpose of the joint meetings seems as much to apply pressure on ministers to act as to obtain information.

A liaison subcommittee—in fact, the Bureau of the defense committee together with a *rapporteur* and the representatives to the Standing Armaments Committee—was set up in 1959 to discuss the activities of the Standing Armaments Committee and obtain information on various problems concerned with joint armaments production. The SAC now meets directly with the chairman and other officials of the defense committee.

Probably the best method of acquiring information has been by the visits of inspection paid by members of the defense committee and its secretariat twice or three times a year to units in the field and military installations. Each year there is a concentration on a certain military activity; in 1963 it was ground forces. These visits have brought parliamentarians and military personnel in close touch, and allowed the former to gain an insight into military activity and problems. In practice there has been a somewhat flexible interpretation of unclassified information and the briefings by military commanders have tended to be far more valuable than those by the Council.

About 75 written questions have been sent by the president of the Assembly to the Council since 1955, and the answers published. Necessarily the kind and amount of information provided is limited. Since 1959 individual ministers of defense have addressed the defense committee in closed session on their national defense problems. The fact that the committee has found these meetings useful and informative has been an additional argument for its demand that defense ministers as well as foreign ministers be on the WEU Council, and that the Council be kept informed of these meetings.

The reports of the Assembly committees have themselves been valuable sources of information on military, political, and economic affairs, testifying to the hard work and seriousness of some members of the Assembly, especially the Committee *rapporteurs*. The reports of the defense committee have played an important part in developing informed opinion on defense problems.

The discussions in the Assembly have generally been on a high level, and have resulted in about 100 recommendations to the Council, very few of which have been implemented. In defense matters the Assembly has proposed, at different times, the creation of a NATO nuclear force, a NATO mobile force and a WEU deterrent. Since the formation of the EEC and Euratom in 1958, the General Affairs Committee has been particularly concerned with, and many Assembly discussions have taken place on, the problems of European integration and on the possibility of the accession of Britain to the communities, a step which the Assembly has always strongly supported. The Assembly indeed has been a constant supporter of all efforts towards further integration and has continually rivaled the Consultative Assembly in urging that WEU be used as a framework for discussions between the Six and Britain. The topics which the Assembly has chosen for discussion in recent years overlap to a considerable degree those considered in the Consultative Assembly. Though some criticism can be made of this duplication of activity, it remains true that a different perspective is given to discussions in a chamber with representatives of seven countries from one with representatives of seventeen.

But the activity of the Assembly has hardly influenced the national defense policies of the governments. The formal procedure for notification of recommendations is for the President of the Assembly to inform the chairman of the Council, which then sends it to the national governments; a reply may be received within four or five months. Dissatisfaction with its own effectiveness led the Assembly in 1957 to set up a working party of 14 to ensure that texts adopted by it would be brought before the national parliaments. The working party selects the texts which are best fitted for discussions in the parliaments and which are most likely to influence governments.

Every national delegation has one member who is supposed to coordinate the work of the delegation with that of the working party, and who prepares questions to be asked in the national parliament. By 1964 the working party calculated it had recorded a total of 82 interventions in the parliaments for the first 90 recommendations, 49 of which were transmitted to the parliaments. But the working party has confessed the inadequacy of its results, and that the majority of representatives in the seven parliaments are insufficiently informed of the work of WEU. This inadequacy is compounded by the fact that, apart from Belgium, there is no committee on European affairs in the seven parliaments, and, apart from the Dutch and the German, there are no administrative secretariats for the delegations to the European assemblies.

The Limits of WEU

The performance of WEU has not been commensurate with its potentialities or with the expectations of its advocates in 1954. It has not undertaken any activity in the economic field, nor has the Council consulted on dangers to economic stability, as the treaty provides. Its cultural activities, which included setting up "European" courses in universities and schools, the making of educational films, traveling exhibits and conferences, were transferred to the Council of Europe in 1959. The Steering Committee on Naval Armaments was transferred to NATO in 1958, and the work on air force equipment was suspended to avoid duplication with NATO. The various other committees it has set up, ranging from a permanent Public Administration Committee to committees dealing with poison in agricultural products, have little relation to its central purpose.

One of its other functions disappeared almost immediately. Under the Franco-German agreement of October, 1954, the Saar was to have a European status within the framework of WEU, provided that this was approved by referendum. The WEU treaty envisaged a Saar commissioner who would be appointed by majority vote of the Council to be responsible for the administration of the Saar, and who would represent the Saar on the Council in an advisory capacity. A commission consisting of representatives from Belgium, Italy, Luxembourg, Holland, and Britain prepared and observed the holding of the referendum in October, 1955. The defeat of the European Statute at the referendum led to the incorporation of the territory into Germany on January 1, 1957, and the ending of WEU responsibility. Similarly, the Tribunal of International Composition, set up to ensure that no one would suffer because of political beliefs expressed at the Saar elections, came to an end.

WEU is not a tidy organization. Its cultural functions overlapped those of the Council of Europe and UNESCO. Its functions over social affairs coincided with those given to ILO, the Council of Europe, and the European Committees. But its most complex relationship is with NATO, clearly the dominant and more valuable organization. WEU became part of the NATO defense system. The forces under Allied Command, Europe, of the BTO were placed under NATO command. The role of SACEUR was increased in 1954 so that he would exercise direct control over the higher training of forces under his command. Proposals emerging from WEU discussions are circulated to the other NATO members, and some WEU projects have been transferred to NATO. In principle the WEU Council is required to fix the level of internal defense forces that states are authorized to maintain. But the NATO Council also must give its opinion on the level of forces for the common defense not assigned to NATO. Since the NATO Council has not given its opinion at any time, the WEU Council has been unable to take any decisions on the matter for nine years.

The Paris Agreements of 1954 seemed to be a revival of the old type of European cooperation which might however be the nucleus for further European integration. WEU was created to have competence not only in defense matters but also with political, economic, cultural, and social functions. But having been the mechanism through which Germany could make a military contribution to Western defense and still be controlled within a European organization, WEU was then, to a large degree, neglected by the seven governments who had given it no executive power.

The underlying problem of WEU is that its ratification coincided with the revival of the Six as an integrated entity in 1955, and the attention of Western Europe has been focused on matters about which WEU, as an organization, could do little. The structure of WEU is purely intergovernmental, and most decisions of the Council are taken by unanimity. Little use has been made by the Council of its ability to make decisions by simple or qualified majority. There is no central organ to represent the interests of the whole as in the case of the Commission of the EEC. Members are not obligated to coordinate their policies.

WEU has made no attempt at integrated activity, and little at coordinated activity. But if it has not been the "real focal point of European integration" that Adenauer anticipated in December, 1954, WEU has intermittently been regarded as a useful link for consultation on developments in the integration movement. After the January, 1963, breakdown, the British argued that WEU was now the obvious place in which to seek for closer European co-operation and consultation in defense and foreign policy, especially in the nonnuclear aspects of defense. Others have suggested that the WEU Council act as a kind of steering committee to review all economic contacts between Britain and the Six. Germany proposed regular contacts on both political and economic affairs within WEU. The Netherlands suggested contacts between the Seven be institutionalized in Brussels through the permanent delegations to the Common Market. The foreign ministers reached a compromise. The quarterly WEU meetings would be restarted within the framework of WEU, the EEC Commission would attend, economic affairs would be included on the agenda, and WEU would be used to prevent the widening of the gap among the Seven. But although France agreed to this compromise arrangement, it did not welcome it with any enthusiasm and has so far prevented it from becoming meaningful. WEU is still an organization in search of a role, and the directorial hand of France seems determined to leave it in the wings of the European stage while the main action goes on elsewhere.

CHAPTER SIX

The First European Community: The European Coal and Steel Community

THE RESUMPTION of the move towards European unity began with the creation of the European Coal and Steel Community. So involved has the activity of the ECSC been with the technical problems of coal and steel that it is often forgotten that it was created for essentially political reasons: the reconciliation of France and Germany, and as a contribution to an organized and vital Europe. The Community was to be the pilot for a new form of international cooperation, not an isolated institution. For Robert Schuman, Europe would be built through concrete achievements which first create a de facto solidarity. The first of such achievements was the placing of the whole of Franco-German coal and steel production under a joint higher authority within an organization open to participation by other European countries. Coal and steel were chosen partly because they are symbols of power and of the historic rivalries between France and Germany, and partly because industrial expansion and the raising of the standard of living depends on them.

In a sense many of the problems of ECSC stem from its obligation to achieve the over-all objectives of contributing to economic expansion, the development of employment, and the improvement of the standard of living in the six countries, while restricted by a double limitation: the limitation to two products, and the limitation of the Community organs to certain functions.

The first limitation was the inevitable result of sector or partial integration. The Community could not control transport and energy matters in general which so greatly affected its own work, and the states still maintained control over general economic policy, taxation, social security, commercial policy, labor and capital mobility. The second limitation was in part the result of the two industries, coal and steel, having been particularly subject to governmental control over prices and production, to private cartels and price fixing, and to nationalized control since the whole of French and part of the German and Netherlands mines are government-owned, as is 42 percent of the total output in the ECSC, while in Italy and Germany part of steel production is government-controlled. The Treaty of Paris imposes restrictions on the High Authority's exercise of its powers. And many of those powers depend, for their exercise, on the opinion and sometimes the agreement of the Council of Ministers, and therefore on the six governments. Moreover, since the ECSC Treaty is one of detailed rules and not of skeleton principles as is the Treaty of Rome, adjustment of the powers of the institutions is a more difficult matter.

The Treaty of Paris creating the ECSC laid down a number of general objectives. In other international bodies such as OEEC and GATT the objective was a gradual negotiated removal of tariffs and quotas. The ECSC went much further in establishing a common market for coal and steel and the raw materials for steel production, iron ore, coke and scrap, which would allow every buyer to obtain supplies without restriction or discrimination. Tariffs, quotas, and exchange controls were to be eliminated since they protect high-cost producers and reduce trade. Inequalities in conditions of production, sale, transport or public subsidies would be ended since they favor certain groups at the expense of others. Common rules of competition would be framed, thus eliminating price discrimination, agreements in restraint of trade, cartels, excessive concentrations, and dominant positions in the market. All this, together with publicity of prices, would enable production to be efficient, to adapt itself to a larger market, to stimulate the modernization of plants and to become more competitive. But for these two industries, peculiarly susceptible to economic fluctuations, production quotas and minimum prices in periods of oversupply, and distribution quotas and maximum price controls in periods of scarcity would be available. The Community would also be concerned with the improvement of social conditions, and with ensuring that the burden of inevitable economic and technological change would not be borne by the workers. The degree of control over the coal and steel industries was left indeterminate; a community basing itself on rules of competition does not inevitably imply a laissez-faire orientation. Qualifications were made to some of these objectives. Temporary subsidies, tariffs and payments to help high-cost producers, such as Italian steel and coke producers, and Belgian coal mines, were permitted in the transitional period to help them compete.

But for its founders, more important than the material or technical objectives of the ECSC was the idea of a Community capable of taking action. The important innovation was that the ECSC was to be a "supranational" body. Supranationality is not synonymous with federalism which implies a coordinate sharing of power between the central and provincial institutions. But it involves a limitation on the sovereignty of the state greater than that normally implied in international agreements and obligations, and the ability of the Community to take independent action on given subjects without the need for consent of the states. In August, 1950, Robert Schuman argued that nations entering the Community must accept in advance the notion of submission to the High Authority within such limits as they themselves will have defined. Although the ECSC was given more limited powers than Schuman or Monnet would have liked, its organs are able to make decisions affecting the citizens of the member countries, to exercise executive authority, to have its own source of income, and to impose penalties on those who have broken the rules. It has its own mechanism of democratic supervision, and its own judicial authority. The members of the Community executive and judicial organs are chosen in their individual right and not as representatives, and they are forbidden to receive instructions from governments or any outside sources, or to take a national point of view. The history of the ECSC, and indeed of the integration process, is one of continual tension between this concept of supranationality and that of the more familiar sovereignty of the nation state.

The Institutions of the Community

The ECSC was established with four major organs: the High Authority, the Special Council of Ministers, the Common Assembly, and the Court of Justice. In view of later European developments, it is paradoxical that it was the French who sought a small High Authority responsible only to the Common Assembly and reluctantly agreed to a Council of Ministers, and the Benelux countries who, fearing the power of the larger countries, insisted on an enlarged High Authority, a detailing of its powers, and a Council of Ministers to protect the interests of the three smaller countries.

Disputes about the structure and functions of the institutions were followed by differences over their location. The Assembly, somewhat reluctantly, took advantage of the facilities already available for the Consultative Assembly of the Council of Europe in Strasbourg. But the site of the High Authority was, in fact, never formally decided, and Luxembourg became its home largely by chance. There was no compromise on the languages to be used; all four languages of the six countries, French, German, Dutch, and Italian, would be equally valid.

THE DOUBLE EXECUTIVE

The ECSC, like its successors the European Economic Community and Euratom, has a double executive, one body of which acts wholly in the communal interest, while the other is representative of the six national interests. The communal body is the High Authority, a body of nine, eight of whom were originally chosen by unanimous decision of the Council of Ministers and the ninth co-opted by the other eight, to serve for six years. After

1959 three retire every other year, and the vacancies are filled alternately by the governments by five-sixths majority and by cooption by the High Authority; the number of those coopted, therefore, rises with each partial renewal. The Council of Ministers, after consulting the High Authority, chooses a president and two vice-presidents for two-year terms. Legally not more than two members may come from the same country; in practice this has meant that France and Germany always have two members. The members have come from and returned to the world of politics, business, the civil service, labor unions, and the academic profession. There have been four presidents, not all of whom have been as strong as the first incumbent, Jean Monnet; the current president is an Italian academic, Dino Del Bo.

The High Authority allocates duties to its members through a system of working parties each consisting of two men and each concerned with one of the specific fields, transport, external affairs, social affairs, economic affairs, coordination of energy, common market of coal and steel, finance, and rules of competition. Each member of the High Authority is responsible for a field and also takes part in one or two of the other working parties. The groups meet once a week and prepare decisions for the High Authority as a whole which acts by majority vote. The High Authority makes three kinds of ruling: decisions which are binding in all respects, recommendations which are binding but allow flexibility in the method used to attain an objective, and opinions which are purely advisory. It is always obliged to explain its action.

The secretariat of the High Authority, about 2,200 members in all, is organized into departments, generally paralleling the system of working parties, but which serve and are responsible to the executive as a whole rather than to the individual members of the working parties. Each department or division handles both coal and steel matters, issues a weekly report and prepares position papers. The High Authority is also advised by a number of committees composed of experts from industry, labor, and government.

The Special Council of Ministers was given the function of coordinating the activities of the High Authority and the six governments, consulting together and exchanging information. Its membership is flexible, but consists primarily of ministers responsible for economic and industrial matters, meeting when necessary. From 1952 until January, 1963, there were 86 meetings. The Council of Ministers is assisted by a permanent group of deputies, the Coordinating Committee (COCOR), consisting of national representatives who prepare the work and the decisions of the Council, ensure continuity, and coordinate the various committees and groups of experts in the different technical fields.

The voting rules of the Council are complicated and give extra weight to France and Germany. Some decisions need unanimity; some need an absolute majority which must include either France or Germany as producers of over one-sixth of the total value of coal and steel produced in the Community; some need a qualified majority with two-thirds or five-sixths assent.

The Council, like the other two councils of the European Community is Janus-faced: it is both an organ of the Community, attempting to reach compromise and making binding decisions in the interests of all six nations, and at the same time it is a group of representatives of the six governments. The Council has been of some significance as a collective group: it reached agreement on limited labor mobility for some Community workers, it signed a Treaty of Association with Great Britain in 1954, it reached agreement on railroad through-rates and ended the penalization of international traffic in 1955, and signed the Rhine Agreement in 1957 by which international rate schedules would be worked out by companies and their customers. Individual governments have sometimes given way before the common interest as when Germany accepted a tax decision it disliked and the French helped end subsidies. In 1956 West Germany agreed reluctantly to help finance the canalization of the Moselle though this would mainly benefit the French steel industry in Lorraine by reducing the cost of transport of the Lorraine steel mills since they would have access, by a cheap water route, to the Rhine and to the ocean port of Rotterdam, while coal and coke from the Ruhr and the United States would get to Lorraine mills more cheaply. In 1964 the canal was opened to traffic. In general, however, the Council has not contributed much to the success of the idea of supranationalism, and its members have not ceased, in any real way, to be the spokesman of their national interests.

A complicated system of public control over coal and steel has come into existence, and there has been a complex relationship between the High Authority and the Council of Ministers in the sharing of executive power. Some functions are exercised by the High Authority only, after consulting the Consultative Committee and/or the Council. Among these are the fixing of the levy, borrowing and lending, advice on investments, readaptation aid, and the defining of price practices that are prohibited. For other functions the High Authority needs the consent of the Council; these include the allocation of funds for research, regulations on industrial concentrations, recommendations to governments on quantitative restrictions, extending certain kinds of loans for the purpose of improving steel production or distribution, and the placing of limitations on exports to third countries. The High Authority is restricted to precise functions and cannot take action effecting national industries outside its immediate jurisdiction without consulting the Council. Sometimes the Council can, if unanimous, veto High Authority decisions; these include ending a quota system and action to deal with a serious shortage.

The Council cooperates with the High Authority to "harmonize the action of the High Authority and that of the Governments." This has meant the exchange of information and consultation between the two bodies, and requests by the Council for the High Authority to examine any proposals and measures it thinks necessary for achieving the common objectives. The Council may also compel the High Authority to make decisions in areas such as the introduction of a quota system if there is a "manifest crisis" or oversupply, or allocations if there is a shortage, or the fixing of maximum or minimum prices. Occasionally the Council has urged the High Authority to take action, as in the 1963 steel crisis when it instructed the Authority to get in touch with foreign steel authorities to try to reach agreement on steel dumping. In some cases, such as the fixing of maximum and minimum levels for customs duties, the Council can act alone after a proposal by the High Authority.

The High Authority has not been the supranational force that

Schuman and Monnet had expected. It has tended to be over-cooperative with the Council and the governments, though at first it took certain steps, such as the removal of ceilings on Ruhr coal prices and the elimination of special railroad rates, over the objections of some governments, and referred its plans to the Council at too late a stage for them to offer suggestions. It is unfair to see the ECSC as the prewar international steel cartel, writ new, with private industrialists dominant over policy making; however, it failed to impose a ceiling price on steel and it has adopted a permissive attitude to concentrations. The Authority has been unable to control what is virtually a steel export cartel which charges outsiders higher prices for steel, and it has tolerated the suspiciously similar internal prices of steel companies. It has relied on the self-regulation of industry, and on the willing cooperation of governments more than on its regulatory powers.

The limits of the powers of the High Authority were clearly seen in the scrap market problem of 1956–1957 and the unsuccessful attempt in 1959 to apply Article 58 of the Treaty, which permits the Authority to establish a system of production quotas in a period of manifest crisis. In the former case the Authority proposed to penalize extra scrap purchases to keep the gap between scrap and pig iron prices from widening. But this required added control of the scrap market and needed the unanimous approval of the Council of Ministers. The latter took over a year during which the Authority proposed ten different formulas before it agreed. In 1959 the Council refused to allow the application of Article 58 to solve the problems posed by the reduction in the demand for coal, and vetoed the plan for reducing imports of coal, limiting production in order to strengthen the structure of the industry, freezing stocks accumulated by producers, and maintaining miners' incomes.

THE PARLIAMENTARY BODY

The original Schuman plan did not envisage a parliamentary body but it soon became clear that such an assembly was likely to favor strongly the supranational role of the High Authority and to support the move to European unity. The Treaty of Paris, therefore, created the Common Assembly; when the EEC and Euratom were created in 1958 the Assembly was enlarged and became the parliamentary body for all three communities, changing its name in 1962 to the European Parliament.

The Common Assembly was set up with 78 members, 18 each from France, Germany, and Italy, 10 each from Belgium and Holland, and 4 from Luxembourg, selected by each country in the manner it chose, though the Treaty provides for direct universal suffrage in the future. The members were largely identical with those of the six countries in the Consultative Assembly of the Council of Europe. Most of the prominent European parliamentarians have become members at some point.

The Assembly organized itself politically and functionally. Politically, the members divided themselves into three parties, Christian Democrat, Socialist, and Liberal, each getting financial support, with a few unattached. Although, as in other European assemblies, the party groups were more significant for the purpose of distributing the official positions than for political homogeneity, they were more important than in the Consultative Assembly. The members sat in party, not alphabetical, order. From 1954 on, a spokesman of each group made the opening speech expressing the party view in debates on the various subjects. Functionally, the Assembly set up a number of committees roughly paralleling the distribution of work of the High Authority, and providing continuity between the meetings of the Assembly.

Jean Monnet called the Common Assembly "the first European assembly invested with powers of decision," but these powers were not very striking. The Assembly had control over its own budget, though none over the general budget of the ECSC, and had an independent secretariat. It had to approve, though it could not propose, amendments to the Treaty by the "little" revision procedure of Article 95. This procedure involves the proposed amendments being approved by a majority of three-quarters of the votes cast and two-thirds of the total membership. Its strongest power, of which it never made use, was to move a vote of censure on the High Authority after discussing the latter's general report. If, after a three day delay, the vote was passed by a two-thirds majority, the High Authority was obliged to resign. But since the Assembly invariably tried to strengthen the High Authority, the likelihood of censure was improbable.

The Assembly also approved changes in the functions of the Authority, sent resolutions to and asked questions of it. The Authority, from the days of Monnet on, tried to cooperate with the Assembly. It provided quick answers to the written and oral questions of the representatives, and information and statistics for the committees. Its members attended both plenary and committee meetings. Though the Assembly was not formally consulted on appointments, René Mayer, when appointed to succeed Monnet as president of the Authority, began a precedent of appearing before it to explain his program. Relations with the Council of Ministers were less close, though ministers also made reports to the Assembly, and, after being excluded, occasionally attended sessions, debating and answering questions.

Not unnaturally the Common Assembly continually pressed for expansion of its own powers, and in 1954 proposed political, as well as technical, control over the High Authority. It also became a focal point for proposals for increased Community action, especially in social and transport matters, and between 1953 and 1958 was the most fervent exponent of further European integration.

THE COURT OF JUSTICE

The Court of Justice, set up by the Treaty of Paris but extended in 1958 to the EEC and Euratom, consists of seven judges appointed for six years by agreement among the governments. One member, the French economist Jacques Rueff, had little previous legal background. The judges organized themselves into two chambers of three judges each, and chose their own president.

The Court was given a number of functions. It was to decide disputes between the member states on the application of the Treaties, between the institutions of the Community and member states or individuals which enabled it to annul the acts of the Community organs, and between the institutions of the Community which allows it to interpret the Treaty. It could compel the High Authority to act if the Treaty so required and it could act as a consultative body for the modification of the Treaty.

Between 1953 and 1958 the Court received 97 appeals; it made 27 judgments on them, 15 appeals were withdrawn, and 45 were carried over into the new Court. Most of the appeals concerned actions by the High Authority, almost all of them being dismissed. Courts affect the operation of any political system. An early decision by the Court in 1954, in the so-called "Monnet rebates" case, helped contribute to a certain failure of nerve by the High Authority. The Authority had permitted steel firms to deviate from their published price list by an average of 2.5 percent without the need to revise it. The Court decision, that any deviation from published prices or conditions of sale was illegal, led to a more cautious attitude by the Authority. The Court also held that the arrangements made by the Authority for the price equalization of imported scrap must be modified because the Authority had wrongly delegated certain powers to Brussels scrap importing agencies. The proposed amendment of the Treaty of Paris by the High Authority and the Council of Ministers was declared unacceptable by the Court in 1959, as contrary to the basic conception of the Treaty; the Authority was obliged to redraft the amendment, meeting all objections of the Court.

In 1960 the Court held the Authority was ultra vires in trying to prescribe the way in which the Dutch government should obey the Treaty obligation to publish tariffs and prices. But most of the High Authority's actions were upheld. The various decisions of the Authority on the changes in the Ruhr coal sales organization were upheld. The right of the Authority to give an unfavorable opinion on an investment plan was upheld. The Court even decided that appeals to the Court do not in themselves have a suspensive effect on the decisions of the Authority. It was during this initial period as an institution of the ECSC that the Court established that its own decisions must be accepted as final.

THE CONSULTATIVE COMMITTEE

The Consultative Committee is an advisory body of 51 members composed of representatives of producers, workers, distributors, and consumers chosen by the Council of Ministers from a list submitted by various designated organizations. The Committee must be consulted on the periodic statements of the Community objectives and on aid for industrial research programs and may be asked by the High Authority for an opinion within ten days. Since 1956 the High Authority has presented its provisional forecasts of coal and steel production and needs for each quarter.

The Committee has not been a very useful or important part of the ECSC. At first it met frequently and was consulted on the establishment of rules. Business organizations thought it might be useful as a convenient point of pressure but soon found it was more advantageous to approach the High Authority directly rather than the Committee, the advice of which can be rejected by the Authority. Coincidentally, labor took a greater interest in the Committee as that of business declined.

The Functions of the European Coal and Steel Community

The ECSC was given the function of establishing a common market for coal and steel. Negatively this involved the removal of a variety of different kinds of discrimination. Its positive functions are to formulate general objectives for production and research, aiding and directing investment, and improving social welfare and living standards.

A COMMON MARKET

The Common Market for coal, iron ore, and scrap was introduced on February 10, 1953, for ordinary steels on May 1, 1953, and for special steels on August 1, 1954. This has meant the elimination of import restrictions and tariff barriers, subsidies, tax concessions to industries, the ending of discrimination in transport rates and in prices charged to consumers, the guaranteeing of conditions of equality to producers for the supply of raw materials, the publication of prices by firms and their adherence to them, the ability of consumers to choose their suppliers and carriers freely, the breaking up of cartels and concerted practices which distort competition, and preventing the occurrence of mergers which are large enough to determine prices, control production or distribution. By establishing these conditions, there would be fair, ordered competition, prices and terms of sale would be applicable throughout the Community, and discrimination on the basis of nationality ended.

The establishment of the Common Market for coal and steel was relatively simple. By the end of the five-year transitional period in February, 1958, customs barriers, currency and quota restrictions, most national subsidies, double pricing for home and export sales, and the discriminatory effects of crossing a frontier on long hauls had been abolished. A harmonized external steel tariff had been established, lower than the average of the six tariffs. Most of the temporary provisions for helping mines with low productivity—Italian duties on imported coke and steel, subsidies for French coal, and special help for Italian coal—were ended.

POSITIVE FUNCTIONS

The positive functions of the High Authority include the promotion of technical and economic research concerning the production of coal and steel, industrial safety in these two sectors, aiding the financing of programs to eliminate redundant labor, granting loans or loan guarantees for industrial investment, granting financial aid to maintain the earnings of workers and for readaptation, and sponsoring housing programs. It can institute a system of production quotas in the event of a really serious glut, or a system of production allocation if there is a serious shortage. It can authorize price-compensation schemes. It can supervise the administration and control of import and export licences for coal and steel for trade with non-Community countries. To fulfill these functions it carries on a permanent study of the market and price trends in the two commodities, draws up programs forecasting production, consumption, exports and imports, sets out general objectives on production and modernization, and gathers material for improving living and working conditions.

Aiding investment. The High Authority can affect investment in three ways: by providing information, advice, and financial aid to investment programs. Information is obtained through an annual inquiry into investments, periodical publications on investment and production programs, and by the general objectives which guide long term planning and allow individual firms to relate their own situation to the probable developments in the demand for steel. The Authority has drawn up three sets of objectives, in 1955, 1957, and 1961, and has worked closely with specialists from the various countries, and with committees consisting of representatives of producers, consumers, workers, and civil servants.

The High Authority must be notified three months in advance of investment programs. Its advice may be negative or given with reserve. Up to the end of 1962, the High Authority had given advice on 715 occasions concerning 1,157 investment projects, and had exerted some influence though its advice might be disregarded. An unfavorable opinion reduces the likelihood of an enterprise being assisted.

Also, by the end of 1962 the High Authority had given loans of $312 million for industrial developments in coal and steel, of which Germany received about half. It has supported the modernization of coal and iron mining, and the development of the capacity of cokeries in particular. But the High Authority has been criticized for its habit of relending a substantial part of its loans to industries in the country where they were raised. Instead of helping to channel funds from low interest areas to high, the High Authority is merely encouraging the sectorization of national capital markets.

Besides these formal mechanisms, the informal contacts between the High Authority and governments and producers have influenced investment especially in coal production where the High Authority encouraged a shift to the more productive mines.

Helping research. The High Authority has encouraged and

coordinated research into the production and use of coal and steel, given aid to research projects, and sponsored research into problems of industrial diseases and into ways of improving the health and social conditions of ECSC workers. It may select directly specialized institutions to perform the work or may make grants to general research centers applying for aid. In preparing research programs and in helping collate the results of existing research, the High Authority is helped by three international committees: the workers' and producers' committee for industrial medicine and safety made up of representatives of the industries, the government experts' committee, and the research committees which run the programs and ensure that the results are publicized.

Sponsoring readaptation. It was expected that technical changes and administrative rearrangements caused by the common market for coal and steel would bring closures and unemployment in certain areas. The Community was determined that technical progress would not be made at the expense of the workers, and the High Authority was therefore given certain powers in the area of social welfare, principally the granting of readaptation aid, helping industrial redevelopment, and aiding housing programs.

Readaptation aid includes the maintenance of workers' earnings for a period of two years at a progressively diminishing level after they have lost their jobs, payment of travel costs for a worker to move to another area, resettlement bonuses and free training for a new job. In 1960 the Treaty was amended to allow aid to firms which have to close down or make basic changes in their operations as a result of profound changes in marketing conditions. During the first ten years of the ECSC, the High Authority, providing 50 percent of the total cost of readaptation schemes, spent $47 million on schemes involving 130,000 workers, of whom 110,000 were in the coal industry. In 1963 its aid to iron ore miners nearly doubled due to the closing of mines caused by foreign competition.

The High Authority has fostered occupational training by supplying information on vocational-training problems, organizing meetings of training officers, publishing statistics showing likely difficulties in recruiting skilled workers and managerial personnel, and organizing study conferences on mechanization.

In 1960 the High Authority organized an intergovernmental conference on industrial redevelopment to speed up plans for the impoverished mining areas, and to prepare alternative employment in these areas before the mines are closed. It has supplied aid for setting up new factories, granted loans for establishing new activities, and taken the initiative in coordinating industrial development. The ECSC also insisted on "negative reconstruction": the closing of uneconomic pits, during the coal crisis of 1958–1959. The High Authority has been especially concerned with the depressed Borinage coal area, and it has helped build aluminum rolling mills, rubber works, and other industries, in Liège and in the French area of Corrèze.

Beyond financial aid, the High Authority in 1964 began making concrete suggestions to businessmen on the location of industry in depressed areas. It asked four specialist industrial research organizations to draw up lists of products for which future demand could be assured and which could serve as the basis for industrial redevelopment in those areas.

Housing and social welfare. To make up for lack of adequate accommodation and to help labor mobility, the High Authority supported a housing program to cover the building of 100,000 homes. By 1964 it had helped finance 75,000 houses, of which over 50,000 have been finished, and granted or loaned $154 million out of a total of $620 million.

The High Authority has a general concern for social welfare although its actions have been more limited than allowed by the Treaty. It cannot fix wages or alter social security provisions or tax structures, but it can prevent the payment of low wages because of inefficient production or to gain a competitive advantage. Where a state imposes a general tax on industry, the Authority may authorize it to grant special assistance to certain firms. In recent years the High Authority has devoted more attention to research on industrial hygiene and mine safety, and published a range of surveys on the conditions of workers in the Community, wages, social changes, employment, and purchasing power.

Since September, 1957, skilled colliery and steel workers have been able to take up jobs anywhere in the Community; this is aided by a chain of employment offices through the Six. The six governments also signed a convention on social security for migrant workers regarding pensions, family allowances, and benefits. But the social program of the High Authority has been more limited than originally intended, and its plans for a community labor passport have not materialized.

The High Authority as Supranational Body

That the Treaty of Paris created the High Authority as a supranational body is shown both by the powers given to it and by its access to its own source of revenue. Its revenue is obtained by a levy assessed annually on the average value of coal and steel production, the rate not to exceed 1 percent without special permission of the Council of Ministers; in 1964 it was 0.2 percent. By the levy the Authority has been able to build up a fund to be used for guaranteeing loans. The High Authority can also borrow and reloan the money to enterprises. Between 1954 and 1962 it lent $373.4 million which helped finance investment projects of nearly $1.2 billion, or 13 percent of the total investment in coal and steel. In addition, the Authority guaranteed borrowing by firms from outside sources up to $30 million.

A number of important powers were given to the High Authority. It can impose fines on industries that have unfairly reduced wages. It can fix production quotas for individual enterprises, or a system of quotas in the event of a serious oversupply. It can authorize price compensation schemes either for collieries in the same coalfield charging the same prices or among collieries in different coalfields. It can frame rules controlling cartels and concentrations. It can fix maximum prices in cases of shortage, and minimum prices in case of "manifest crisis." It can forbid private investments needing subsidies. It can make recommendations where wages and pensions are substandard.

But it is questionable whether the High Authority has made or been allowed to make strong use of its powers. Some examples of its lack of power can be seen in the fields of price publicity, subsidies, price alignment, cartels and concentrations.

Price publicity. To help prevent unfair competition or discrimination, enterprises are obliged to publish prices while the High Authority prescribes the conditions under which firms must publish their prices. But the Authority has not received as much information as it would have liked. Moreover, the decision of the High Authority in 1958 that the Dutch government had not complied with its request for the publication of information about road transport tariffs and prices partly because the information had gone to the Dutch government and not directly to the High Authority, was declared *ultra vires* by the Court in 1960, since the Authority could not prescribe the way in which the Treaty obligations should be carried out. In a later case in 1962, however, the Court upheld the right of the High Authority to point out where the requirements of publicity had not been met, and called on governments to do what is necessary.

Although the Treaty calls for steel firms to fix their own prices, in practice there has been considerable intervention by governments, especially that of France. Between 1954 and 1958 the French government laid down the amounts by which prices should rise and the time when these prices should take place.

Subsidies. Subsidies are legally incompatible with the existence of the common market in coal and steel, except that certain governmental assistance is allowable, while Article 37 provides for special measures to be taken in the event of disturbances in the national markets. But in fact the Belgian mines have been subsidized, though to a decreasing extent, throughout the life of the ECSC. France has been allowed to grant credits to coal mines to equalize regional differences in family allowances. Germany has subsidized coal transport, and the Dutch frontier was virtually closed to coal imports. The High Authority was compelled to sanction Community subsidies of the coal industry, a Community subsidy to enable displaced workers to be retrained, and French government price control over oil products.

In some cases the subsidies have been disguised. The French Charbonnages de France has been allowed to lose money every year and the loss per ton has progressively increased. Germany was allowed to pay part of the social security taxes of coal companies. In 1961 the Court held that the financing of a shift bonus to underground miners out of the budget of Germany was a subsidy and consequently illegal, although the High Authority had allowed it.

In order to be able to deal with the true problems of energy in the Community, the High Authority, for the last two years, has proposed that existing national subsidies be subjected to joint Community scrutiny, and that control of subsidies is necessary. It has argued for a revision of the Treaty of Paris which would include allowing subsidies for regional development, to combat unemployment and help consumers, the formulation of a common foreign trade policy for coal, and the alignment of rules of competition for all energy, coal included.

Price alignment. In the ECSC a firm is allowed, within certain limits, to undercut the price listed in its own schedule and to bring prices down to the lowest level offered by firms outside as well as those inside the Community in order to compete. But the flexibility allowed by this system of price alignment has been greater than expected. In 1954 the High Authority, through the "Monnet rebates," allowed a 2.5 percent variation in price above or below the published figures; the Court in December, 1954, decided this was illegal.

With the steel crisis of 1963, caused by the 40 percent increase in imports in the previous two years and consequent price reductions, there was an almost total breakdown of internal price discipline in the ECSC. In recent years the tonnage of Community steel on which price alignments have taken place is often larger than that of the imports on which its prices have been aligned.

Cartels and concentrations. In Articles 65 and 66 of the Treaty, the Six drew up what Monnet called "Europe's first anti-trust law." Article 65 deals with cartels and bans agreements between enterprises and concerted practices which distort competition by sharing markets, fixing prices or restricting production, investment and development. Agreements for specialization to encourage more efficient production, and some small-scale joint selling agreements which do not result in market control, are allowed to continue.

In the first ten years of the Community, 214 cases were investigated under Article 65: 27 agreements were authorized, 6 prohibited and 8 were ended by the firms themselves. At the start of the ECSC, there were five powerful joint selling and buying organizations for coal. The High Authority dealt with Oberrheinische Kohlenunion (OKU), a large coal sales organization in South Germany, by prohibiting it from apportioning customers within South Germany among its members. But it has been less successful with the other four. It has not interfered with the Charbonnages de France, established in 1946 to administer the nationalized French coal industry and which has continually been subsidized by the government. The Association Technique de l'Importation Charbonnière (ATIC) was the sole French buyer of imported coal, though the High Authority has attempted to control it and ruled in 1957 that its functions as sole purchaser be abolished, the French government in a series of objections and appeals to the Court, succeeded in producing a compromise which left much of the activity of ATIC intact, including the control of imports from the other ECSC countries. The Comptoire Belge des Charbons (COBECHAR) controls a substantial part of the open-market sales of Belgian producers, but the High Authority has generally approved its operations. It is with the Gemeinschaftsorganisation Ruhrkohle (GEORG) that the High Authority has had most trouble in this area.

GEORG, in 1955, controlled six sales agencies handling all coal produced in the Ruhr, and could, therefore, allocate deliveries as it wished. The High Authority held that a single sales organization was incompatible with the Treaty. In 1956 GEORG was dissolved and replaced by three sales agencies, a joint office for coordination and for allocating supplies among large consumers, and a common sales agency for export to non-member countries. But it was soon apparent that the three sales agencies were in collusion on sales and prices. The High Authority held that the joint office must be ended after March 31, 1960, and that the agencies must base their activity on independent decisions by the firms. In return the sales agencies argued that competition would not produce efficient operation of the coal market, and requested the formation of a single agency.

After the High Authority had rejected two proposals for a single sales organization, the Ruhr agencies appealed to the Court which upheld the Authority and held that a single agency grouping all or most of the Ruhr companies is not compatible with the Treaty since it could determine prices and would affect the balance of the coal market. In November, 1962, the Ruhr owners decided to amalgamate the existing three companies into two. Although the two organizations were to continue their export activities in one organization, and each of the two would include one large firm, owned by the government, which would allow coordination of policy, the High Authority approved the establishment of the two agencies in principle in January, 1963.

The High Authority has approved joint selling by firms in all mining districts where coal is produced by more than one firm, and has authorized common purchasing arrangements among wholesalers in South Germany. In 1953 it refused to interfere with an export cartel formed by steel producers to fix minimum export prices for third countries, arguing that it had no authority over cartels that did not influence competition in the ECSC. In a number of fields, such as the international tube and pipe market, cartels have remained uncontrolled.

Article 66 of the Treaty allows the High Authority to authorize new mergers and to veto them if they are large enough to determine prices, control production or distribution, or restrict competition in the market. Concentrations are permitted if they do not affect freedom of the market or if necessary for modernization or reorganization of production.

The High Authority has examined nearly two hundred proposed mergers both on its own initiative and on application by the firms themselves, and has not vetoed any, nor has it dissolved any existing concentrations. In agreeing to steel mergers the Authority has held that a concentration is permissible if it does not exceed the size of the largest firm in the Community, and that most of the concentrations have promoted efficiency. But measuring the output of a particular concentration in proportion to that of the Community as a whole, as the High Authority does, rather than to that of its immediate area, almost inevitably implies approval.

Occasionally the Authority has made its approval of mergers dependent on certain conditions such as the elimination of interlocking directorates, of financial participation in other firms, or the severing of connections with other groups. In other cases it has insisted that it be consulted over future expansion projects of the new merger.

The dilemma of the High Authority is that it deals with two industries which are not naturally competitive by virtue of their technical needs and methods of financing, and the markets of which are oligopolistic. In addition, the coal industry is subject to increased competition from other sources of energy, and suffers from instability of employment, while readaptation of its workers is difficult. Piero Malvestiti, while President of the High Authority, argued that the ECSC had no objection to concentrations as such, provided they were justified on technical and economic grounds. Indeed, the ECSC itself has caused the formation of a number of steel concentrations because of the threat of competition, while in coal the need to protect some mines and to stabilize miners' incomes has weakened any tendency to competition. The authorization by the High Authority, in 1962, of a joint venture in which a number of Belgian, Luxembourg, and French companies merged into a new steel concern, Sidmar (which produces about 15 percent of flat products in the ECSC), was an explicit recognition of technological trends in steel necessitating very large capital expenditure and investments and larger concentrations.

The ECSC has been successful in ending any large-scale discrimination among classes of consumers, and has imposed some limits on the price policies of producers. But in steel, prices have, to a large extent, been set by a combination of informal agreement and price leadership. In all six countries a small number of groups now dominate steel production, and the High Authority has overtly or tacitly allowed concerted action among the steel producers in each country. In coal, the Charbonnages de France have set a uniform price, and the Ruhr agencies in Germany have essentially done the same.

The Problem of Partial Integration

Some of the difficulties of the ECSC arise from the fact that it is a community of partial integration. As yet the general economic policies of member countries remain unharmonized, and the High Authority is unable to control or mitigate any undesirable impact such policies may have on coal and steel. The ECSC is affected by, but cannot interfere with, changes in monetary and fiscal policies, taxes, wages, general inflation or deflation, trade cycle policies, external trade, or social security. Moreover, the Treaty explicitly recognizes that the national methods of fixing wages and social benefits shall not be affected. In some cases economic developments have bypassed the ECSC, as the considerable migration among the Six has rendered totally ineffective the qualified rules that the ECSC can make for the free circulation of workers. The difficulties of the ECSC in this regard have been increased by the creation, in 1958, of the other two Communities, the interests of which overlap with that of the ECSC. These problems can be seen by looking at three areas: commercial policy, transport, and energy.

Commercial policy. Commercial policy has only a marginal place in the Treaty of Paris, and there is no provision for a common commercial policy. The High Authority has the right to see commercial treaties before the state signs, and it calls attention to any problems involved. The states administer the system of export and import licenses, but the High Authority can supervise them and suggest that the control is too restrictive. But the High Authority complains that while the EEC can fix a common external tariff and looks for and to a common foreign trade policy, the Treaty of Paris stipulates only the harmonization of external tariffs and makes no provision for a joint policy on imports. The lack of power was particularly noticeable in the 1958–1959 coal crisis and the 1963 steel crisis. Only under the stress of the latter crisis did the Council of Ministers empower the High Authority to consult with the traditional foreign steel suppliers of the Community. In the 1958–1959 coal crisis, the High Authority proposed that governments should take concerted action to reduce imports from third countries, and recommended the use of Article 58 of the Treaty which authorizes the use of import quotas by the Community as a whole and Community-wide production quotas, as well as proposing the creation of a fund to help the industry finance the building up of stocks. But the six governments refused this extensive use of authority and the High Authority was obliged to rely on more flexible rules to allow it to deal with the coal situation.

Transport. The Treaty limits the control of the ECSC over transport to what is necessary for the efficient working of the common market in coal and steel. Primarily this has meant publication of prices and nondiscrimination to make equal treatment possible. Discrimination based on country of origin or destination of products carried was ended, as were terminal station fees which involved unnecessary costs for outsiders. For international transport, one tapering rate was to be payable over the whole run instead of the more expensive separate charges. On May 1, 1955, through-rates for coal and ore, and on May 1, 1956, for scrap and steel products, were introduced. After study by groups of experts, a partial harmonization of rates took place on January 1, 1958. In July, 1957, an agreement on the Rhine river freight rates adjusted the regulated internal rates of the different countries to the free international rates. By international agreement direct tariffs have been extended to Switzerland and Austria. The ECSC has also tried to control special rail tariffs which allow concessionary rates to some users. Those special tariffs that were in operation before the creation of the ECSC have been subject to review and modification by the High Authority; those introduced later require prior authorization from the High Authority, which regards them as unjustified if they protect the interests of particular firms or industries, but allows them if they are part of measures to help a region, or if they are competitive.

Because of the importance of transport prices on the final price of coal and steel, the ECSC has been concerned about them.

But control over transport carriers is outside the jurisdiction of the Community. There has been little real progress toward harmonization of the different transport policies and rates for rail, and almost none for road and inland waterways. There are no uniform schedules, special rates are still granted internally, several of the countries began concealing the freight rates charged on their railroads in 1961, and the ending of discriminations has not necessarily meant a general lowering of rates. Moreover, the ECSC soon found that part of its difficulty lay in the fact that prices and conditions of transport are, to a considerable degree, determined by noneconomic considerations.

Energy policy. The Treaty of Paris was based on the assumption that coal supply would continue to be insufficient, that oil would not be of major significance and, therefore, that consumers ought to be protected through a free and competitive market and the elimination of cartels and subsidies. But if coal production was insufficient in 1950, it was overabundant a decade later. In 1950 coal provided 74 percent of the energy supplies of the Six; in 1963 it provided only 43 percent, though consumption has remained constant at about 250 million tons. For the first time since the Industrial Revolution, coal constitutes less than half the energy used in the Six. Oil is providing 39 percent of the total in 1964, compared with 10 percent in 1950; natural gas, now accounting for 3.5 percent, is likely to expand substantially in the near future. In 1964 imported coal and oil covered over 40 percent of the needs of the Six; imports of energy have tripled since 1950.

Control over energy has been difficult partly because each of the three Communities regulates some energy source: the ECSC covers coal, Euratom atomic power, and the EEC oil and natural gas. But the Six are also divided in their interests. Germany, France, and Belgium are coal producers; Italy, Luxembourg, and Holland are coal consumers and are more interested in natural gas and oil; France is also concerned with the gas and oil products of Algeria. The ECSC soon realized the inadequacy of partial control over energy. In October, 1957, the High Authority was given responsibility for coordinating the separate power policies of the Six. It was to exercise general guidance over a European energy policy, and to collaborate with the new organizations, the EEC and Euratom.

A common energy policy has been under discussion for seven years. Agreement has been difficult to reach because of the principles, sometimes conflicting, on which such a policy must be based: cheap energy supplies but security of supply, increasing recourse to imported energy but maintenance of European coal mines, subsidies for coal mining on a degressive basis, harmonization of the conditions of competition. In 1959 the interexecutive working group, containing representatives of the three Communities, was set up, the High Authority being responsible for making proposals. Meeting once or twice a month, it formulated preliminary reports and interim notes which were submitted to the Six, and in June, 1962, presented a memorandum which suggested, among other things, standardization of rules governing competition in markets for coal and oil, a system of subsidies for coal, and the adoption of a common policy for trade in energy with nonmember countries. In 1963 a Special Committee on Energy Policy, composed of senior officials from the member countries and representatives of the three Communities was set up, with the High Authority representative as chairman, after the Six had failed to agree on the June, 1962, memorandum.

After a vigorous appeal by the new President of the High Authority, Dino Del Bo, the Six agreed in April, 1964, to enact a common energy policy. While no details were fixed, the Six agreed that the common policy must be based on three themes: a common commercial policy for supplies of energy, a unified system of subsidies, and conditions and rules of harmonized competition between the sources of energy. This would eliminate the danger of individual states being able to provide subsidies to coal and regulate energy markets and prices, thus striking at the very principle of a common energy policy.

Crises in Coal and Steel

Any appraisal of the ECSC is complicated by the fact that the Community coal industry was subject to severe competition in the

1950s, that the place of coal in the total energy picture changed drastically around 1958, and that steel was faced with major technical changes, needing large investments, and then with increased competition from third countries. Problems of this magnitude were not foreseen when the Treaty was drafted, when it seemed essential to avoid delays in production and to contribute to general economic expansion. The safeguard clauses in the Treaty were available to deal with emergencies, but not with the consequences of major structural or economic changes. For the High Authority the only long term solution would be Community control over appropriate structural development, and a concern with specialization and lowering of costs rather than with the development of production. But the powers given to the ECSC are not appropriate for this, and the Treaty limits very strictly the scope for initiative by the institutions. This was shown in 1961 when the Court denied the attempt of the High Authority to relax some of the clauses on cartels to permit the temporary approval of rationalization agreements going beyond what the Treaty ordinarily allows.

The High Authority has been restricted in its attempt to deal with the coal difficulties. The Belgian coal industry has been in constant crisis. Between 1953 and 1958 it received $53 million in reorganization aid from German and Dutch mines, and an equal sum from the Belgian government. Since 1958, due to the heavy buildup of stocks, reductions in production and short time operations in Belgian coal fields, its problems have been aggravated. But the Council of Ministers refused to allow the High Authority to make use of Article 95 of the Treaty which permits amendment of the rules for the exercise of the Authority's powers where unforeseen difficulties have been revealed, or where there have been profound changes in the economic or technical conditions directly affecting coal and steel. Instead, the High Authority was obliged to use Article 37, which allows certain special interventions to correct a situation in which there are fundamental and persistent disturbances in the economy of a state. It isolated the Belgian coal industry from the rest of the Common Market by means of restrictions on imports of coal into Belgium from non-member countries and other Community coal fields, and also on exports of Belgian coal. In return the Belgian government agreed to cut production and close the most uneconomic mines gradually over a four year period. These temporary measures were extended until 1963 when the High Authority considered that the continued isolation of Belgium from the common market of coal would hinder further recovery. In addition, the High Authority authorized the payment of subsidies to the Belgian mines, and permitted an extension in time to prevent disturbances in the Belgian economy, to provide partial compensation for losses resulting from wage increases awarded Belgian miners in 1962, and to compensate for structural changes. But the High Authority's demand, in 1963, for special measures relating to production quotas, price levels, and distribution of orders to apply to Belgian coal was not met.

The structural problem of coal is complicated by political difficulties. Under a liberal energy policy, about half the mines of the Community could stand competition because of cost conditions, and there would be a progressive closing down of unproductive mines. But since most of the productive mines are in in Germany, there has been no agreement on this. Because of partial integration, the High Authority has no control over products competing with coal until a common energy policy has been agreed.

In recent years the steel industries of the Community have been handicapped by high coal costs, expensive but low-grade iron ore, rising foreign competition, especially from the Soviet bloc, and by structural problems.

Between 1960 and 1963 the production of steel stagnated. The sellers' market, which had existed since the beginning of the ECSC, had ended, the demand for heavy capital goods had declined, and there was an overcapacity of steel production. The steel crisis of 1962–1963, caused by the tremendous increase in world production of steel that far outstripped demand, and by the 40 percent increase in steel imports in the ECSC, led to a price war among steel producers with discounts on the list price up to 40 percent, and the cutting of profit margins, expenditure, and investments. The Community steel producers complained they were hampered by the rules on price publicity and nondiscrimination, while the noncommunity producers benefitted from low production costs and favorable government policies. The French producers complained that they were largely tied to the highly protected French coal, while the other five ECSC members benefitted from cheaper fuel and power. The French steel industrialists asked the ECSC, in 1963, to raise steel tariffs and minimum price levels, and asked the French government for a 5 percent reduction in the price of French coke, and for the import of coal from abroad.

The Six were divided over the French demand, and troubled at the French threat to take unilateral steps to protect itself, which seemed to endanger the whole concept of a community. Holland, an importing country with low tariffs, argued that an increased tariff would lead to higher prices. Italy, with the highest ECSC tariff at 9 percent, objected to the removal of the differential between its own tariffs and those of the other five. To some extent there was a conflict of interest between the older, high-cost, inland steel plants grouped around the Ruhr-Luxembourg-Liège-Thionville area, and the new coastal plants using high-grade imported ores.

The steel crisis necessitated a Community solution. In June, 1963, the Council of Ministers agreed to coordinate the policy of the Six on steel imports from the Soviet bloc. The Council of Ministers could not agree unanimously on the creation of a uniform steel tariff at the Italian level. Therefore, in January, 1964, the High Authority, with unaccustomed forcefulness under its new President, made binding recommendations to help settle the crisis: steel tariffs were to be raised and aligned with the current Italian tariff of 9 percent, and a specific duty of $7 a metric ton was to be imposed on foundry pig-iron imports. Through these recommendations the Six were able to make a temporary increase in the level of the ECSC's external protection. The Council approved a ban on price-cutting by ECSC producers to meet competition from the East until December, 1964, and renewed quota restrictions on steel and pig-iron imports from the Eastern bloc. Also an agreement was made between the Six and Great Britain that neither would sell below cost price in the markets of the other.

But the problem of surplus production remains. France has asked for concerted action by international agreement to reduce production and investment. Other ECSC members have asked for international pricing agreements, theoretically not allowed, while nonECSC countries have criticized the price alignment mechanism as an excuse to lower ECSC prices. However, steel remains a world problem and in 1964 the OECD was considering the possibility of calling a world conference to discuss it.

A related problem for the ECSC is the reduction in Community iron-ore production. This is partly explained by the relative stagnation of steel, but it is largely the result of the opening up of overseas sources of iron ore which is richer in iron content than Community ore, and by low cost transport provided by the new large cargo ships. This has encouraged both the development of coastal steel works and a 50 percent increase in imported ore since 1953.

These crises and structural changes have influenced the work of the ECSC. The reduction between 1959 and 1964 in the number of coal miners by over 200,000 has created a major problem of readaptation, increased by the unemployed iron-ore miners. It has also meant more concern with commercial, transport, and social policies, and a greater need for coordination of activity with the other two Communities.

The Record of the ECSC

The record of the ECSC during its first ten years is one of mixed success. Steel production increased 74 percent, iron-ore production 41 percent, and supplies of scrap by 50 percent. Apart from 1958 and 1962 the record was one of continuous expansion in steel. Steel prices were held relatively stable, rising only 3 percent; during the 1962–1963 crisis, they fell by 15 percent. Intra-

Community trade increased remarkably; over 7 times in scrap, 5 times in steel, and 3 times in iron ore. However, between 1958 and 1963 the share of the ECSC in world steel trade dropped 10 percent. The productivity of each enterprise increased about 82 percent in steel, and about 50 percent in coal. Coal output has declined since 1957 and was 5 percent lower in 1962 than it had been in 1952. Intra-Community trade rose by only 8 percent; prices have risen 5 percent. Output per man-hour rose 47 percent in coal, and 73 percent in steel.

The Six have invested $9 billion in steel during the last decade, towards which the High Authority lent $400 million. The High Authority has contributed to the retraining of 160,00 workers and to a number of redevelopment programs, and has helped the building or planning of 75,000 houses.

Naturally enough the home market has remained the center for each national industry and the hopes that French ore would go to German blast furnaces and German coal to the mills of Lorraine have not altogether been fulfilled. However, it has become easier for the Six to export to each other, and strong trade links have developed between the different countries.

The High Authority has contributed to this record in a multitude of ways. It has ensured that trade barriers will not be automatically reimposed to meet domestic problems, it has achieved the end of double pricing, and of national discrimination in most transport rates affecting coal and steel, which often meant banning special concessions in favor of individual firms. It ordered the abolition of the "administrative tax" imposed by Italy on imports, and the import duties on pig iron. The Belgian tax exemption on deliveries of domestic coal and steel to public bodies was condemned and stopped. The High Authority got the German government to revoke a tax-exempt miners' bonus and to stop paying the social security contributions of the mine owners, which it considered to be government subsidies.

The High Authority has occasionally represented the Six in tariff negotiations with nonmembers, as in 1956, when it negotiated tariff concessions for France, Germany, and Italy with the

United States and Austria on trade in steel at the GATT conference. It has signed transport agreements with nonmember countries.

The High Authority has sometimes taken the initiative in dealing with a problem over which it had no specific powers. In August, 1956, after the Belgian mine disaster at Marcinelle, it called a conference of the governments of the Six to study the state of safety in mines, an enquiry which led to the creation of the Mines Safety Commission. In 1959 it recommended to the French government that it take action to counteract the effects of France's devaluation on its steel prices in 1958. In October, 1964, it initiated and sponsored an International Congress on Steel Utilization which examined the latest techniques on the modern uses of steel.

The High Authority tried to regulate scrap extensively. It authorized a Community-wide organization of scrap consumers to replace the previous regional organizations concerned with the purchase and distribution of foreign scrap and with the operation of a price equalization scheme, financed by a levy on domestic scrap, to reduce the cost of imports. Unfortunately, this scheme encouraged rather than discouraged the import and use of scrap, and the High Authority failed in its attempt to encourage the use of pig iron as a substitute. In 1959 the scrap equalization fund was discontinued and the scrap market freed.

Nations, industries, and groups in the Six have wavered in their loyalty and commitment to the ECSC. The six governments supported the High Authority's maximum price policy for coal which lasted until 1956, and even aided the negotiations between producers and the High Authority since their objective, low coal prices, was a common one. But on other matters they have been less sympathetic to the Authority. In the Gaullist period France has been most critical. In 1959 it argued that the supranational activity of the High Authority ought to be reduced; French use of oil from the Sahara made High Authority control over Ruhr coal less necessary. During the 1963 steel crisis French industrialists, with some governmental approval, proposed a controlled entente among European producers, and the abolition of the High

Authority, to be replaced by a looser association among European steel companies. But other nations have also slowed the work of the ECSC. Germany, in general, has been reluctant to see High Authority regulation of industry. In 1963, the Netherlands, otherwise a strong supporter of the idea of integration, vetoed the proposal for degressive subsidies to coal mines, and so prevented agreement on a common energy policy. The High Authority has not always insisted on its prerogatives, but in 1962 it successfully protested against the setting up by Belgium of a joint administrative board with powers of decision and control over the collieries, on the grounds that the Community, not the national states, was responsible for prices, production, and sales in coal and steel.

If the attitude of governments and business to the ECSC has been ambiguous, that of the trade unions has been invariably favorable. Both the International Confederation of Free Trade Unions and the International Federation of Christian Trade Unions have representatives and committees in Luxembourg who keep in touch with and are consulted by the High Authority, which itself has always included at least one trade unionist. Labor also has 17 of the 51 members of the Consultative Committee, and thus keeps closely in touch with the daily problems of the Community. The trade unionists have always pressed for the extension of social powers in the Community, for raising the standard of living, for greater supranationality in the ECSC so that the High Authority can take independent action on readaptation schemes and on the uses of Community finance, and for the increased power of the Assembly.

The High Authority has been criticized for being overly cautious, for leaving too much authority to the governments, for attempting to obtain the unanimity of the Council even when the Treaty did not require it, and for consulting the Council where this was not prescribed, and for unduly desiring to placate the different interest groups. Like the six governments the High Authority has been faced with difficult choices: the desire for low-cost energy but the protection of coal, the right of consumers to choose among competing sources of energy while not relishing

the decreasing use of coal. In the relatively easy matters, like helping research, compilation of statistics, and aid for rehabilitation,
the record of the High Authority has been good. In more difficult
matters, its success has been qualified.

The Missing Link

The ECSC is almost *Hamlet* without the Prince of Denmark.
Great Britain, whose coal output was equivalent to that of the
Six together, refused to join a supranational organization, giving
as reasons the problem of the Commonwealth, a possible incompatibility with the rules of GATT, a possible danger to full employment in Britain, and the difficulty of reconciling nationalization of coal in Britain with the ECSC. Although it would not
join an organization which could "close down our pits and our
steel works," Britain was prepared to enter into an association
with it. On becoming President of the High Authority, Jean
Monnet arranged for cooperation between the Six and Britain
which set up a delegation in Luxembourg. In 1955 a Council of
Agreement was established consisting of four members of the
High Authority and representatives of the British Ministry of
Power, Board of Trade, the National Coal Board, and the Iron
and Steel Board. The Council has normally met twice a year,
as have its three subcommittees which meet before the Council
meetings. Reports are prepared and mutual market problems
discussed, but the Council is essentially a place for exchange
of information, consultation, and liaison, not for policy making,
though its activities have led to a mutual lowering of tariffs.
Besides this link with Britain, the ECSC has also entered into
agreements with 16 other countries, as well as special agreements
with Switzerland and Austria.

In March, 1962, Great Britain made its official application to
join the ECSC, but the negotiations were conducted not through
the Council of Association or even the Council of Ministers,
but by the six governments and Britain. Before the EEC-British
negotiations failed in January, 1963, Britain had agreed to the

abolition of all incompatibilities in steel, and the British steel manufacturers were preparing a basing-point pricing system to fit in with that of the ECSC. But France objected that the large size of the British industry produced difficulties, that it might gain the market of Northern France, that its system of subsidies might make competitive pricing difficult, and that the National Coal Board's joint selling operations were unacceptable. The negotiations remain suspended.

CHAPTER SEVEN

The European Economic
Community

NAPOLEON advised that constitutions be short and obscure. The Treaty of Rome setting up the EEC for an unspecified period is a long, ingenious, and reasonably clear document containing 248 articles, 4 annexes, 9 declarations, 2 conventions, and 13 protocols. It provided for the creation of a common market, the automatic reduction of internal tariffs and the establishment of a common external tariff. A transitional period of from 12 to 15 years was laid down, divided into three stages during which tariffs would be gradually ended. Each stage was to last four years and the move to the second stage was conditional on the Six agreeing that sufficient progress had been reached. Duties on intra-Community trade were to be abolished by the end of the period. A common tariff on imports from nonmembers was to be set up by the end of the transitional period at an approximately arithmetical average of the tariffs in force in the Six on January 1, 1957. Quantitative restrictions on trade were also to be ended in stages.

The economic arguments favoring the creation of a single common market were based on the view that freedom of trade in a larger market would lead to greater output, more economical production and distribution, the elimination of some marginal producers, mass production and greater specialization, modernization of equipment, promotion of the flow of capital, lower prices, greater real incomes and the increase of trade. The size of the market is not the only factor preventing economies of scale. But many of the factors that have hindered economic progress in Europe—too much product differentiation, too many firms, restrained competition, high profits on low turnovers, marginal producers—are diminishing.

The EEC is popularly known as the "Common Market," but the popular term is, in a sense, a misnomer, and any parallel with the nineteenth century German Zollverein a mistaken one, for the reduction of trade barriers, significant though this is, was to be only the starting point for the Community. The idea of a large single national market is at the heart of economic integration, but the EEC is more than a customs union. Economically, its over-all objectives are to increase prosperity, encourage expansion, and raise the standard of living of the citizens of the Six; politically, it is to establish the foundation of an ever closer union among the European peoples. The EEC is, therefore, concerned with the removal of all discrimination, correcting the "distortions" of the conditions of competition, framing common rules forbidding cartels that are socially undesirable, the free movement of labor and capital and the free establishment of business, common agricultural policies, common foreign-trade policies of the Six, the harmonization of monetary policies, the harmonization of legislation in a large number of areas, the coordination of over-all economic and social policies, retraining workers and improving the opportunities for employment of workers, common transport and energy policies, aid to the underdeveloped regions of the Community and to the overseas countries with which it is associated.

Certain compromises were written into the Treaty of Rome. The special problem of the Italian economy was recognized. France was allowed to maintain temporarily its system of export aids and special charges on imports in the franc area. The other five states were obliged to adjust their systems of overtime payment and rates to that of France. Germany was allowed to maintain its existing pattern of trade with East Germany, the former colonial powers to continue their preferential treatment for imports from their former possessions, and Luxembourg to keep certain quotas on agricultural products.

The Treaty of Rome, in spite of its length and technical details, is a *loi-cadre* (framework law) which has continually to be amplified. It is specific largely for the transitional period, otherwise it sets out general aims and lays down procedures. Whereas in the Treaty of Paris the main lines of common policy are defined and the High Authority is supposed to decide only on implementation and application in individual cases, the institutions of the EEC are left to decide on common policies and rules. The Treaty of Rome, partly because of the resurgence of some nationalistic tendencies and the tempering of idealism in the Six, and partly as a result of the experience of the ECSC, is more cautious in its allocation of powers than the previous Treaty. The Community was given no power in those areas that are the core of political decisions: defense, foreign affairs, finance, and police matters. The states still largely decide to what degree and under what conditions the common institutions can make decisions; there is no specific power to act to secure the objectives of the Treaty. The states still largely control the rule-making and Treaty amendment powers of the Community. Where the ECSC Treaty explicitly spoke of the supranationality of the High Authority, the Treaty of Rome deliberately omitted any such reference. The operation of the EEC is financed by the member-governments, rather than by any direct Communal levy: France, Germany, and Italy provide 28 percent each, Belgium and the Netherlands 7.9 percent each, and Luxembourg 0.2 percent.

Clearly, the EEC is not a federal organization, but it is considerably more than an intergovernmental agreement or commercial arrangement. It aims at integration, not cooperation, at a fusion of interests, not a balance of power. But it is sui generis since its institutional structure and procedural rules do not allow it to be placed in one of the known categories of regime in political science. The voting arrangements, allowing some decisions by a simple or weighted majority in the Council of Ministers, provide a procedural device by which national sovereignty is qualified. Similarly, the obligation on the members to take specific common actions and decide on common policies impose some limitations on sovereignty. The states are committed to a gradual transfer of legislative jurisdiction in areas such as agriculture, transport, and commercial policy; here the Treaty provides for common policies.

Their legislative power is also limited by their commitment to achieve coordination of economic or monetary policy or harmonization of the turnover tax or social legislation. Collaboration is called for in some subjects, such as social affairs. Within specified limits the Community organs make decisions which are binding on the states or are directly applicable. Community regulations have direct effect on states as does domestic legislation. The method of the Community is to try for communally devised solutions to problems in certain areas rather than individual or bilateral state action, coordination of national policies in other areas and for the implementation of rules by the Community institutions.

The Institutions of the Community

As in the ECSC, there are four major institutions in the EEC, the Council of Ministers, the Commission, and the Court and Assembly, both of which were already in existence.

THE COUNCIL OF MINISTERS

The Council of Ministers consists of one delegate from each member state, the actual composition depending on the subject of the meeting. It is thus a body with changing membership, lacking some of the continuity and coherent policy of national cabinets. As a group of foreign ministers it normally meets twice or three times a month, about six days in all; the Ministers of Agriculture have, in 1963 and 1964, been meeting about twice a month. The sessions of the Council are numbered progressively no matter which ministers are attending; several ministers can take part in one meeting or different ministers can make up a different Council at the same time. Occasionally, for less important subjects, the Council is composed of Secretaries of State rather than Ministers.

The Council was given a more dominant role in EEC than in the ECSC. It has the functions of ensuring the coordination of the general economic policies of the member states and "disposing of a power of decision." The Council acts as a political unit, capable of making decisions which are binding and immediately applicable. This differentiates it from meetings of ministers at international organizations or intergovernmental conferences, even when it acts unanimously. Some see the Council as a legislative body or normative institution since it must approve the rules and norms to be applied and is thus the enacting body of the Community; others see it as one of the two executive bodies in the Community.

The voting rules are significant and unusual: the Council can vote by unanimity, simple or qualified majority. Almost all important decisions are made by unanimity. Unanimity is required for decisions on the harmonization of fiscal systems, modification of the common external tariff, the extension or curtailment of the second or third stage, the harmonization of legislation on the turnover tax and acts that constitute modifications of the Treaty. During the second stage there are now 38 specified times when the Council decides by unanimity. Where a qualified majority is used, the votes are weighted according to country: France, Germany and Italy have 4 each, Belgium and the Netherlands 2 each, and Luxembourg 1, the qualified majority being 12 of the 17 votes. When the Council decides on the basis of a proposal of the Commission, the 12 need include only three states: when it wishes to act without a proposal of the Commission, the 12 must include at least four states.

Even during the first stage, the Council could decide by qualified majority vote in twelve cases such as the application of the principles governing competition, the granting of tariff quotas to a state in certain cases, the prohibition of state aids and the adoption of the budget of the Community. During the present second stage the Council can decide by qualified majority on more occasions, including decisions on the implementing of the right-of-establishment program. After the second stage, decisions on commercial, agricultural and transport policy will be made in this way. As an increasing number of decisions are made by qualified majority during the transitional period, the progression of the

Community itself becomes mathematically easier. The move from the first stage to the second, which took place on January 1, 1962, needed unanimity on a proposal by the Commission; the move from the second to the third is automatic unless the Commission proposes that the move not be made and this is accepted unanimously by the ministers. The more the Council acts by qualified majority rather than unanimity, the more it becomes a Community instrument.

The Council has a secretariat of about 400 in Brussels, headed by five director-generals, responsible for internal market affairs, external and general affairs, energy, and administration. The experience of the Committee of Coordination (COCOR) in the ECSC had shown the need for some organ to prepare the meetings of ministers. In the EEC this is done by the Committee of Permanent Representatives which consists of the heads of the delegations of the states to the European Communities in Brussels. The permanent representatives, diplomats with the rank of ambassadors, meet at least once, and generally three or four times, a week to prepare the ground work and decisions for their ministers. There is normally a division of labor, the ambassadors meeting to discuss the problems with political implications, and their deputies dealing with more technical matters. The representatives are assisted by a number of working parties consisting of medium level civil servants from the competent ministries, and by eighteen permanent groups, and some ad hoc groups of experts who prepare material for them.

The permanent representatives play a vital role in the work of the Community since the ministers are dependent on their advice. For convenience the agenda of the Council is divided into two kinds of problems, "A" and "B." On the first group the representatives have reached agreement and the Council simply registers its assent. The second group raise political problems which the representatives cannot resolve and which, therefore, go to the ministers for solution.

The representatives illustrate the unique nature of the European Communities for they are on the one hand the representatives of their countries to the Communities, and on the other they are a community organ attempting to harmonize the different national points of view and acting as mediator between the states and the Communities. By their physical proximity to each other and to the European Commissions, their constant negotiation and social contact, they are able to play the latter European role as well as that of national representatives.

THE COMMISSION

The major administrative and executive body, and the pivot around which the work of the EEC turns, is the Commission. It consists of nine members serving a four-year term who are "chosen for their general competence and . . . indisputable independence" by the states, and who pledge not to accept instructions from member governments or any outside source. The three larger countries provide two members each, and the Benelux countries one each. The president and three vice-presidents are chosen from among the members by the Council for two-year terms. In 1964 the Commission consisted of the President, Walter Hallstein, former German foreign-office official, three Vice-Presidents, Robert Marjolin, former French civil servant and Secretary-General of OEEC, Sicco Mansholt, former Dutch Minister of Agriculture, and Lionello Levi Sandri, former Italian professor and administrator, Jean Rey, former Belgian Minister of Economic Affairs, Hans von der Groeben, former German civil servant, Lambert Schaus, former Luxembourg diplomat and minister, Henri Rochereau, former French politician, and Guido Colonna di Paliano, former Italian Deputy Secretary General of NATO; five were civil servants and four were politicians. Among the nine it is apparent that the diversity of ability and the distribution of function has given rise to a powerful inner circle of three, Hallstein with his marked diplomatic skill, Mansholt with his astute political sense, and Marjolin with his creative talent for new ideas. The President as such has no special status, but the personality of Hallstein, his function as chairman, and his responsibility for general administration has made him at least primus inter pares.

The work of the Commission is divided into nine subjects: agriculture, economic and financial affairs, internal market, external relations, anti-trust, transport, social affairs, the development of overseas territories, and administration. The commissioners are divided into groups of three to deal with each subject. Each commissioner is responsible for the administration of a department run by a director-general, who is of a different nationality from himself. As the work load has increased, the commissioners have been spending less time on their two minor concerns and have concentrated on their own department. In addition to the nine departments divided on vertical lines, the Commission is also partly responsible for the three service departments—legal, statistical and information—common to all the three Communities.

The Commission is served by an executive secretariat of about 60 who are responsible for internal coordination, organizing meetings and preparing the agenda and the working documents of the Commission, advising the Commission and maintaining relations with the other institutions of the Community, especially the parliament and the permanent representatives. The secretariat, drawn from the worlds of politics, labor and commerce, and the civil service, are appointed very deliberately on national lines: its head is a former French civil servant and his assistant a German foreign-office official.

The Commission is also responsible for the recruitment and promotion of its staff, now 2,700. Originally the staff was seconded from national administrations or appointed from nongovernmental bodies. Now there are also periodical open competitions for recruitment. The budgetary contributions of the states determine approximately the numbers of the staff and their allocation by nationality. In 1964 the numbers of those from Germany and the Benelux countries were disproportionately high and those from Italy particularly low. Very few of the civil servants come from nonmember countries. About 600 form the top administrative level, while the majority are translators and secretaries. In general, the national governments have been loath to increase the staff, numerically or materially, both for financial reasons, and to prevent too many good graduates from entering the European, rather than the national civil service. The first strike of the employees of the Community in 1964 demonstrated the solidarity of the staff and the Commission in face of the intransigence of the Council of Ministers. The staff, popularly known as "Eurocrats," are a remarkably gifted and hardworking group, whose linguistic ability is formidable.

In French and Belgian political style, each commissioner is also assisted by a cabinet, three or four men who serve as his personal staff, who advise and who represent him on the Commission. The members of the cabinet are of the same nationality as the commissioner and help keep political contact with their own country. The cabinet is particularly concerned with the political, rather than the administrative aspects of the problems confronting the commissioner. The nine *chefs du cabinet* normally meet every day to prepare the preliminary discussion and to seek agreement on subjects before they go to their superiors.

The Commission itself meets once a week and theoretically takes collegiate decisions by majority vote, though it tries to get unanimity for important decisions. In practice the making of decisions has become so complicated that individual commissioners have resorted to the "written procedure." By this procedure a proposal is adopted if there are no objections by the other commissioners in a given period; some fifteen decisions a day are taken in this way.

Walter Hallstein has spoken of the Commission as a watchdog seeing that obligations are carried out and capable of taking offenders before the court, a motor stimulating and initiating Community action by its right of proposal, and an honest broker trying to get agreement among the six member states.

As guardian of the Treaty, the Commission is responsible for seeing that its provisions and the Community decisions are correctly applied. The Commission can ask a state to justify an action within a specified period, and can issue a reasoned statement (*avis motivé*) if it refuses. If the state does not comply, the Commission may bring the case before the court, as it has done on sixteen occasions. The Commission has exclusive power to execute the Treaty, to apply the rules to particular cases and to allow safeguard clauses to be invoked by a state or firm. Its powers of drafting and applying the detailed measures for implementing decisions include the suspension or modification of the common external tariff, granting import quotas, approving agreements between firms, investigating firms and fining them, issuing regulations on violation of the anti-trust provisions, and applying the agricultural regulations, especially the determining of the variable levies. As the Community moves into its later stages, the Commission's power to make decisions of this nature will increase.

The Commission can make four different kinds of rules. (1) It can make regulations which have the effect of legislation, are binding on states and become part of their law, and do not have to be ratified by national parliaments. (2) It can issue directives which are binding for the result to be attained, but not as regards the form and manner in which they are enforced. This is left to the states which may amend their legislation, modify governmental regulations or issue completely new measures. The directives are binding only on the states concerned. (3) It can make decisions addressed to a particular person, firm, or state which are binding on those to whom they are directed. (4) It can give opinions or make recommendations to the Council, or publish its point of view on issues where it has no strict competence.

The Commission's most important function is to initiate proposals since the Council is unable to act without them. This right of proposal is even more significant since proposals can be amended only by unanimous decision of the Council; in most cases, therefore, the Council will either accept or reject, and the Commission virtually retains the power to amend its own proposal. After January, 1966, when the Council will make nearly all its decisions by simple or qualified majority, the influence of the Commission will be even stronger.

The Commission operates in a different way depending on whether it is framing proposals or applying a policy already agreed. In the former case the Commission carries on consultations at every stage with representatives of governments and of private organizations, many of which now have lobbyists in Brussels, as well as with its own staff. In the latter case, the departments of the Commission are advised by meetings of national experts appointed by their governments; over 100 such meetings are held annually. When the proposals or memoranda of the Commission are sent to the Council, they are examined by a committee of senior officials or a permanent working party, the operations of which are coordinated by the Committee of Permanent Representatives, before going to the ministers. The Commission members have the right to attend and speak at the Council meetings in which the proposals are discussed. The proposals are then sent to the European Parliament and to the Economic and Social Committee for an opinion. At any time, however, the Commission can make changes and send a new working paper to the Council.

The Commission acts not only as mediator of the different national attitudes, but also as spokesman for the Community interests as distinct from the national interests. The commissioners are politically oriented, no less than the Council. Through their formal and informal relations with the Council and the permanent representatives, the commissioners have developed a fine sense of what is politically possible in the interests of the Community, and this is reflected in the individual proposals they make, in their appeals for support to individual governments or groups, and in the package deals which they have proposed as a way of reaching agreement. A spectacular example of the success of the Commission was the marathon negotiation on agriculture in December, 1963, during which the Commission, acting as skilled arbiter and possessing technical expertise that none of the six individual nations had, could formulate an acceptable settlement that reconciled purely national interests and the general interest of the Community. The Commission is, in fact, a seventh partner in the Community, with its own interest and with its own political support. It has taken every opportunity to move the Community forward, to accelerate its program, and to get agreement on common policy.

The Commission sometimes represents the Community in formal relations with member states and third parties. Besides the permanent representatives of the member states, there are now 59 ambassadors of nonmember states accredited to the Community in Brussels who remain in close touch with the Commission. From a strictly legal point of view the Council is responsible for the negotiations on association or commercial policy with third countries. But in practice the role of the Commission, though varying, has been greater than that of mere participation. In the negotiations with Greece, Turkey, and with the African and Malagasy States, the Commission bore a considerable part of the burden, aided by national experts who set up working parties to deal with the various problems; its role in the negotiations with Great Britain was more limited. The Commission took an active part in the work of three special committees set up by GATT in 1958 to expand international commerce. The hope of the Commission that it could present a common approach for the Six in the United Nations Conference on Trade and Development in Geneva in the spring of 1964 was not realized. But in the GATT negotiations which formally opened on May 4, 1964, as in the Dillon Round of 1960–1962 the Commission negotiated on behalf of the Community on the basis of directives issued by the Council in December, 1963.

The relationship between the Commission and the Council of Ministers is probably the most intriguing and uncertain feature of the Community structure, a reflection of the tension between the communal and national elements and interests in the Community. According to the Treaty the Council is responsible for "the achievement of the objectives laid down" in the Treaty, while the Commission ensures "the functioning and development of the Common Market," but decision making is shared between them. The Council and the Commission are connected through a multitude of committees in which experts, national and communal, discuss problems. The Commission is a technocracy which is in continual consultation with experts on both general lines of policy and particular issues.

THE COURT OF JUSTICE

The Court, created in Luxembourg by the Treaty of Paris, now serves all three Communities. It consists of seven judges appointed for six years, assisted by two court advocates. A judge, if he wishes, may be reappointed. The judges appoint one of their members—currently, Charles Hammes—as president for three years. They come from different backgrounds, from the bar and universities, as well as the national bench.

The Court operates through both a written and an oral procedure. After a case is brought, the judges read the relevant documents before they decide to hear witnesses. An advocate-general assists at the hearing, and helps with the questioning. Any of the four official languages may be used, although French is the common language. The advocate then writes a "conclusion" and makes a recommendation. The Court deliberates without him, and need not accept his advice; it has done so only about half the time. The Court renders one judgment as a collegiate body, without dissent being registered. It usually takes 8 or 9 months to settle a case.

The Court can hear suits of member states against each other after the Commission has tried to settle the matter. It hears cases by one Community institution against another. The Commission can appeal against states which it believes to be defaulting their Treaty obligations or violating its provisions. The Court also hears appeals by private persons against the action or inaction of the executive bodies; in the case of the EEC this includes the Council, as well as the Commission. If asked, the Court can give a preliminary decision on the interpretation and validity of the executives' acts if they are challenged in the national courts, and the domestic court is obliged to observe the Court's decision in its own ruling. However, the Court cannot compel a national court to submit issues of Community law to it, nor can it review the national court's decisions on such issues.

The Court is more than an international tribunal. It is also an administrative court, a disciplinary tribunal, a constitutional court, and an arbitrator. The Court has not tried to shape the economic policies formulated by the Community executives, and it cannot review economic or political reasons for decisions. But it has tried to insist on strict adherence to the treaties, and it has annulled regulations or decisions via this strict adherence. By 1964 the

Court has made 185 decisions in the 320 cases brought before it since 1953; 101 cases are still on the docket. Of the 62 opinions delivered by the Court by 1961, 9 concerned complaints by employees of the Community, and 53 concerned the validity of action proposed or taken by the ECSC. Since almost every major decision of the High Authority has been challenged in the Court, it has had the opportunity of deciding on the principle activities of the Authority.

The operation of the three Communities has given rise to a complex relationship between the developing Community law and the laws of the states. The Treaty of Rome, in so far as it is self-executing, has been incorporated into the municipal law of the Six. The Court can determine Treaty violations by states that the national courts cannot review. It sees that the Treaty and the regulations made under it are given a uniform interpretation in the national courts. It passed on the legality of certain agreements and economic concentrations among firms. It held, in the Van Gend case in 1963, that the Treaty grants private rights to individuals, and that the national courts must enforce those rights even against member governments, for the Community law forms a part of the domestic law of the Six, and member states have surrendered certain rights to the newly formed juridical regime.

The Netherlands and Luxembourg both amended their constitutions to provide for the supremacy of international treaties over national constitutions or legislation, and for acts of international bodies to prevail over municipal laws.

In France, Germany, and Italy, the constitutions allow for transfer of some sovereign powers to international organizations. In all six countries the acts of the Community organs are accepted as valid, and the local courts cannot examine them.

The Court at first refused to adjudicate on the acts of member states. But, in a case in 1960, it held that it could declare a legislative or administrative act of a state to be contrary to the Community law. In 1964 the Court ruled that the Six do not have the right to enact laws that are incompatible with their obligations to the Community. The Commission has argued that the formation of the Community must lead to the creation of

Community law, directly applicable in the national courts, that will prevail over conflicting national legislation even if subsequently enacted. Though the Court has not fully accepted this view, it has gone beyond the view of the governments: that the Treaty establishes only the states' obligation without internal effect on their subjects. In an important case, that of NV Algemene Transport, in 1963, the Court held that the "Community constitutes a novel juridical order of international legal character, for the benefit of which the states, though only in limited areas, have limited their sovereign rights, and the subjects of . . . [the juridical order] are not only the states, but also their nationals." Since a firm can sue in the Court for damages on account of an act of a Community employee or institution, the Court has the opportunity to develop a "Community law," not only in administrative and constitutional law areas, but also in the area of private law.

THE EUROPEAN PARLIAMENT

The supporters of European integration were determined there should be no new parliamentary assembly added to those already existing: the ECSC Assembly, the Consultative Assembly of the Council of Europe, and the WEU Assembly. With the signing of the Treaties of Rome, the ECSC Assembly was converted into the common assembly of all three communities. Its membership was increased from 78 to 142: Germany, France and Italy provide 36 members each, Belgium and the Netherlands 14, and Luxembourg 6. The members are chosen by the national parliaments in the manner they decide; the members are always parliamentarians although this is not a requisite of the treaties. They attend in their individual right, and their expenses are paid by the Community, not by the states as with the Consultative Assembly. The name of the body was changed to the European Assembly, and is now known, in all four languages, as the European Parliament.

The Parliament elects a bureau, the president and eight vice-presidents. However, the choice is circumscribed by the unwritten rule that the president of the three European assemblies—the

Consultative Assembly, WEU Assembly, and the European Parliament—shall come from a different political group, and, where possible, from a different nation. The seven Presidents chosen so far—Paul-Henri Spaak, Alcide de Gasperi, Guiseppe Pella, Hans Furler, Robert Schuman, Gaetano Martino, and Jean Duvieusart—make up a distinguished and experienced group of European politicians. The eight vice-presidents include representatives from all six nations, and from all political groups. The task of the bureau is to supervise the administration of Parliament, to help select committee members, and with the assistance of the Conference of the Presidents of Committees, and political groups, to prepare the agenda of the Parliament.

As in the other assemblies, the members are divided into three main political groups, Christian Democrat, Socialist, and Liberal. The rest, principally the French UNR, were planning, in 1964, to organize themselves into a fourth group. No Communist has been chosen as a representative. The members sit together in political groups, not in alphabetical order as in the Consultative Assembly and the WEU Assembly. Since the three principle political groups support, in differing degrees, the idea of European integration, the nationalist French Gaullist UNR tends to form a kind of automatic opposition. The Socialist group, numerically dominated by Germans, is the most united ideologically, the strongest supporter of integration, and the most critical of the Council of Ministers. It is organized in working groups and, through an efficient secretariat, maintains liaison with the Socialist parties of the Six. The Christian Democrats form the largest group but are more likely to divide on substantive economic and social issues than are the Socialists. They, too, have working groups studying issues; the groups meet together as a whole from time to time. The Liberals are the smallest group, but include members from fourteen different parties, seven of which are French. Not surprisingly there is little political cohesion in the group, and it does not have any working parties. Nevertheless, even this group votes together more often than national delegations which, except in an exceptional case—as in 1962, when all the Italians voted against protection for energy producers—will never do so. The groups participate in the working of the Parliament, in choosing the members of the bureau, drawing up the agenda, choosing spokesmen in debates, choosing oral questions to be debated, and selecting committee members.

As in most continental systems, the committees play an important part in the working of the Parliament. They are particularly significant because of the complexity of the issues with which the Parliament has to deal, and because they provide the most satisfactory method to influence executive action. There are 9 large committees of 29 members and 4 smaller committees of 17, the members of which are apportioned approximately according to political and national representation. Committees tend to include experts in the subject with which they deal; the *rapporteurs* of the committees are generally appointed for their individual qualities. Unlike the procedure in the Consultative Assembly which partly follows the British pattern, the first discussion of proposals takes place in the committee. Debates in the Parliament invariably take place on the reports of the committees, and, in particular, are based on the resolutions of the committee. Meeting at least once a month between sessions of the Parliament, the committees invite the executives of the three Communities who often attend, and members of the Council of Ministers who attend less frequently.

The Treaties require that the Parliament hold an annual session, but it now meets eight or nine times a year for about thirty days as well as having a two-day joint meeting with the Consultative Assembly, and, since 1961, occasional meetings with over 100 parliamentarians from the African associated overseas territories. The Parliament is geographically diffused. It normally holds its meetings in the Council of Europe building at Strasbourg, although it has also met in Brussels and Rome, but its secretariat is in Luxembourg, and about half the committee meetings are held in Brussels.

The three committees differ in their budgetary rules which complicates problems since the Parliament gets one-third of its budget from each of the Communities. In the ECSC the Parliament is given control over its own budget, whereas it can only propose draft estimates for the other two Communities. Though the ECSC Assembly was consulted on some financial matters, such as the levy system, over which it had no formal jurisdiction, the Parliament generally has been dissatisfied with its lack of influence over the formulation of the budgets for Community affairs as a whole which are decided by the Council of Ministers.

Primarily the Parliament is a consultative group which technically must be consulted on specific matters. In practice it has been consulted more widely than this, and on detailed regulations as well as on general policy proposals. Though the High Authority was obliged only to send it an annual report, it soon began sending proposals to the committees both to solicit their opinions and to garner political support. All three commissions now frequently consult the parliamentary committees before formulating their proposals. Often the EEC Commission has sent the texts of proposed regulations or directives to the Parliament simultaneously with the Council, although this should be done at a later stage by the Council. But the fact that the Commission can amend its proposals at any time means that the Parliament may be by-passed. The EEC Commission, like the High Authority, has tended to use the Parliament to strengthen its bargaining position. But since the Commission is the initiator of policies, as well as executive agency, the Parliament might be more critical than it has been of the Commission's activities. It is difficult to evaluate how much influence the opinion of the Parliament has on the final text of regulations; in some areas, such as anti-trust regulations and social affairs, it is larger than in others, such as agriculture. At all times the Parliament has supported a greater role for the Commission and a wider interpretation of the Treaty. In addition the Parliament has been able to bring issues to the attention of the Community as a whole by passing resolutions, such as those in 1960 and 1963 calling for a merger of the three executives, and by issuing reports on problems with which the Community is concerned, such as transport, anti-cartel regulations, and external relations.

The Parliament, however, has few powers of control over the operation of the executives. The strongest power is that of censure.

By a two-thirds majority the High Authority can be censured during the debate on the annual report, and the Commissions of EEC and Euratom can be censured at any time. Although the Socialist group in 1962 suggested censuring the High Authority because of its inactivity, it is, at the moment, difficult to foresee situations in which censure would be desirable or necessary, especially since the Parliament has no control over the replacement of the executives. The Parliament takes no part in the approval of the appointment of the Commissions, and has asked that it be given an opportunity to do so. Nevertheless, the President of the High Authority on his investiture, has made a practice of appearing before the Parliament and explaining his policies.

The Parliament can ask both oral and written questions of the executives and occasionally of the Council of Ministers. About two hundred written questions a year are raised. Oral questions take a number of forms. They can be asked in advance—a week for the Commissions and six weeks for the Council of Ministers—with supplementary questions following the answers. They can take the form of the interpellation in France, with a short debate ending with a resolution and a vote following the question; they can be put in committee meetings attended by the executives.

Other opportunities for discussion of Community affairs occur in debates on the annual reports and in the annual "colloquies." Since 1962 the Parliament has had a general debate on each Community; it also discusses the EEC Commission reports on the economic situation and on social affairs, and the bi-yearly Council summaries of its activities. Since 1957 there has been an annual "colloquy" each November. This is a debate on two subjects in which the Chairman of the Council of Ministers and members of the Commissions participate. But since no vote is taken, the impact of the discussion is reduced. The Parliament remains dissatisfied and somewhat frustrated at its lack of influence, especially over the Council of Ministers, and with the lack of progress to further European integration and to the creation of an Atlantic partnership. In January, 1963, the Parliament proposed an expansion of its powers in six chief ways: parliamentary participation in the appointment of Community executives; consultation between the Parliament and the Council on all important items; parliamentary opinions, adopted by a two-thirds majority, to be binding on the Council unless opposed by unanimous decision of the Council; parliamentary ratification of the international agreements made by the Community; greater parliamentary control over the finances of the Community; and parliamentary nomination of judges for the Court of Justice from lists provided by the states. A major problem in the Community still remains the lack of democratic control over the executives.

Both Treaties provide for direct election of the Parliament. In February, 1960, after a study group report, the Parliament unanimously proposed a Parliament elected by direct universal suffrage. But France, unsympathetic to the idea, has so far blocked progress on the subject.

THE ECONOMIC AND SOCIAL COMMITTEE

The Economic and Social Committee is an advisory body of 101, comprising 24 each from France, Germany, and Italy; 12 each from Belgium and the Netherlands; 5 from Luxembourg. All are chosen for four years by the Council of Ministers on the nominations of the states. According to the Treaty, the members are representative of producers, farmers, transport operators, traders and artisans, the professions and the general interest, and they are not bound by any instructions. In fact, the members are divided into three groups: representatives of industry, trade unionists, and a heterogeneous group consisting of professional people and those representing consumers. There is no fixed number of each group: in the fall of 1964 there were 27, 33, and 41 respectively. Members of the different groups frequently meet together to discuss a common approach before meetings of the Committee. The bureau of the Committee is carefully divided both on national and group lines. In 1964 it consisted of a President, an Italian industrialist, two Vice-Presidents, one French and one Belgian, and twelve other members, four from each group and two from each country. Every two years the office of the President goes to a different nationality and group.

The members are divided into nine specialized sections for different subjects, each of which is divided into three working groups which prepare the work on a proposal and report back to the section. The Committee as a whole meets every two months in Brussels as do most of the groups. Members of the Commission are sometimes present and speak at the plenary sessions while their officials frequently attend meetings of the working groups and specialized sections of the Committee.

The function of the Committee is to give advice to the executive organs on their long-term planning and on their proposals for implementing the treaties. On some subjects it must be consulted.

Though there is no treaty obligation, the High Authority has also consulted it on a number of subjects. The advice of the Committee is constructive in showing the points of agreement and disagreement between the different interests, and therefore indicating to the Commission the way to a possible compromise. To the majority opinion is appended an addenda in which the minority point of view is made known.

The Economic and Social Committee was set up as an institution of the Community because the Benelux countries and the trade unions of the Six wanted an additional organ in which they could be represented. But the role of the Committee is circumscribed. Although it has had some influence on matters such as agriculture, cartel policy, the European Social Fund, and on basic health standards in the atomic energy sector, it has no right of initiative. It cannot, unasked, give an opinion on the implementation of the Treaties, it can meet only at the request of the Commission or Council of Ministers, and it cannot even decide on its own procedure. However, the Committee has often asked to be consulted and normally the Commission has agreed. Also, when the agricultural proposals of the Commission were being formulated in 1961 and 1962, a new procedure was evoked, that of information reports by the sections and the Committee as a whole on various aspects of the proposals. From 1958 to June, 1964, the Committee gave 101 opinions, 56 of which were obligatory, 33 of which were optional, and 12 of which were information reports.

Though there are no formal ties between the Committee and the Parliament, there has been an informal exchange of documents between them, and normally the Parliament awaits the opinion of the Committee before itself discussing a proposal. There is no real duplication of function by the two bodies since the Parliament is a forum for criticism and recommendations, and the Committee an advisory body only.

THE EUROPEAN INVESTMENT BANK

The Bank was set up with a subscribed capital of $1 billion to aid capital investment within the Six, and to guarantee private lenders. The Bank is an autonomous organ headed by a Board of Governors, the Finance Ministers of the Six, who meet annually and set the general policy. Under it is the Board of Directors, a group of 12 with 12 alternates, 3 each from France, Germany, and Italy, 2 from Benelux, and 1 from the EEC Commission; they are mostly bankers, industrial managers, and directors, meeting bimonthly to approve every loan. The daily administration is carried on by a management committee consisting of the President and two Vice-Presidents of the Bank.

The Bank aids three types of investment. The first are those projects helping the underdeveloped regions of the EEC such as Southern Italy, Sicily, Sardinia, South West and South East France, and certain regions in Benelux. A second type are European projects such as modernization of railroads and roads, which could not be financed by a single state. A third type are conversion projects when workers have to be reintegrated in other employment as a result of the reduction of duties and elimination of protective measures. The Bank finances only a part of each project, on average about 20 percent, and largely acts as an incentive. Generally, prospective clients must have tried other banks before first approaching the Investment Bank.

Of its $1 billion capital, only $250 million has actually been paid in by the states. In addition, the Bank has borrowed $215 million from the capital market. Up to January 1, 1964, it had approved $358 million in 67 loans. Its largest loans inside the

Six have gone to help development in South Italy, and Italy as a whole has accounted for about two-thirds of all loans. The loans are limited to the European territories of the members and foreign firms located in the Six are eligible, but they can also be granted to countries outside the Six by unanimity of the Board of Governors.

The Activity of the Community

The work of the Community can be conveniently, if not exactly, divided into five main categories: the creation of a common market, the first measures towards the formation of common policies, the beginning of a common agricultural policy, the association with the African countries, and external relations.

THE COMMON MARKET

Creation of a common market involves the removal of barriers to a single market including not only the ending of obstacles to free trade in commodities and the elimination of customs and quota barriers, but also ensuring the free movement of workers and capital, the right of free establishment and services, the establishment of fair competition, and formulating a common external tariff.

The removal of tariff barriers has been so easy that the original timetable has been considerably accelerated. By 1965 there had been seven internal tariff reductions on industrial products, making the tariffs 30 percent of the pre-Common Market level in 1957. The tariffs are to be completely eliminated by January 1, 1967, three years earlier than expected. The Commission has continually favored larger and speedier cuts in the tariffs as a means of binding the states. But the cuts have also partly been the result of the tension and trade rivalry caused by the creation of EFTA.

As a gesture of goodwill the tariff cut of January 1, 1959, on industrial goods and on nonliberalized agricultural produce was extended to all GATT members, and the quota increase was partially extended to all OECC members. The cut on July 1, 1960, was extended by the Benelux countries to nonmembers for products on which the duty levied was higher than that of the common external tariff. The French tariff cuts in April, 1961, were also applied to all countries.

Quotas on industrial goods were also reduced much more rapidly than originally imagined, and by December 31, 1961, they were abolished within the Community, eight years ahead of schedule. However, a large part of the nonliberalized sector is outside Community control because of the existence of a state monopoly of a commercial kind, or a national marketing organization, or because of the introduction of a minimum price system. Also, as with tariffs, there has been much less progress on agricultural products. The Community again made gestures to nonmembers. In 1959 it proposed the reciprocal abolition of quotas on imports of industrial goods from all countries. In 1962 the Six signed the cotton agreement by which they doubled their quota of imports of textiles, and also agreed to extend the most-favored nation clause to Japan. To reduce discrimination in supply, the members are obliged to modify any national trading monopolies. Both the French and Italian governments have accordingly modified their tobacco monopolies to allow greater imports of cigarettes, and the Italian government has adjusted the monopolies in salt, cigarette paper, lighters, and quinine.

There are, however, a number of safeguard provisions in the Treaty which allow obstacles to free trade. A country with balance-of-payment problems may place restrictions on imports from nonmembers, and, to a lesser degree, on imports from its partners. If a region experiences persistent difficulties, the country can ask the Commission for permission to take protective measures. Thus Italy aided a number of industries, including sulphur, chemicals, raw silk, lead, and zinc. Italy was also exempted from enlarging import quotas for wine because of its own surplus production. Germany was allowed to levy a temporary tax on bread coming from the Netherlands and on paste from Belgium and the Netherlands. In addition, there are internal and external nontariff barriers. The first include administrative and technical regulations such as food and drugs legislation which, although passed to protect citizens from harmful and adulterated products, may be an obstacle to free trade. Also, states can adopt minimum prices for certain commodities if the Community policies result in prices that may endanger a country's agriculture. If prices fall below these levels, imports can either be suspended or reduced. This has been done for fruit and vegetables. The Community countries have been protected, to some degree, against nonmembers by tax laws against foreigners, unfair methods of calculating the value of imports, and the provision of government funds for protecting companies launching products in a new market. But after the transitional period, some safeguard measures will no longer be applicable.

One of the chief features of the common market, the keystone of its foreign trade policy and a main differentiating feature of the EEC from the rejected Free Trade Area is the common external tariff, CET. Indeed its early significance was such that the Commission President said "We have no flag, no common language, and no emblem, nothing to establish our identity except our common external tariff." In February, 1960, the common tariff on 2,893 items into which the individual tariff positions had been condensed, was fixed on the basis of the arithmetical average of the national duties of January 1, 1957, except for a group of about 70 items known as "list G," and some other items which were determined later by the Council of Ministers. The effect of the change was, roughly, to double the Benelux tariffs, to halve those of France and Italy, and to leave those of Germany at approximately the same level.

The CET conformed to the rules of GATT that the average level of the common tariff should not be higher than the average of the various national tariffs it was replacing. Some critics, however, argue that the volume of trade was not taken into account and that a simple arithmetical calculation led to a generally higher tariff rate. As another gesture to nonmembers, the first alignment of the national duties toward the CET, with the exception of some list G products, was made on January 1, 1961, a year earlier than intended, on the basis of the common tariff reduced by 20 percent, a reduction which was offered during the GATT negotiations in 1960, and will be kept until 1966. The members adopted the CET immediately if their own tariffs on goods were not more than 15 percent different from the CET, and reduced the difference between their remaining national tariffs and the CET by 30 percent. On July 1, 1963, a second 30 percent alignment was made. By the end of the transitional period, the CET will have replaced the existing tariffs on imports from nonmembers. But again there are certain qualifications. The Commission can grant waivers from the CET if the Community output of certain products is insufficient or if a member's supply depends on imports from nonmembers. About 50 tariff quotas at reduced duties have been granted in these conditions.

Since the breakdown of the EEC negotiations with Great Britain in January, 1963, the United States and other countries have become increasingly concerned at the possibility of their exclusion from the market of the Six. It is not yet clear how much of a barrier the CET will be and therefore how protectionist the Common Market will become. The real effects of tariff discrimination in Western Europe will probably only be felt when both EFTA and EEC have completely ended their internal tariffs. The Common Market is supposed, according to the Treaty, "to contribute, in conformity with the common interest, to the harmonious development of world trade." But some economists have doubted that a custom union, reducing internal tariffs, inevitably constitutes a move to free trade and the maximization of world welfare. A customs union diverts trade as well as creating it, and the predominating impact will depend on a variety of factors such as the size and diversity of the union, the level of the external tariff, the degree of prior protection, the differences in costs of production in different parts of the union, and the tariff levels of outside countries.

As a result of the CET almost all the high tariff rates in the individual countries have been greatly reduced; less than one fiftieth of the duties are over 30 percent. The tariffs on list G were fixed at a much lower level than had been feared. But there are also few items on the free list. The Commission has authorized protection in a number of cases, and the EEC was quick to respond to increases in U.S. tariffs against Belgian carpets and glass in 1962 by raising its duties on plastic products, paint, and synthetic textile fibers. All EEC countries levy additional taxes on imports. The degree to which the common agricultural policy and the levy system will be protective depends on the final price level which, if set too high, will accelerate French production and reduce the quantity of imports, especially of temperate foodstuffs. The semifarcial "chicken-war" between the EEC and the United States in the summer of 1963, caused by the loss of United States exports due to the EEC levies, seemed an omen of the future. Another indication of the same kind in 1963 was the action of France, forbidden to import Dutch pork because of the swine fever in the Netherlands, in buying from the dearer Belgian pig farmers rather than cheaper third countries.

The Commission has defended the EEC against charges of protectionism. The trade deficit of the Common Market rose from $245 million in 1958 to $3,000 million in 1963, and its deficit with the United States rose from $712 million to $2,500 million. Its agricultural imports have increased 21 percent in five years, as compared with the increase in world trade in agricultural products of 11.6 percent In July, 1962, the Community agreed to tariff reductions of 20 percent on trade totaling over $5 billion a year, which were extended to all GATT members. This reduction will be maintained until at least 1966 even though the Community did not receive reciprocal concessions. In 1964 the Community also reduced its CET by up to 40 percent for a wide range of tropical products; duties on tea, tropical woods, and some other products have been suspended altogether. About a quarter of the imports from developing countries are in the form of industrial raw material on which there is no duty. The EEC does not regard a Free Trade Area with North America as economically feasible, or agree that agricultural trading arrangements should be global, or that there be a maximum limit on the system of variable import levies.

A related problem, about which elemental national emotions, especially in France, have been aroused, has been created by the growing U.S. investments in Europe, particularly at the heavy concentration in automobiles, agricultural machinery, food products, and tires. Since 1958 almost 2,500 United States ventures have been started in Europe, 70 percent of which have been in the Six. In all there is some $18 billion of American direct investment in Europe. The recent American investment has essentially been by large companies, in the growth sectors of an expanding Europe and in technologically advanced industries. Among the Six, Germany has the most American capital and France the most new operations. This has led to a certain European economic nationalism, reinforced by French reservations derived from their desire to plan their economy which becomes difficult with the presence of large American companies.

The free movement of persons, services, and capital. Free trade in goods has been accompanied by steps to free the movement of persons, capital, and services. Regulations of September, 1961, and March, 1964, have laid down the rules by which citizens of one country can stay and work in another, and vacancies can be filled. Priority was at first given to nationals, but since March, 1964, vacancies can be filled immediately with any worker in the Community; the priority is now against non-Community citizens. After four years a noncitizen will be treated in the same way as a national. Workers need specific job offers before they can move, and the states have designated official employment agencies whose work is coordinated by the Commission which is also advised by a consultative committee composed of representatives of labor and management as well as governmental delegates. In addition, rules on migrant workers, covering a million persons, have been in force since January 1, 1959, enabling these workers to retain benefit rights when they move to another Community country.

Important though these rules are, they have been less meaningful because of the shortage of labor in the Six which has obliged all members to import labor from nonmember countries, and from Italy. The Commission has devised schemes which have allowed and even encouraged this transfer. Between 1958 and 1962 the net emigration from Italy was 716,000, and the net immigration into Germany 1,600,000.

Removal of all restrictions on capital movements is expected by 1967. Directives, based on proposals of the Commission, came into effect in June, 1960, and April, 1963. These rules permit free movements of capital when they are connected with freeing trade in goods, the movement of persons, direct investment, and commercial loans. Governments cannot restrict the purchase and sale of foreign stocks. But controls still exist on short-term capital movements because of their speculative, or "hot money" character.

Integration in this area is complicated by the different banking systems of the Six. In the Netherlands and Germany, a few large banks dominate the capital markets, in Italy much of the industrial long term capital is supplied by government lending agencies, while in France most of the new capital issues are distributed by nationalized deposit banks. Moreover, stock exchanges are primarily national in character, almost all groups underwriting capital loans involve banks of one country only, and governments often afford preferential interest rates for capital going to domestic needs.

Less progress has been made in free establishment for independent activities. The Treaty calls for the removal of all obstacles to the movement of services, insurance, banking, finance, distribution, personal services, and the exercise of liberal professions inside the Community by 1969. After then, each state is supposed to grant citizens and firms of other countries the same treatment as its own nationals. The Council of Ministers, in December, 1961, approved the general program for the gradual removal of restrictions on establishment drawn up by the Commission, but most industrial and commercial activities will not be liberalized before the end of the second stage.

Competition policy. Since the ideological differences between Germany and the other countries could not be resolved, the philosophy behind the Treaty of Rome is neither one of planning nor of laissez-faire. The Treaty does not provide for "free" competition, nor regard competition as an end in itself. Rather it calls for "fair" or "normal" competition which will reduce private barriers to trade by international cartels, while at the same time containing a number of loopholes which limit control of restrictive practices, and recognizing that specialization agreements and measures of industrial rationalization are inevitable in the modern economy. To establish fair competition—the prevention of distortions of all kinds—which will keep costs and prices down and stimulate technical innovations, the Commission has made proposals in a number of fields: cartels and mergers, dumping, state aid, harmonization of legislation and taxation, and conditions of transport.

The articles in the Treaty on cartels and mergers reflect the traditional European habit of tolerating desirable cartels and monopolies and the existence of state monopolies rather than the American opposition to bigness as such. Agreements preventing, distorting or restricting trade among states are made unlawful, but they are allowed if they promote efficiency benefiting the public interest. Enterprises are prevented from taking improper advantage of a dominant position in the Common Market, but are not forbidden from attaining a dominant position.

The Commission held that two articles were legally binding in the states simply by virtue of the ratification of the Treaty, but that another needed regulations to get effective implementation. The first directive implementing the articles, based on the proposals of the Commission of October 1960, was approved in December, 1961. Applying to agreements effecting trade across frontiers, its objective is to prevent firms from fixing prices, restricting production, or dividing markets. Its premise is that the Treaty ban on cartels is automatically operative in the absence of authorization. The regulations made require compulsory notification of agreements if firms wish to be exempted from prohibition. To allow a firm to ascertain its position, it can apply to the Commission for "negative clearance." The Commission has the right to gather any necessary information from governments or firms, it can make investigations of individual firms or can make a general inquiry concerning the restriction or distortion of competition, it can decide that infringements have taken place, it can impose penalties on firms for infringements of the Treaty or for supplying incomplete or inaccurate information. In reply to its demand for firms to report all agreements affecting interstate trade which might violate the Treaty, the Commission received some 37,000 notifications.

In July, 1963, the Commission published the details of its "negative clearance" procedure. By applying for negative clearance on agreements made with other firms, a firm can be assured by the Commission that it is not guilty of anti-trust violations. Theoretically, the Commission can examine the books and records of a company, can require reports or demand explanations, but the problem of examining some 37,000 agreements makes the task of the 30 responsible experts in the Commission somewhat forbidding. In 1964 the Commission proposed a system of group exceptions, which would simplify matters by allowing agreements to be grouped into categories for purposes of examination and approval, but the Council of Ministers has so far refused to agree.

The administration of the Community anti-trust laws remains divided. Institutionally, there is cooperation between the states and the Community, which has included general conferences outlining policy in working groups on different industries and cases, and collaboration between the Commission and the cartel authorities in the states. Before the Commission makes a decision, it must consult these national authorities and the Advisory Committee, composed of one civil servant from each of the Six. For the Commission the problem is complicated partly because of the different system of anti-trust rules in the Six. At the time the Treaty of Rome was signed, only three of the countries, France, Germany, and the Netherlands, had cartel legislation and administrative authorities to carry it out.

It is doubtful there has been much effective control as yet. There have clearly been many price agreements and market-sharing arrangements which are theoretically forbidden by the Treaty. There has been no interference with agreements between firms in the same industry in different countries. In 1963 the Commission turned to the question of mergers and began arranging for a number of independent studies to explore the definition of a "dominant position" and other matters, and for the first Community census of production which might help identify trends leading to industrial concentration. But so far thousands of mergers, associations and pooling of resources have taken place.

Since 1963 the Commission has made two decisions in this area, approving exclusive dealing agreements, and requested changes in another case, that of the Faience walltile monopoly.

Since the start of the Common Market there has been a rapid development of business relationships between firms in the Six, involving joint research, the use of joint distribution outlets, and the creation of joint subsidiaries. If, at the same time, there has been an increase in competition within the Community, this has been due more to the growth of discount houses and supermarkets, and to the reduction of resale price maintenance in France and Germany, than to the effect of the Community regulations.

The Commission also has powers for controlling dumping. It can address a recommendation to a firm asking it to desist. If the firm continues the Commission can authorize the state concerned to take measures which it defines. Of the twenty complaints examined by the Commission by 1963, eight were dismissed as unfounded, six became groundless since the firms concerned ceased their dumping practices, two were withdrawn, two gave rise to recommendations, and two were still being examined.

The Treaty requires that state trading monopolies must gradually end any discrimination in the Community, and the Commission has urged that the Italian and French tobacco monopolies, the French match and potash monopolies, be reduced. State aid is forbidden if it distorts competition by unfairly helping some firms. The Commission has ended certain aids such as those to German synthetic rubber producers, French textile manufacturers and investment goods industries, and Italian automobile manufacturers. A state, contemplating a new subsidy, is obliged to notify the Commission which can refuse to permit it; in 1963, there were 60 cases in which such refusal occurred. State aid, however, is allowed if it promotes economic expansion or regional development in certain sectors, or benefits the Community as a whole. Thus aid has been allowed to the shipbuilding industry of France and Italy because of Japanese competition, and to the film industry of France, Germany and Italy to harmonize their position.

Besides government subsidies, state assistance can also take other forms such as discriminatory internal taxes, codes, rules for company establishment, commercial law, and health, industrial safety and hygiene regulations which may be used to hinder competition. The states are responsible for harmonization, and the Council of Ministers for the coordination of municipal laws in fields such as the mutual recognition of diplomas and certificates, and restrictions on the right of establishment of foreign nationals.

The Commission has pressed for the harmonization of national legislative and taxation policies which might affect the condition of competition and prices. It set up a coordinating committee to study the problems involved in working out a European law for patents, trade marks, designs, and models. The most important of the harmonization policies are those relating to turnover taxes. The Commission set up a commission of economists and national experts to examine existing disparities between taxation systems in the Six and ways of harmonizing them. Five of the Six have the cumulative tax system in which a given percentage tax is added at each stage of production. This may distort competition since it favors the large vertically integrated firm. The Commission favors the adoption by all of the French added-value system, which levies only a fixed percentage on each type of product. But, while generally indirect taxes on exported goods are refunded, imported products are often subject to compensatory taxes. Some critics argue that, by supporting the French system, the Commission may also be forced into supporting the French protectionist view of a compensatory levy against third countries.

COMMON POLICIES OF THE COMMUNITY

The removal of obstacles to the creation of a Common Market and the ending of tariffs and quotas have been comparatively simple. But since the EEC is more than a customs union, it is required to work out common policies in agriculture, trade in agricultural produce, foreign trade, and transport; agreement on these has been more difficult to obtain. Moreover, nations and the Commission differ on whether the Treaty of Rome applies, in principle, to all economic activity and whether the underlying objective is to bring about the complete integration of the economies of the states. Certainly, the Commission has taken the maximilist view and proposed policies on economic growth, trade cycle policy, monetary affairs, energy, commercial policy, and social matters, as well as on the objects named in the Treaty.

Commercial policy. A common commercial policy is supposed to be in existence by December 31, 1969, by which time all trade with third countries will be conducted in accordance with agreed Community policy, and trade negotiations, agreements, and general import and export policy will be handled by the Commission under mandate from the Council instead of by national governments. Under the Commission's first proposals which came into effect in October, 1961, the Six agreed to consult before opening trade negotiations or concluding agreements with non-member states and before modifying quotas, and decided that no bilateral trade agreements should run beyond 1969. But the Commission has complained that it has not been consulted on major trade developments in the Six, such as the large imports of Russian petroleum by the Italian Ente Nazionale Idrocarburi (ENI). Under a second program adopted in July, 1962, the Community will, in 1966, begin examining all existing bilateral trade agreements and start drawing up single Community quota lists and common protection against dumped goods.

But there are still over a hundred items which, if imported by a member from a third country, are not accepted in one of the other five countries as being eligible for entry on EEC terms. Half of these relate to goods from East Europe and another thirty to Japan.

In 1964 the Commission expressed concern about the slow progress on a common trade policy and began concerning itself with differences in liberalization of the Six towards Japan, and the Eastern bloc. The latter subject is politically perilous since the economic trade policy of Germany is an important political matter for the Communist countries. In April, 1964, the Council agreed on a number of measures for trade liberalization with non-Community countries including removal of quota restrictions, harmonizing export aids, standardization of export restrictions, conversion of bilateral agreements into Community agreements, as well as harmonizing commercial relations of the Six towards Japan and the Eastern bloc.

Economic and monetary policy. According to the Treaty, the Six are obliged to maintain equilibrium in their balance-of-payments, confidence in their currency, full employment, and stable prices, and the Commission has the task of coordinating their policies. In the favorable economic climate of 1958–1962 these obligations did not create any particular difficulties. Not until the rapid price inflation of 1963–1964 did the need for action appear overwhelming to the Six.

The Commission has been rather coy in its approach to economic controls for fear of offending industrialists in general and Germany in particular. But it has argued that the modern state must be responsible for the state of employment, a balanced rate of economic growth, an incomes policy, and that these must be under Community "discipline." The Commission has always avoided the word "planning," and instead spoke first of "programmation" and then of the coordination of policies. In 1963 its Action Program proposed the drawing-up of a program for 1966–1970, holding that this was essential for working out common policies, for guiding the plans of the members, and for regional development. The Six were not yet prepared to accept all the implications of the Commission's proposals for a single labor market, free movement of capital, single monetary policy, harmonized tax systems and wage policies. But in April, 1964, the Council of Ministers agreed to set up a committee on Medium Term Economic Policy, which the Commission had proposed the previous year, composed of senior national officials who will advise the Comission.

The Commission has produced annual economic forecasts, quarterly economic surveys, and monthly business surveys, has made both general and specific recommendations to the Six on policies, has studied the different techniques of economic management in the Six, has collected statistics of the Six on a wide variety of subjects and formulated them on a comparable basis, and tried to improve the coordination of policy between the responsible economic authorities. It also has helped a committee of independent experts prepare the base for a medium term Community economic policy.

For purposes of coordination, the Ministers of Finance of the Six meet together four times a year with the Commission to discuss economic problems. A Trade Cycle Committee, including representatives of the Six and the Commission, studies the instruments of trade cycle policy available to the Community countries to maintain economic growth. An Economic Policy Committee, composed of three representatives from each state and three from the Commission was set up in March, 1960, to analyse the way in which the instruments of economic policy were used, and to advise the Commission on the proposals it makes to the Council on economic matters.

The Treaty of Rome refers specifically to the need for developing Europe's less-favored areas. Little action has been taken in the field of regional development. Together with a group of national experts, the Commission has tried to define regional problems and agree on regional boundaries. The Community has been divided into 54 regions, and the Commission proposed that the needs of the underdeveloped regions be treated on a European level, acting at first in cooperation with national governments and then with regional development agencies. After a conference on regional development organized by the Commission in December, 1961, three working groups were set up to study different aspects of this problem. In the fall of 1964 the Commission was formulating proposals on the basis of recommendations made by the groups.

The Community recognized the interrelationship between trade and monetary matters: the greater the reduction in tariff barriers, the faster the impact of inflation or deflation. The Monetary Committee has concerned itself with monetary problems of interest to the Six. Composed of two representatives of each state from the Central Banks and the Finance Ministries and two from the Commission, it has met about once a month to discuss the monetary and financial policies of the Six and also the international monetary system. But the consultation was not as close as desired. In March, 1961, Germany revalued its currency without previously consulting its partners on the Commission.

Since 1962 the Commission has made a number of proposals to coordinate monetary policies. By 1964 the galloping inflation in Italy made the Six realize that all their economies were likely to be affected, and that if even one country was out of line it would endanger the possibility of common prices and create difficulties for the coordination of policies. The states can grant mutual assistance to fellow members troubled by balance-of-payments difficulties if the Council of Ministers by qualified majority approves the Commission's proposals. During 1964 the Commission was particularly active in making recommendations to the Six on how to deal with their inflationary problems.

If one of the Six is in financial difficulties, the initiative must come from the Commission which proposes action to the government concerned. If this is not sufficient the Commission, after consulting the Monetary Committee, can propose mutual aid to the Council of Ministers. If the latter refuses, or if the aid is found inadequate, a member is entitled to invoke the exceptions procedure in the Treaty, and the Commission may fix appropriate safeguards.

In April, 1964, the Community took a significant step when the Six agreed on a common effort to stabilize price levels and production costs though a short term anti-inflationary policy. In addition, the Council also approved the Commission's proposals for coordinating economic policies through a Medium Term Economic Policy Committee, a Budgetary Committee composed of senior officials and the Commission which would discuss the wider impact of budgets on economic activity, and a Committee of Governors of Central Banks which would meet periodically to exchange information on the central bank policies. In the eyes of the Commission the logical end of such monetary coordination would be a single monetary authority with a unified policy for the Six, a common currency, a pooling of the gold and foreign exchange reserves, and a common external balance-of-payments account. However, every specific decision of the Council in April, 1964, was qualified. And the fact that, on the very day the

Monetary Committee of the Common Market was meeting, the Governor of the Bank of Italy was in Washington negotiating for a dollar loan rather than consulting his colleagues, indicated that cooperation was still at only a formative stage.

Transport policy. Community progress in the field of transport has been slow because of differences on the powers of the Community, differences in the transport systems of the Six, and differences between the various modes of transport. Some nations, such as France and Germany, take the view that the powers of the Community in transport are limited to the rules outlined in the Treaty, and to the establishment of common regulations applicable to international transport. The Commission argues that, since transport pervades the whole of economic activity, the general rules of the Treaty, especially those on competition and the right of establishment, are equally applicable to transport, that it is necessary to end the obstacles hindering competition, to abolish unjustified measures of aid and support, to achieve nondiscrimination and free circulation, and to create an integrated transport system meeting the needs of the Community.

The transport systems are the heritage of nineteenth century policies. It is difficult to reconcile transport policies regulated in some states, especially Germany and France, on the basis of the common interest—uneconomical for social and military reasons—with those states such as the Netherlands and Italy dealing with transport in the same way as other industrial and commercial sectors. Generally, France, Germany, and the Commission emphasize the special public service aspects of transport, while the Netherlands, in particular, has insisted on liberty in international transport and on transport as an ordinary business activity. Because of these differences, the Treaty dealt only in a vague way with the general principles for transport: the need for common rules, nondiscrimination on national grounds, the removal of government aids to firms or industries with certain exceptions.

For the Commission, a common transport policy has three objectives: the elimination of obstacles which transport may put in the way of establishing the Common Market as a whole, the integration of transport on the Community level, and the general organization of transport in the Community to ensure the optimum use of resources.

The elimination of obstacles implies ending any form of discrimination in the rates and conditions of transport, such as aid to certain enterprises or industries or adjustments when crossing frontiers or differences based on the nationality of the firm, and the application of the rules on monopolies and understandings to transport.

The Commission plans the elimination of discrimination before the end of the transitional period. Some discrimination has already been ended. From July 1, 1961, discrimination by a carrier on the grounds of country of origin or destination of goods was ended. Special rates in favor of a particular industry or region were ended in January, 1962, although a number of exemptions have been made by the Commission, especially for South Italy. In July, 1963, discrimination based on country of origin or destination of goods, or the nationality of the consumer was ended. Governments must notify the Commission of any differential freight and transport conditions. The Commission is making an inventory of all state aid to see if it is compatible with the principles of competition in the Treaty. Different national regulations on fiscal, health and other matters remain a discriminatory factor.

The integration of transport requires common rules applicable to international transport and establishing conditions under which carriers in one state shall have access to transport activities in another state on the same terms as citizens. In principle, the general organization of transport is to be based on competition but this will be severely qualified because of the needs of regional economic, commercial, and agricultural policy.

All this implies equality of treatment between enterprises and means of transport and between users, freedom of action for enterprises to fix rates and to have access to the different transport markets, free choice for the users and the coordination of investments.

But the proposals made by the Commission in this area reflect a compromise between the conflicting national points of view, and a limitation of the principle of competition in the attempt to avoid ruinous competition on the one hand and exploitation of dominant positions on the other.

Social policy. In the Treaty the social aims of the Community are stated to be the improvement of the living and working conditions of the peoples of the Six, while particular mention is made of some topics such as equal pay for women and the maintenance of the existing equivalence of paid-holiday schemes.

The Commission has argued that the social provisions do not simply serve an economic end of reducing distortions of competition, ensuring the best combination of the factors of production, or leveling production costs, but are also important in themselves as a means to social justice and an essential part of the ultimate political objective of the Six. In this view, the abolition of discrimination in employment is regarded as an aspect of common European citizenship, training schemes as an example of genuine equality of labor rights, and the harmonization of social systems as an instrument of social progress.

But social policy has been low in the priority of interest of the Community. There has been little economic compulsion, in a Community of over-full employment, to oblige action. The Commission itself has only vague powers as compared with those given to the High Authority. However, regulations have been made on a number of topics, such as the free circulation of workers, and the right of establishment for the self-employed. By the end of 1964, pay discrimination based on sex will be ended: the 1961 deadline was postponed. The Six have agreed to allow migrant workers to participate in the national social security benefits and to carry over rights accrued in another country. A common policy of vocational training has been framed, which allows the different national systems to remain in operation, and in 1964 a vocational training consultative committee was created. European conferences were held on social problems such as hours of work, hygiene, security, and social security. In 1964 the Six agreed to encourage the exchange of young workers among the six countries. The states, in framing their employment policies, are pledged to take account of the situation of the labor market in the other states. But the Commission has not pressed very strongly its argument for income policies to bring social betterment, leveling of wages, and better equilibrium between agricultural and industrial wages.

The European Social Fund was set up both to ensure employment against the risks arising from economic integration and to promote the expansion of employment. It assists in resettling and retraining workers, encourages vocational training centers, and promotes the mobility of workers, paying half the expenses incurred while the states bear the other half. It began to operate in 1961. By 1962 the Fund had made grants of over $12 million and had helped 183,000 workers to find new jobs. In 1964 the Commission overruled the advice of the Fund Committee for the first time and held that the Fund existed to help workers, not companies. It thus rejected the request of the Ford Company for a special payment from the Fund to workers thrown out of work by the reconversion of its Antwerp factory.

Energy policy. The Treaty does not contain any special provisions for the introduction of a common energy policy, but the fact that each of the three Communities deals with a different form of energy has necessitated some coordinated policy. A number of difficult problems have arisen. The demand for energy has risen by 62 percent between 1950 and 1960, and by 1970 is expected to increase by 140 percent. The share of coal in the energy demands of the Six has fallen from 70 percent in 1950 to 43 percent in 1964: correspondingly, the share of oil has risen from 10 percent in 1950 to 39 percent in 1964. The price of coal of the Community producers compares unfavorably with that of outside suppliers. This combination of factors—increasing demand for energy, increasing proportion of imported energy, and lower price of much of the imported energy—has made the Six keenly aware of the insecurity of their energy supplies. For military as well as social reasons, the Six may keep up domestic production of coal at a higher than economic level to reduce dependence on outside sources, while policy is framed for the supply of imported fuel.

The problem is handled by the Interexecutive Energy Committee consisting of three representatives from the EEC Commission, three from the High Authority, and two from the Euratom

Commission, meeting once or twice a month. From 1960 on the Committee made recommendations for coordinating national policies on energy, so that commercial policies and rules of competition would be brought into line, and fiscal and administrative measures changed if they produced price distortions. Its proposals for free movement of crude oil and oil products within the Community, for Community quotas for oil imports from the Communist bloc, and for subsidies for Community coal, aroused more controversy. Strong national differences were revealed. Germany was opposed to subsidies for marginal coal mines, and Belgium to low prices for fuels since she had a high cost fuel output. While Italy was opposed to quotas on imports of Communist oil, the other five favored them since they felt that unrestricted imports might be dangerous to any long range plan that would assure a plentiful supply of low-cost energy. However, in July, 1961, the Six agreed to consult each other before entering into trade agreements with the East.

In April, 1962, the mandate of the Committee was broadened from proposals for coordination of national policies to that of recommending a common energy policy. The Committee has worked in collaboration with two committees set up by the Council of Ministers, a committee of national experts under the chairmanship of the High Authority, and a group of high officials to discuss actual policy. A new set of proposals was made in June, 1962, suggesting, among other things, the creation by 1970 of an open market in the Six for fuel and power, not subject to restrictions and national protection, the fixing of maximum levels of aid to internal production, the definition of a common oil policy, and the adoption of a definite timetable for different phases of the transition period, at the end of which a common policy would be evolved.

The Six reached agreement in April, 1964, on the outlines of a common energy policy, based on cheap power, security of supply, free choice for the consumer, fair competition in a single market, and price stability. In particular, the governments accepted the principle of subsidies for coal, although they would be gradually reduced. Oil and natural gas supplies will be as widely diversified as possible, and the Six will attempt to formulate a common policy for stocking crude oil and gas, and a harmonized taxation system for petroleum products.

COMMON AGRICULTURAL POLICY

The setting up of a common agricultural policy is dealt with only in a general way in the Treaty, which left the details to be filled in as the Community progressed. Agriculture, as always, has presented special difficulties for the Common Market, and the nations differ widely on how to deal with it. In the 450,000 square miles of the Six, there are 9 million farms, of which 5.5 million are less than twelve acres in size. While a relatively small number of farms obtain good incomes, the general level is low. Economically, the position is aggravated by a certain underemployment of resources, and socially by the aging of the agricultural population. With a farm population of nearly 13 million workers, the Six have one worker per 2.7 acres as compared with an average in the United States of one per 53 acres. But in the Six, as in the whole of Western Europe, the total farm population is diminishing, both absolutely and relatively, to the total population.

But, despite the decreases in farm population, the agricultural areas are all overrepresented in their national legislatures, and they exert an influence on the policies of their governments greater than their numbers warrant. This has tended to make national differences, especially between France and Germany, more pronounced as the Community attempts to frame a common policy. France, with its balanced economy, efficient agriculture, half the arable land in the Common Market, and the lowest wheat prices, is anxious to expand the European market for its food surpluses, and has been the keenest supporter of the Commission's drive for a common policy. Germany, with its inefficient and high-cost agriculture, and high wheat prices, is less self-sufficient than France and needs to export to pay for its food. Politically, the ruling Christian Democrat party in Germany depends to a considerable degree on the farmers for its electoral support. Therefore, while France insisted on an agreement on the beginning of a common agricultural policy before agreeing to the move from the first to the second stage of the EEC, Germany has been more interested in keeping its high wheat prices, in keeping the Community open to third country supplies, and in liberalization of trade on industrial items. Differences exist between France and the Netherlands which are interested in agricultural exports, and Germany and Belgium more interested in maintaining high prices for their own farmers indefinitely, with Italy in a middle position, selling fruit and vegetables but wanting to protect its high priced cereal production. Hence, different attitudes have been taken to the pace of tariff reductions and quota increases in agriculture and to the level of over-all intra-Community preferences. Free trade in agriculture must result in a common price level throughout the Community. But although all Six want a Community-wide price support system, they differ on the level of the price to be set which, if too high, would lead to overproduction and surpluses and, generally, to higher prices for the consumer.

According to the Treaty the objectives of the common agricultural policy are increasing agricultural productivity, ensuring a fair standard of living for the agricultural population, stabilizing markets, guaranteeing regular supplies and ensuring reasonable prices to consumers. The Community will also integrate agriculture into general economic development, bring industry to the land, and improve the rural infrastructure such as transport, education, and electricity supplies. No dates were laid down for implementation, but the common agricultural policy was to be developed during the transitional period.

The Commission, helped by advice from groups of national experts and after consulting the different farmers' organizations, began framing its proposals. After months of technical argument and ministerial debate, a series of day and night sessions, 137 hours of Council meetings and 214 hours of subcommittees, the examination of 582,000 pages of documents, the stopping of the clock to pretend that 1961 had not yet ended, agreement on common marketing arrangements for some products was reached at 5 a.m. on January 14, 1962. The common agricultural policy was to be established gradually over the seven-and-a-half years from

July 30, 1962. By 1970 prices, marketing, competitive conditions, and legislation will be harmonized. Regulations established common machinery for organizing markets in cereals, pig meat, poultry, eggs, fruit and vegetables, and wine, commodities which accounted for over half the agricultural produce of the Community and almost half of its internal agricultural trade.

Most of the old protective devices for these products were abolished on July 30, 1962, and the rest will be replaced before the end of the transitional period by Community controls or a levy system. Variable levies will be adopted during the transitional period for intra-Community trade. These will foster free circulation within the Common Market while providing adequate guarantees to farmers and consumers and effective support for the market. Export subsidies help a Community country with a higher price level to export its agricultural produce to the other five. Both the levies and the subsidies will be gradually reduced and will end with the common price level to be established by 1970 at the latest.

Another system of levies on imports from non-Community countries will protect the Common Market against the outside. These levies will be higher than the intra-Community levies and will be permanent, thus allowing preferential treatment to Community produce. From 1970 there will be a common variable levy against third countries, as well as a commonly financed support system and a common price for agricultural commodities in the six. The variable tariff levy will in effect allow imports only when there are internal shortages.[1] A system of Community export aids will also be set up. In a step toward harmonization of prices, the Council of Ministers decided to fix maximum and minimum prices for the marketing of wheat, barley, and rye for the year beginning July 1, 1962. Since then the target prices for each year have been set on the preceding September 1.

In the transitional period, the states may also fix minimum prices for various products, after notifying the Commission and the other states before the price is fixed. However, if an interven-

---

[1] The "target" price is the internal price in the largest deficit area, plus the cost of distribution to that area. The levy is the difference between the EEC price and the world price. The "intervention" price is the price at which public authorities will intervene to buy surpluses.

tion price has been set, the state cannot fix the minimum price at more than 10 percent of this price. Minimum import prices have been fixed in most states for particular products, including pork, poultry, and eggs. For fruit and vegetables there are common standards of grading and supervision of quality which will keep imported goods up to certain standards, as well as rules of fair competition which may lead to quantitative restrictions against third countries. Although national subsidies are to be abolished except in special cases to be decided by the Commission, both France and Italy have maintained some subsidies of fruit and vegetables, under the control of the Commission.

Agreement on further steps in the common agricultural policy was delayed by the British negotiation, and by the deliberate obstruction of the other five in protest against the French uni-lateral action. After a series of marathon negotiations mingled with French threats at the dire effects of failure, agreement was reached by the Ministers of Agriculture in December, 1963, on proposals of the Commission for regulations for dairy produce, beef, veal, and rice, general guide lines for fats and oils, and on the rules of the Agricultural Guidance and Guarantee Fund which will govern the financing of the common farm policy of the Community. The December, 1963, agreement was both a remarkable success for the Commission, and an illustration of the procedure through which it has been obtaining agreement by proposing package deals.

But the most ambitious and radical proposal, a common price level for cereals, was defeated by Germany. The keystone of the whole agricultural policy is its price policy, which will largely determine both production and protection and therefore the balance between internal production and imports. The establishment of a Common Market depends on the harmonization of prices. In January, 1962, it had been agreed to move to a common price for wheat and feed grains in six yearly stages. The low French prices would rise while the high German prices would fall. But because of German opposition, the initial move was deferred. Since the Six were stalled, the commissioner for agriculture, Sicco Mansholt, proposed breaking the deadlock by moving immediately to a single price, halfway between the French and German prices. To avoid the risk of overproduction, government supports for farmers would be frozen, but compensation would be paid to German, Italian, and Luxembourg farmers for their loss of income. After a threat by de Gaulle that France would cease to participate in the Common Market if a common grain price was not decided, and the creation of an atmosphere of crisis, Germany agreed in December, 1964, to accept a single price system for cereal grains to go into effect on July 1, 1967. The EEC agreement, a major step towards the completion of the common agricultural policy, was the result of another package deal in which Germany agreed to lower its grain prices in return for French cooperation in the Kennedy round of the GATT negotiations.

After considerable differences of opinion, agreement was reached for a three-year period on what to do with the money obtained from the levies. This is to go to the Agriculture Guidance and Guarantee Fund which will partially finance export rebates, price supports, and structural readjustments. Market intervention, when prices have dropped below the support price, will be by the Community, as well as by national authorities. The export rebates will cover the difference between national prices and world prices. Since Germany and Italy as food importers did not want their contributions to the Fund to be used solely for subsidizing the exports of France and Holland, the Fund will also aid and facilitate investment for the rationalization and modernization of farming in the Six, the adaptation of production, improvements in marketing, and development of outlets for farm produce.

Though little has been done in this direction, the Commission has emphasized the need for structural changes in agriculture which would involve encouraging amalgamation of holdings, rural industries, afforestation, technical education, and the provision of services to the countryside. In dealing with this problem it is now aided by a Structural Committee.

The states contribute to the Fund partly in proportion to their share in the general budget of the Community, and partly in proportion to the value of their imports from third countries. The Fund will be administered by the Commission, advised by a committee which will include national finance and other officials.

Both the formulation and the execution of the common agricultural policy are shared by the Community institutions. The original proposals of the Commission were examined not only by the Economic and Social Committee and the European Parliament but also by a Special Committee for Agriculture set up by the Council of Ministers in 1960, before being sent to the Council. There is now a complicated sharing of responsibility between the Council and the Commission for the administration of agriculture, while the states implement the regulations. The Council still agrees to the proposals of the Commission unanimously during the second stage (1962–1965), and by qualified majority in the third stage on subjects that need political decisions such as the harmonization of grain prices, the Community rules for the operation of the markets, the fixing of the levies and certain commercial transactions. But now the Council can make other decisions by qualified majority once the regulations are in force in certain fields. The Commission can act alone for the execution of measures which are not of a discretionary nature. This includes the daily fixing of the variable levy, among other things. After consulting the states, it has sole power to decide what agreements, decisions, or practices are permissible according to the rules of competition. The Commission is also responsible for coordinating the various policies concerned with the modernization of agriculture in less developed areas, such as Southern Italy.

To give advice to the Commission and to help prepare measures for them, five management committees, composed of representatives of the states presided over by a representative of the Commission, were set up to deal with grain, pig meat, eggs and poultry, fruit and vegetables, and wine. The Commission, after drafting a proposed regulation, consults the relevant committee which votes by qualified majority. The Commission then decides on the measures. If it differs from the committee, the application of the measures is postponed for one month. The Council of Ministers, by qualified majority, is able to make a final decision. Sometimes, however, the Commission can make decisions without consulting the management committees and which the Council cannot alter. These include decisions as to whether agreements between or practices followed by agricultural producers are incompatible with the Common Market.

The Commission is also aided by advisory committees, including representatives of the different pressure groups such as farmers' organizations, dealers, workers, and consumers, which were set up to give advice to it on the different aspects of the common policy for agriculture.

There are safeguards in the agricultural policy to allow a state to close its frontier to imports to prevent national markets from being disrupted. The Commission has the power to decide within four days after such measures have been taken whether they were justifiable. If it does not, states can generally appeal to the Council which decides; in some cases, however, there is no appeal from the Commission's decision.

Critics of the common agricultural policy argue that it continues protection of the Community farmers who will get prices above the world price level and is unfavorable to imports. Moreover, since governments may buy surpluses and the refund system allows exports to sell below the world price, the Community producers not only have a preference within the Community, but also have a special advantage on the world market as exporters. The European Agricultural Guidance and Guarantee Fund helps further protection and supports the subsidy of exports. On a number of occasions the states have taken advantage of the escape clauses and imposed minimum prices.

Against the charge of being protectionist, the Community argues it will still largely import commodities such as coarse grain, beef, high-grade wheat, vegetable oils, and fats. Commissioner Mansholt has argued that, while it is true that the United States will not be able to increase imports greatly, this is the result of greater European productivity, which has led to greater European self-sufficiency, rather than protection.

THE ASSOCIATION OF THE AFRICAN STATES

It was not at first anticipated that the Treaty of Rome would deal with the dependent territories of the Six. But the French, against the opposition of Germany and the Netherlands, insisted that these areas be associated with the Common Market. Previously assured of outlets and guaranteed prices for their goods by France, these areas would be granted commercial preferences by the Six and assisted in their economic development, while close economic relations would be established between them and the Community as a whole.

Although some areas in Oceania were included in the Convention of Association, about 98 percent of the population of the Associated Countries live in the former French West Africa and French Equitorial Africa, the former Belgian Congo, Madagascar, and Italian Somaliland. The Convention provided for a gradual elimination of duties and quotas by the Associated Countries on goods from the Six though they could not discriminate in favor of any one state, while their exports to the Six benefited from the same tariff reductions and elimination of quotas as did the Six themselves. Moreover, preferential rates were given under the CET for some sensitive products of these countries such as coffee, cocoa, vegetable oils, bananas, and hardwoods. On January 1, 1963, customs duties on imports of certain tropical products from the Associated States were abolished, and replaced by the CET reduced by a certain percentage. In addition, the Treaty allowed the States to levy customs duties needed for their development and industrialization or which could contribute to their budgets. This was done by Senegal when the breaking of relations with Mali threatened difficulties for Senegalese industries: Senegal imposed both customs duties on competing imports from the Six and import quotas. The Associated States applied among themselves the same customs and quota reduction measures which they applied to member states, but they did not form a customs union applying a common external tariff to nonmember countries. The States were also helped by preferential treatment by the Six who imposed high duties on imports of coffee, cocoa, and bananas from nonassociates, and by long term marketing arrangements.

The African States also benefited from the European Development Fund set up with a total of $581 million to assist projects of an economic or social nature submitted by the governments of the recipient countries who retain full responsibility for planning their own development. After a slow start, the Fund began approving a large number of projects. By October, 1962, it had approved 277 projects involving over $360 million expenditures.

Besides financial aid, the Six have also provided technical assistance of a substantial kind. This has taken the form of planning and regional development surveys, or general surveys of natural resources. The Commission has organized cooperation between European research institutions in the study of certain technical problems such as afforestation or soil conservation experiments. To help overcome the shortage of trained personnel a scholarship program was started in 1959 to train statisticians and is financed out of the ordinary budget of the Commission. Since then, training in economic, agricultural, and technical subjects has been offered, and aid given to civil servants who serve a traineeship in the various departments of the Commission.

Initial fears of the Associated countries that the Association arrangement might become a semi-colonial relationship have long since disappeared. At first most of the relations with the Associated countries were carried on via the metropolitan capitals, particularly Paris and Brussels. In 1960 most of the Associated countries became independent, and all, except Guinea, asked that the Association be maintained. Since then, relationships between the Associated countries and the Community have been direct, and the countries submit investment projects directly to Brussels. A series of bilateral arrangements was created. The Six have not allowed the Commission to establish representatives in the Associated countries, but representatives of the latter meet regularly with the Commission for consultation.

The Common Market has been criticized, in this area, for three main reasons: that it might impede the industrialization of the Associated countries, that it will lead to diversion of trade at the expense of outside countries, and that it tends to divide Africa into political blocs. But in fact the Associated countries are specifically allowed to protect their infant industries, and they retain full freedom with regard to tariffs and trade. Trade figures do not bear out the second criticism. While the EEC's imports from the Associated states increased by 7.5 percent between 1957 and 1961, the increase in imports from nonassociated countries rose

15 percent. The preferential treatment did not change the terms of trade.

In June, 1961, the joint meeting of the European Parliament with over a hundred African parliamentarians in Strasbourg recommended that the Association be continued for a further period after December 31, 1962. In December, 1961, discussions began for the negotiation of a new Convention, France wanting the same kind of relationship, while Germany and the Netherlands favored extending preferential treatment to other African nations, to avoid discrimination. The Commission planned to increase the competitiveness of the Associated States and enable them to develop and diversify their economies, to rationalize production, encourage new crops and to promote industrialization. But it also wanted to make a gesture towards the non-Associated tropical producers.

After a series of five Eurafrican ministerial conferences, agreement was reached in December, 1962, on the new Yaoundé Convention. But the Convention did not come into operation until June 1, 1964, partly because of the resentment of the other five for France's unilateral action against Great Britain, and partly by the mechanical difficulty of getting ratifications by 24 countries. The Yaoundé Convention creates a free trade area between the Six and the 18 African nations, makes certain concessions to nonmembers, increases the amount of financial aid, and creates a number of institutions.

There is no provision for a common European-African tariff or a common trade policy. The African states continue to get the benefit of the Common Market internal tariff reductions and of duty free entry for the nine major tropical products, including coffee, cacao and tea. The Africans will reduce tariffs on products originating in the EEC, and grant all members of the EEC the same treatment in trade policy, but they can also impose duties or import quotas to protect infant industries, and make trade arrangements with other countries, thus enabling them to participate in other regional groupings. But at the same time, as a gesture to nonmember countries, the Common Market reduced its CET on tropical commodities by 25 percent to 40 percent, thereby decreasing discrimination, and completely removed tariffs on tea and tropical woods. The possibility was also open to the African nations of the Commonwealth to become signatories of the Convention in the future, or to become associated with the Common Market.

However, the EEC agreed to make available over the next five years, $500 million in development capital and $230 million for the diversification of the African economies, and promotion of efficiency in tropical agriculture, while the dependent French and Dutch territories will get $70 million. Of this Community fund, France and Germany are each to supply $246.5 million, Italy $100 million, and the European Investment Bank $50 million. The new fund allows more diversified methods of investment aid such as long term loans, and also provides help to the Associated countries in adjusting the prices of their commodities to the world-market level. In the first five-year Convention, social projects were approved by the Commission, and economic projects by the Council of Ministers. In the new Convention, all projects will be approved by the newly created Council, based on partnership.

The Yaoundé Convention differs in an important way from the preceding Association by setting up four new institutions. The Ministerial Council of Association is the supreme body. It consists of the EEC Council, a representative of each associated government, and the EEC Commission; each side has one vote and must reach agreement on its own first. It will meet once a year, alternately in Europe and in Africa. The first meeting of this Council took place in July, 1964. Although the Africans pressed for a strong secretariat for the Council, a simple administrative committee was set up. To obtain permanence in the organization there is a Committee of Association composed of representatives on both sides at ambassadorial level. After the 1961 Strasbourg meeting of the European and African parliamentarians, there were further meetings of joint committees of representatives of the two sides at different places in Africa and Europe. The Convention sets up a Parliamentary Conference, consisting of an equal number of representatives from the European Parliament and the parliaments of the Associates. The fourth institution is a

Court of Arbitration of 5—a president chosen by the Council of Association and four by the partners—to settle disputes.

The Common Market trades almost as much with the non-Associated states in Africa as with the Associated. Although France naturally trades far more with the latter than with the former states, the converse is true of the other five. During the negotiations with Great Britain in 1962, the EEC discussed several possible solutions for dealing with the British Commonwealth countries in Africa: association, agreements like those concluded for Franco-Moroccan trade and for trade between Surinam and Benelux, and commodity agreements. But France has always been hostile to the inclusion of the English-speaking countries in the Association. After the breakdown of the negotiations in January, 1963, some of the Commonwealth African countries were inclined to look on the new convention with suspicion as neo-colonialist. But fear of being excluded from the markets of the Six led several of them in 1964 to open their own negotiations with the EEC. Nigeria, Kenya, Tanganyika, and Uganda are all interested in a commercial link. As a package deal in June, 1964, France dropped her opposition to the EEC opening negotiations with Nigeria in return for Belgium, the Netherlands, and Italy modifying their hostility to conversations with Spain.

RELATIONS WITH THIRD COUNTRIES

The Treaty of Rome provides for the addition of new members, and for the association of nonmembers with the Community. Membership is open to European states and association to any third country. But though the EEC has no set philosophy on the matter, it is probable that applicants for membership must be economically strong, be democratic in nature, and be prepared to enter into common political and military arrangements in the future. There are no given conditions for association, but in general only those countries able or willing to become members are thought likely candidates. Association is more than simply a commercial treaty or a mere bilateral trading arrangement, it implies a structural link with the Community. This has made the Commission hesitant about admitting neutrals since they might not accept all the political implications of the Community. But in 1964, Austria, in spite of its neutrality and EFTA membership, was negotiating for association with the Common Market with which it trades three times as much as with its EFTA partners. At the same time the illiberal regime in Spain caused four of the Six to reject the suggestion of France that Spain be considered for more than a commercial agreement.

The Community has been carrying on four sets of negotiations: discussing applications for membership, discussing association, reaching trade agreements, and participating in general negotiations.

Applications for membership. During 1961 and 1962 a number of countries applied for some relationship with the EEC. Three of the EFTA countries—Great Britain, Denmark, and Norway—and Ireland applied for membership. Austria, Sweden, and Switzerland asked for varying kinds of association; Portugal and Spain were interested in an agreement.

On July 25, 1961, Britain decided to apply for membership in the EEC. The three major issues in the negotiations were agriculture, the Commonwealth, and relations with the EFTA countries.

The main agricultural preoccupation of Great Britain was to move gradually towards the Community common agricultural policy through a longer transitional period in order to avoid a sudden increase in prices and an immediate end to guaranteed prices and deficiency payments. It also wanted special arrangements for British horticulture, which would be most affected by entry, and supplementary guarantees for the producers of livestock products. The Six held that Britain should drop the system of deficiency payments immediately on entering the Common Market, and that to compensate for the rise in internal prices, Britain should introduce a system of consumer subsidies to be reduced gradually during the transition period.

Britain promised her EFTA partners that their interests would be protected during the negotiations, and that she would not enter the Community unless there were assurances that there would be no trade discrimination against them. The Six would not agree to relax tariffs against the imports of EFTA until all negotiations were concluded.

But the main disputes concerned the Commonwealth. The Commonwealth is a group of sovereign states, differing widely on important issues, with tenuous links between them. It is not a military alliance, nor a single trading area. It is now a voluntary multi-racial association of 18 nations loosely bound to each other because they were all in the past administered in some form by Britain. They share a common language, a common educational, legal, parliamentary, and commercial system, and participate in a network of diplomatic interrelationships. Economically the Commonwealth benefits from preferential treatment from Britain, economic and technical aid, and easy access to the London financial market.

But both the nature and the trade pattern of the Commonwealth have been changing. To the original five white nations have now been added seven African, two West Indian, and four Asian states, comprising over a quarter of the population of the world and a quarter of its surface. The preferential arrangements dating from the Ottawa Agreement in 1932 have become less significant, especially those advantages formerly enjoyed by British exports in the Commonwealth markets, some of which have reduced preferential margins or imposed substantial tariffs. The preferences for Commonwealth products in the British market, especially temperate agricultural goods, raw materials and some manufactured goods, were to be one of the most contentious issues of the EEC talks. For Britain, trade with the Commonwealth, although still very important, was decreasing in value. Its prewar imports from the Commonwealth were 35 percent of its total trade; in 1963 it was 30 percent. Between 1953 and 1962 total Commonwealth imports, excluding Britain, rose 46 percent, while its total imports from Britain rose only 12 percent. Between 1954 and 1961 British exports to Western Europe exceeded those to the Commonwealth. If this change in the pattern of trade was partly responsible for the British decision to apply for membership, it did not prevent the other Commonwealth countries from ex-

208

pressing anxiety, and in some cases hostility, to the British action.

The British application was subject to an obligation to work out some special arrangements for British imports originating in the Commonwealth. This included requests for alterations in the CET on basic industrial materials on which the British tariff is very low or at zero, taking account of the dependence of the less developed members on Commonwealth trading arrangements and an analysis of the problem of both tropical and temperate agriculture. The most difficult problem, in the highly complicated and technical negotiations, was that of temperate foodstuffs since they compete with Community production.

The role of the Commission in the negotiations was a crucial one since, with one exception, all the texts on which agreement had been reached were based on its proposals. In July, 1962, it suggested a world conference be called to discuss agreements on temperate agricultural commodities; in December, 1962, it set up a committee under Mansholt to examine the economic effects of the different proposals for British agriculture. M. Spaak, as Chairman of the Council of Ministers at the end of 1962, tried to push for agreement and hurry along the negotiations. Great Britain had accepted the principle of a common external tariff, and the abolition of the Commonwealth preferential system, and had fully accepted the Community position on free movement of workers, the right of establishment, services, capital, transport competition regulations, tax provisions, the harmonization of legislation, cyclical policy and social policy. It had also agreed that, on joining the ECSC, some powers exercised by the Iron and Steel Board such as price fixing and vetoing investments would have to be modified.

The Commission believed that the chance of success was considerable enough to justify the continuation of negotiations when on January 14, 1963, the French President intervened in his Paris press conference. General de Gaulle has never greatly concerned himself with the economic details of government, which he quaintly terms "the baggage train" and would evidently find the prolonged discussions on canned salmon and kangaroo meat by the "borough councillors, not statesmen" who were negotiating little to his taste. But though he was interested in having the EEC maintain its preferential treatment for the ex-French colonies —which might be lost with British entry and the extension of such treatment to the African Commonwealth countries—his action in unilaterally ending the negotiations was motivated less by economic than by military factors.

In December, 1962, a meeting between de Gaulle and Macmillan at Rambouillet had failed to produce political or military agreement. A few days later President Kennedy met with the Prime Minister at Nassau to discuss the American decision to cancel the development of the Skybolt missiles which had been promised to Britain in March, 1960, to extend the life of its V-Bomber force and its nuclear deterrent. As a substitute the United States agreed to make Polaris missiles available to Britain. Britain would construct the submarines in which these weapons would be placed. This force together with an equal U.S. force, would be made available for inclusion in a NATO multilateral force. A similar offer was made to France who rejected it. For de Gaulle the Nassau Agreement was another example of "Anglo-Saxon" military domination of the West, of the British preference for the United States rather than for the European Community, and of the British undermining of the Community. His veto of the British application was an assertion of his belief that France and Europe should not remain dependent on the United States.

The Commission deplored the manner in which France had interrupted the negotiations. The other five nations retaliated in various ways; they held up the Association Agreement with the African states, they refused to admit special treatment for Algeria, they blocked any agricultural agreement that would help dispose of the French dairy surplus.

Germany proposed formal contacts with Britain at the level of the permanent representatives, but this was opposed by France who argued that this might lead to Britain indirectly participating in the formation of Community policy. Since the French veto there has been some activity through bilateral contacts between the Six governments and Great Britain, through meetings of the joint economic committees, and through the meetings of the

WEU Council of Ministers, and a wide variety of proposals for reconciling and even unifying the seven countries. One of the minor ironies is that since the veto British trade with the EEC has considerably increased.

As for the Community, the British negotiations obliged it to deal with a number of new problems. The problems of the Asian Commonwealth countries brought up the question of aid to the developing countries and future Community policy to low-wage manufactured goods. Those of the African countries brought up the question of markets for tropical products from all parts of the world, including Latin America. The temperate agricultural difficulties led to concern with the world problems of agricultural surpluses, and the proper organization of production.

The Community has also been perplexed by the problem of the European neutrals. They are prepared to accept the provisions of the Treaty of Rome, but ask for some freedom of action as to trade policies with third countries while also retaining the possibility of withdrawing from the Community in the event of an international crisis. But on the other hand an association agreement is difficult because they are fully industrialized nations, and their association would give them an unfair trade advantage.

Applications for association. Negotiations with the EFTA nations for association collapsed with the January, 1963, breakdown. But the EEC has agreed on association for Greece and Turkey. Their status as members of NATO helped give their case a degree of priority they might not otherwise have obtained.

Greece was admitted as an associate on March 30, 1961, and the 22-year agreement went into operation on November 1, 1962. All import duties and quantitative restrictions on imports from Greece will be completely abolished by the end of 1969. Greece will abolish duties on imports from the Six within a period of 22 years for some manufactured goods and within 12 years for others. It will also accept the common external tariff of the EEC. Greece will be guaranteed markets in tobacco and raisins, she will be allowed to maintain tariffs on some infant industries needing protection, while the European Investment Bank will provide a $125 million low-cost long-term loan. The two sides are supposed to consult each other on the coordination of trade policy towards nonmembers. After the 22-year transitional period, Greece is expected to become a full member of the EEC.

Internal political strife in Turkey held up the agreement with the Common Market, but it too signed an agreement of association in September, 1963. Unlike the arrangement with Greece, the Turkish association and its future depends on the success of its economy. There is to be a five-year preparatory period during which Turkey will get $175 million in easy loans from the European Bank, receive preferential treatment for tobacco and dried fruit, and will try to put its economy on a sound footing, so that its average annual income of $180 can be raised. The provisions for introducing a customs union between Turkey and the EEC after the initial five-year period have deliberately been left imprecise although eventual Turkish membership in the Community is anticipated.

For both Greece and Turkey similar institutional arrangements have been made. Decisions are made by the Association Council, consisting of ministerial representatives of the Turkish or Greek Government on one side, and the Council of Ministers and Commission on the other, each side having one vote. The Council of the EEC and Greece set up an Association Committee in 1962, which meets about three times a year to assist the Council and prepare its decisions.

Commercial agreements. The first bilateral commercial agreement between the Community and third countries was made in September, 1963, with Iran. It did not involve a customs union or technical assistance by the EEC, but provided for nondiscriminatory reductions of the CET and tariff quotas for exports of goods of particular importance to Iran, such as carpets, caviar, and dried grapes and apricots.

Negotiations with Israel extended over a three-year period, primarily because of the desire to avoid offending the Arab nations unduly. A three-year trade agreement, finally signed in May, 1964, gave Israel some advantages in both industrial and agricultural products, involving temporary tariff reductions in the CET for 21 products, lowering of some other tariffs by about 20 percent, and some alignment of the national tariffs of the Six in the direction of the CET for seven products including oranges and citrus fruit juice. But the economic advantages for Israel seem slight compared with the political success of reaching agreement.

A noticeable feature of the external policy of the Common Market is that until 1963 all agreements were concluded with Mediterranean countries, Greece, Turkey, Iran, and Israel, and negotiations continue with Lebanon and the Magrab. This has led Italy, a trade rival of all these countries, to propound the theory that association is possible for a European country only as a preparatory step to full membership. Otherwise a Convention like Yaoundé or a trade agreement must be made. But the other five have not agreed on such an interpretation. After the breakdown of the British negotiations some of the Commonwealth countries themselves began discussions with the EEC. In October, 1963, India was granted a series of tariff concessions on a unilateral basis when some twenty duties in the Common External Tariff were provisionally suspended in whole or in part, and nil duties applied to a number of products.

General negotiations. There are now 59 nonmember countries which have Ambassadors to the Communities, but, apart from an ECSC Ambassador in London, the Communities have no diplomatic representatives abroad, since the French objected to EEC representation in Washington or London.

There are procedural differences in the various kinds of negotiations undertaken by the Community. In application for membership it is the Council which is responsible; in application for association it is the Community as a whole, which thus allows the Commission to be concerned. During the Greek talks the Commission alone negotiated; for the Turkish discussions the Council assisted as observer. Generally, the Commission is responsible for exploratory conversations with foreign nations after which the Council decides what kind of relationship should be established. The Commission can then carry on negotiations with the foreign country on the basis of the mandate given to it.

In the last two years the Six have become more conscious of their obligations to the less developed world. But they still differ on their main responsibility. The French, and to a lesser extent the Italians, see the Community as essentially European but which should also concern itself with the developing nations of Africa who had been their former colonies. The Germans and the Dutch see the Community as equally concerned with all developing nations, thus encouraging world commerce. The Commission takes part in the work of a number of OECD bodies including the DAC, the DAC working party on technical cooperation, and the OECD Technical Cooperation Committee.

A European Education

An interesting side product of the integration movement has been the beginning of a European school system. Since a school was founded in 1953 in Luxembourg for the children of the personnel of the ECSC, five others have been established, now open not only to the children of officials of the three organizations, but also to other children. The curriculum is a general synthesis of the syllabuses of the Six countries. In addition to a child's native language, either French or German is used as a second working language, and English is taught from the eighth grade. The schools grant a European Baccalauriat which is accepted both as a school-leaving diploma and for entry to a university.

In May, 1958, the Council of Ministers agreed to appoint a special committee to draw up proposals for a European university which is envisaged by Article 9 of the Euratom Treaty. The Euratom Commission in July, 1959, presented proposals for a university to prepare graduates as administrators and technicians and which would award a doctorate from the European university. The intention is that subjects will be studied there from a specifically European angle, and that the university will become a vital European center. But though in July, 1960, the Council of Ministers decided it would be set up in Florence, no further action has yet been taken.

A declaration on cultural cooperation by the heads of state and governments at Bonn, in July, 1961, provided for the creation of a Council consisting of the Ministers of Education and for negotiations of conventions on university exchanges. But again these plans have not yet been fulfilled.

A Striking Success

Economists differ on whether the EEC has stimulated the rate of economic growth, or whether the greater increase in production and trade in the Six than in other European countries, led to the success of EEC. Some contend that the economic gains from integration in getting considerable economies of mass production are debatable, that there is no inevitable close relationship between market size and rates of economic growth, and that in fact there has been no acceleration of economic growth after 1957. The Commission itself has said that the expansion of trade among the Six is partly, and perhaps primarily, due to the attitude of businessmen determined to seek new outlets.

Certainly the Community has been fortunate to develop during a favorable business climate. But by any statistic computation the EEC has been a great success. The annual increase in the gross national product has been over 4 percent. The Common Market is still far behind the American level, but the general rise in prosperity has been progressive, and the general standard of living in the Six has increased by 29 percent since 1959. In the 1958–1963 period, intra-Community trade rose 130 percent, imports from nonmember countries 51 percent and exports to nonmembers 35 percent, as compared with the general increase in world trade of 31 percent. In 1958 30 percent of the EEC imports came from EEC countries: by 1962 this had risen to 37 percent. The EEC imports of agricultural products rose 22 percent in the same period.

The reduction or disappearance of the former protection in the home market has led to modernization, the spread of an export mentality, joint selling and production arrangements in the Six, a large number of industrial and commercial EEC-wide organizations, a number of European banking consortia, as well as a general expansion of industry and trade.

Perhaps the most eloquent testimony to success has been the attitude of outsiders to the EEC. Not only did it receive a rush of applications for membership, association, and commercial agreements; it has also been the reason for the setting up of EFTA, and been imitated in varying fashion by the Communist Council for Mutual Economic Assistance (COMECON), and the Treaty of Montevideo setting up a free trade zone for seven states. In 1964 five Middle Eastern states and four West African states were contemplating the possibility of a common market in their respective areas.

Towards a Community

The work of the EEC has inevitably been uneven. It has concentrated on the internal market and agriculture, neglected social affairs, and been stalled on energy and transport. It seems impossible for it to deal with more than one major problem at a time or both the Commission and the national administrations would be swamped. Perhaps, not unfairly, it can be said that the Community has staggered successfully from one crisis to another. Because of the built-in timetable and the mythology of the calendar, the Community, as the French Minister of Agriculture Pisani has said, is condemned to succeed. The EEC is, in a sense, trapped by its success, and has been forced to deal with problems, partly because of the British negotiations, sooner, or less logically, than it might otherwise have done. It has been obliged to enter important trading conferences, such as the U.N. Trade and Development Conference and the GATT negotiations before it has decided its own commercial and agricultural policies.

The Commission has continually tried to hasten progress, the acceleration of the original timetable and the development of common policies, in the face of a reluctant or unwilling Council of Ministers. Underlying its attitude is the belief that political decisions lie at the heart of economic ones, and that some degree of political unity is resulting from the increasing number of economic arrangements, common policies, and economic integration of the Community which are essentially political decisions committing governments at the highest level. Though the process of integration is neither automatic nor inevitable, the growing interpenetration of the economies of the Six creates an inherent logic by which dealing with one subject leads naturally to an interest in a related field.

Sovereignty is being pooled in innumerable facets of the life of the Six. The Commission is aware that once the common agricultural policy has established common prices, unilateral changes in individual exchange rates will become difficult. Harmonization of legislation on taxation, social insurance, and labor legislation could lead to similar national budgets and the merging of central banks. The Community's interest in expansion of trade necessarily intensifies its concern for a solution to the international liquidity problem. The nations of Western Europe have been compelled by economic necessity and military need, if not always convinced ideologically, to accept the fact that their problems are common ones, that no nation can now solve these problems by itself, and that the creation of common institutions is the only feasible democratic alternative. But at the same time it is not historically true that a customs union leads inevitably to political union. More important is a political will to union.

The Community and the common institutions are now a going concern with vested interests of their own in their continuance. Since 1958 the idealism has perhaps been tempered, and the original enthusiasm become subdued amid the prosaic activity. Immersed in difficult technical problems and with its central preoccupation continually changing, the Commission is not the standard bearer for permanent radicalism. But its value has been accepted even by those who have referred to it in derogatory fashion as "mere technicians."

The French veto of the British application in January, 1963, especially the manner in which the decision was made known at the press conference of General de Gaulle, seemed to endanger the whole principle of taking communal decisions. Holland, and to a lesser degree Belgium, spoke of "reprisals," and held up the signing of the Convention with the Associated African nations until July 20, 1963. The idea of "synchronization" put forward by the German Foreign Minister, Gerhard Schroeder, in April, 1963, reacting against the French veto, implied that internal and external progress must proceed simultaneously in a series of mutual compromises. The implication that tangible and immediate benefits would be obtained by each of the Six seemed to break with the Community method. The danger arose of each country putting forward prior conditions for decisions necessary to the progress of the Community.

But the Community has weathered the crisis of confidence, and patience has again become a political virtue. In May, 1963, the Council of Ministers agreed on the outlines of a program of work for the next year which included agricultural regulations on dairy produce, beef, and rice, definition of a common approach to the Kennedy Round in GATT and the fixing of the price of cereals. In turn the Commission planned the Action Program for the Second Stage to ensure the balanced implementation of the Treaty. Offstage from another press conference of General de Gaulle on July 29, 1963, came the warning that the Common Market might disappear if the Six did not effectively accomplish what had been agreed in May. In December, 1963, important agreement was reached on many of the outstanding agricultural problems, and in April, 1964, the Council agreed on closer co-operation in monetary matters.

The governments agreed in principle to a merger of the executives on January 1, 1965, and to the merger of the three Communities themselves by January 1, 1967. Cooperation between the three Communities has taken place in a number of ways. The Presidents of the three Communities have met every two or three months to discuss administrative problems. There are interexecutive groups on energy, transport, external relations, economic and financial policy, and joint participation in the social field and in the committee for social security of migrant workers. The three Communities jointly share the statistical, legal, and information services. In the discussions of the merger of executives a number of problems emerged. There were differences on the number of members of the new executive. The Commission, joined by the larger powers, argued for a small executive body of nine to ensure the continuance of collegial decision making; the smaller powers argued for fourteen. Luxembourg was loath to surrender its capital as the seat of the High Authority, and asked for some other institution to be located there in its place. The ECSC budget was approved by the Committee of Presidents (the Presidents of the High Authority, the Council of Ministers, the European Parliament and the Court), although that of the other two Communities was approved solely by the Council of Ministers. The High Authority was financed by the levy while the other Commissions depended on a pro rata contribution by the governments. All agree that, in some way, the powers of Parliament should be expanded. After prolonged discussion, the Council of Ministers agreed to merge the three executives on January 1, 1966. The headquarters of the future joint commission will be in Brussels.

In the early years of the EEC, Walter Hallstein was fond of saying "We are not in business, we are in politics." The Commission considers that political integration has already begun in the field of economics, while other areas, such as cultural policy, foreign policy, and defense are left in the hands of the states. But the biggest gap in the work of the Community has been the lack of progress to political union.

The philosophical differences that existed a decade and a half ago between "federalists" and "functionalists" are now irrelevant in a Europe with the three Communities existing and exercising functions. Differences today are of two kinds, concerned with ideology and with foreign policy. Ideologically, the struggle exists between those favoring a European Community, a Europe of the peoples against those supporting a *"Europe des patries,"* based on the states. Equally divisive are the differences on foreign policy between those emphasizing a global trade policy, an integrated Atlantic nuclear defense and some kind of Atlantic partnership, and those stressing a more regional policy and a strong Europe capable of playing an independent role in politics and defense.

The inequalities in power and status of the six nations have also affected the move to union. To regard the EEC, as Walter Lippman has done, as a bargain between French agriculture and

German industry is to neglect unduly the idealistic element in the Community. Nevertheless, the EEC can hardly progress unless both countries are substantially agreed, as was shown by the stalemate in 1964 when Germany insisted on a liberal trade policy and a concern for relations with third countries, and France pressed for the completion of the common agricultural policy. By definition, the Community is, or should be, the negation of all hegemony, a union, not a concert of powers orchestrated by the leading nations. But the smaller nations, aware of the possibility of a Franco-German hegemony over Continental Europe, have pressed for the inclusion of Great Britain to act as a political stabilizer before moves are made to political union. The Commission, too, has been worried that the Franco-German pact of 1963 might detract from the existence, functioning, and momentum of the Community. But neither the Treaty of Rome nor the Treaty of Paris includes any provisions linking the objective of political union with the institutional structure of the Communities.

In July, 1959, the French proposed a secretariat be set up in Paris to coordinate the foreign policies of the Six, but both the Commission and the Benelux countries were opposed to the idea itself and especially to the proposed location. In November, 1959, the Six foreign ministers agreed to hold meetings every three months on the "political extension of the European Communities." Three such meetings took place in 1960 followed by the first meeting of heads of states and governments which was held in Paris in February, 1961. A committee was set up to present concrete proposals for meetings of heads of states, and governments, and foreign ministers. Though most governments approved such regular meetings. the Netherlands was opposed. A second meeting in Bonn in July, 1961, set up a committee, with the French diplomat, Christian Fouchet, as chairman, to draft a charter for the political union of the peoples of the Six.

The Fouchet Committee reported in November, 1961, presenting essentially a Gaullist plan for a Union of States with a common policy on defense and foreign affairs in three main proposals:

1. Council meetings every four months at the level of heads

of state or governments acting by unanimity to coordinate foreign policy.

2. An intergovernmental European political commission, composed of senior officials in the national foreign services, located in Paris and responsible for assisting the Council and preparing policy proposals.

3. An advisory European Parliament to address recommendations and questions to the Council.

But neither this, nor certain amendments suggested by France, were acceptable to Belgium and the Netherlands in a Union from which England was absent. This, together with differences on the scope of the contemplated political union, brought about the failure of the negotiations. The work of the Committee virtually stopped with the beginning of the British negotiations and has not since been reactivated.

Symbolic of the two different approaches to the Community and its future are the two Frenchmen, General de Gaulle and Jean Monnet. The politics of de Gaulle are as inscrutable and ambiguous as the smile on the face of the Mona Lisa. His speeches and effects are carefully contrived, but sibylline and oracular in nature which have led to contradictory interpretations.

His politics are a curious mixture of the archaic, in his appeal to a hardly relevant emotional nationalism, and the novel, sometimes radical, approach. But it is difficult to judge whether his experimental, pragmatic, and frequent changes of political direction are the result of a profound sense of historical destiny and appreciation of contemporary reality, which few other statesmen possess, or whether they are largely opportunistic. Perhaps it is not unfair to apply to de Gaulle those qualities he himself described as necessary for leadership: egotism, pride, aloofness, and trickery.

But at bottom there are two interrelated premises underlying de Gaulle's actions. The first is his belief that only the nation-state can be the basis for political action, and that nationalism is the strongest of political emotions; the world is seen as a Hobbesian international anarchy. The second is his preoccupation with the grandeur and strength of France and its ability to play an independent role in politics. As a result, the attitude of de Gaulle to Western European problems revolves around a nuclear deterrent for France, a protectionist agricultural policy based on autarky, and a Community which is not supranational but which can act as an important force in world affairs.

The concept of a supranational Europe is for de Gaulle a Europe without political reality, incapable of its own defense, in which France would be sacrificed to an institution which would be little more than a dependency of the United States. The Commissions have their technical value, and have been useful to France in helping expand the market for French farmers and for supplying aid to West Africa, but they do not have political authority and consequently cannot be effective. They are international experts, not true executives. Yet, this conclusion is not inevitable if de Gaulle's premise about the nature of the state is rejected, and his argument limits the concept of politics to his own interests and excludes much of the substance of political life. A European union for de Gaulle can be at best a confederation of states in which France must remain responsible for her own defense, rather than transfer its sovereignty to an "international Aeropagus," and to an integrated entity. Europe must be an organized, regular concert of the responsible governments supervising the work of organizations specializing in each of the common fields and subordinated to the governments.

At the same time the new Europe must be strong enough politically and militarily to act independently and as an arbiter between the Anglo-Saxon and the Soviet camps. Soon after his return to power in 1958, de Gaulle suggested a triumvirate, the United States, Great Britain, and France, to formulate the defense policy of the West, and to make joint decisions on strategy. When this was rejected, de Gaulle turned to the idea of the Community as an independent power bloc. Great Britain must be excluded from the Community because of its maritime activity and outside links with the Commonwealth and the United States, which would lead it to act as the Trojan Horse bringing world influence to bear on European policy-making.

After the refusal of the other five to accept the proposals of the Fouchet Committee in 1962, de Gaulle turned to Germany and held a series of meetings, significant both politically and symbolically, with Chancellor Adenauer, resulting in the Franco-German pact of January 22, 1963. It remains to be seen whether this is a marriage of convenience or of love. The heads of states and governments meet at least twice a year, the foreign ministers every three months, and regular meetings are supposed to take place in the fields of defense, education, and youth. Activity so far has been largely limited to an office for youth, but in none of the other fields, in cooperation in the manufacture of armaments, or in prior consultation on foreign policy, has much progress been made, except for the decision in October, 1963, for joint Franco-German production of the Transall C160 transport aircraft. In July, 1964, de Gaulle himself proclaimed that the Treaty was ineffectual, blaming Germany which did not yet believe in a policy for Europe that was European and independent. Not for the first time a Frenchman may be working unknowingly for *le roi de Prusse*. Moreover, the possibility of a revival of nationalism in Germany, now economically strong and the most important industrial power in Europe, haunts both East and West. For Germany the idea of an integrated Europe, has been a plausible alternative to a reunited or nationalistic Germany. But the breakdown of the progress to political union and the policies of de Gaulle have lessened the likelihood of a Germany submerged in a larger entity, and the exaltation of nationalism in France may have an intoxicating effect on its neighbor.

Opposed to the conception of a *"Europe des patries,"* and representative of the case for closer integration, is Jean Monnet and his Action Committee for the United States of Europe, one of the most influential pressure groups in contemporary Europe. Monnet, a mixture of idealism and hardheaded practicality, a believer both in the value of ideas and in a pragmatic approach, and insistent on the need to create common institutions, has changed his front and tactics, but never his ground or belief in the need for states to surrender certain powers to the community institutions and for concrete accomplishments to establish the community firmly. The community method must be the basis for the solution of economic problems, and the common involvement must eventually lead to some form of political association. What is new and challenging, and almost Rousseauesque in character, is the concept of the communal executive speaking and acting on behalf of the general interest, rather than representing the sum of the national wills.

The EEC is a good example of the political adage that not moving forward may mean slipping backwards. The customs union has been developed faster than originally intended and should be in existence by January 1, 1967. But there has been no easy transition by the Six to an economic union, and even more difficulty in agreeing on the first steps toward political union. The European Community is still searching for a means to stem the counterrevolution of nationalism symbolized by General de Gaulle.

The nature of the European Economic Community and the direction in which it should move still remain contentious. Philosophically the argument is whether European unity should be built around an alliance of sovereign states or through common institutions; economically, between the champions of a basically self-sufficient economic unit and those insisting on an outward looking trade community; politically, between those wanting to keep the Community limited and those arguing that British membership is vital, and between those insisting on European independence and others urging a closer relationship with the United States.

CHAPTER EIGHT

Euratom

THE LESSER KNOWN and publicized of the two Communities set up by the Treaties of Rome is the European Atomic Energy Community (Euratom). Yet during the negotiations of the Treaties, the proposals for Euratom gained more immediate support and interest than those for the Common Market. Anxiety that conventional power sources and domestic energy supplies might be insufficient to satisfy the increased demand for energy in the Six, a belief that the real cost of conventional energy would rise, leading to higher production costs in general, apprehension that the 1956 Suez Crisis might result in a threat to European oil supplies, and alarm at a future atomic energy program in Germany, were coupled with appreciation of the advantages of the communal benefits to be derived from coordinated atomic research and development and jointly financed programs which needed an investment and scientific knowledge beyond that of the individual states.

Realizing that the six states would not agree to a complete integration of their national atomic industries by one supranational body, the Spaak Report of 1956 suggested that Euratom concern itself with developing research and disseminating nuclear knowledge and techniques, establishing nuclear safety standards, facilitating atomic investments that were beyond the resources of individual countries, ensuring the supply of atomic ores and fuels, and establishing a common market for special nuclear materials and equipment. By these functions Euratom would help develop the production of power and would create conditions allowing both a growth of nuclear industry and the application of nuclear techniques to other industries.

Ironically, in view of the later French position, the Treaty signed in March, 1957, was, among other things, a compromise between the French desire for a strong political body to control German atomic development and to own nuclear materials, and the German preference for private ownership and a free market for source materials and ores. The French case for a common nuclear technology for both power and weapons was rejected, partly because of the strong opposition of the United States and Great Britain, and Euratom was restricted to peaceful activity. But individual states were allowed to continue their development of weapons outside Euratom, which thus had no control over French production or use of atomic weapons. The Community was given the exclusive right to ownership of special fissionable materials and the right of option to other nuclear materials. But the French demand for building an isotopic separation plant in order to reduce the dependence of the Six on imported nuclear fuels was rejected, party because the United States could supply enriched fuels cheaper than could Europe, and partly because of the military possibilities of such a plant. Euratom was limited to the same six nations as the EEC. Britain argued that it did not want to endanger its exchange of information with the United States. It preferred multinational cooperation through OEEC, and was reluctant to risk losing its nuclear lead by merging a part of its resources with Euratom.

Euratom, set up on January 1, 1958, was to guide the Six into the atomic age and provide supplies of energy to keep up with their growing industrial and commercial needs, to create the conditions necessary for the speedy establishment and growth of nuclear industries which would provide the needed supplies of energy and make up for anticipated coal deficiencies and inadequate new sources of fuel. Euratom was to help the modernization of technical processes through encouraging nuclear investments and coordinating nuclear research programs, while trying to prevent duplication of research in the Community. Economically, it was to contribute to the well-being of the peoples of the six countries; politically, to help achieve a united Europe. Essentially, Euratom was to develop the civilian nuclear technology of the Six, in which all except France were backward, by a joint Community effort, supplementing and complementing that of the individual states. A common approach would be established to problems of safety, health protection, nuclear potential, and raw materials. Euratom would buy the nuclear ores and fuels in the Community and supervise the regular and equitable supply of all users in the Six, thus preventing discrimination and allocating nuclear supplies when demand was greater than the supply. It would also guarantee by adequate controls that nuclear materials were not misused. In addition, Euratom was given the function of supplying atomic information on industrial matters in which the Community was involved, and controlling the exchange of nuclear knowledge by a member state with nonmembers.

The Institutions of Euratom

Euratom has four institutions, and three others which are advisory groups. Executive power is shared between the Commission and the Council of Ministers. The Court of Justice and the European Parliament serve all three Communities. Advice is given by the Scientific and Technical Committee and the Consultative Committee for Nuclear Research as well as by the Economic and Social Committee.

The Council of Ministers consists of different ministers, usually those of science, finance, or foreign affairs, and its meetings normally immediately precede, or follow, those of the Council of Ministers of the EEC. As in the Common Market, the Council is responsible for making decisions which are then directly binding. Most decisions are reached unanimously, such as those approving the five-year budget, and setting up the Commission, usually by majority vote, but it can amend those proposals only by unanimity. As in the EEC, most of the preparatory work is done by the permanent representatives in Brussels.

The Euratom Commission is a body of five members named by the governments for four years, with a President and Vice-President chosen from the five for two years. Since the President of the EEC Commission is German and the President of the High Authority since 1958 has been Italian, it is seemingly inevitable that the President of the Euratom Commission has always been French; Louis Armand was succeeded by Etienne Hirsch and Pierre Chatenet, former Minister of the Interior under de Gaulle. Of the five current commissioners in 1964, two have scientific backgrounds, two have backgrounds in politics, and the fifth is a former economist.

The Commission acts as a collegiate body, meeting once a week. Two commissioners are responsible for supervising each of the nine directorates into which the work of the Commission is divided, with each member primarily responsible for at least one of them. The Commission makes regulations, directives, decisions, and recommendations in similar fashion to the Common Market Commission. Under it there are 2,700 officials, of whom 2,100 are research workers mostly working at the research centers of the Community.

Its functions are to implement the Treaty, to formulate recommendations and advice, and to act when the Council of Ministers gives it authority. It is responsible for drawing up proposals for the research programs, both the five-year program and the details of each annual program, assuring the diffusion of technical knowledge, establishing safety norms for the health of the population, facilitating investment, guaranteeing that nuclear material is used only for the purposes specified, providing for equitable distribution of nuclear material by all users of the Community, and representing the Community in the negotiation and conclusion of international agreements.

The Commission is assisted by the Scientific and Technical Committee, an advisory body of twenty scientists, appointed by the Council after consultation with the Commission. It is primarily responsible for examining research proposals for the following years. In 1961 the Council set up the Consultative Committee for Nuclear Research to bring together national civil servants including financial and budgetary experts, and members of the Commission under the chairmanship of the President of the Commission. The Committee thus provides a link between the Commission and the states. Representatives of the two advisory Committees have carried out a joint examination of some problems of Euratom.

There is also the Supply Agency, consisting of Euratom officials directed by Fernand Spaak, which is financially and legally independent of Euratom, but which acts for it in the area of nuclear supplies. The Agency has the right of option on all nuclear ores, raw materials, and fissionable materials if produced in the Community, maintains the general principle of equality of access to supplies of source and fissionable materials, and negotiates contracts for fissile materials with third countries. The Agency is advised by a consultative committee composed of experts, and representatives of users and producers.

The Activity of Euratom

At the beginning of 1959, Euratom created a common market for all nuclear material and equipment, removing any existing internal trade restrictions, ending tariffs on raw and fissile materials, keeping import duties down to minimal levels, and setting a common external tariff for specific nuclear goods and products. Free movement of qualified nuclear workers was established in March, 1962, and free circulation of capital for atomic investment is provided for in the Treaty.

When the Treaty came into operation, there were divergences among the existing regulations on health and safety of the member countries. In 1959 Community standards were laid down specifying maximum doses of radiation to which atomic workers and the public could be subjected. The Community is also responsible for coordinating radioactive monitoring and for examining some of the new projects for nuclear investment from the point of view of safety. The basic health standards are binding on the six states.

Through the Supply Agency, Euratom has an option on all ores, raw materials, and special fissile material produced in the states, and ensures that fuel material will go to consumers on the basis of equal access to resources. All special fissile materials are the legal property of the Community. The Commission keeps a check on nuclear installations and materials through a team of inspectors, and guarantees that the materials will be used only for the specific purpose set out in the contract. All enterprises must make declarations to the Commission about their installations, stocks, and movements of materials, which are checked periodically. The Commission has not yet found it necessary to impose sanctions for infringements.

Firms and governments must file, three months in advance, notice of investment projects in the field of nuclear energy. Euratom has had some influence on investment, but not as much as originally hoped. The Commission was given the responsibility for forecasting the energy needs of the Community. Through its Information and Documentation Center, the Commission acts as a clearing house for nuclear information, publishes periodicals, and issues reports on Euratom research to outside parties as well as to the Six. Euratom can assist the national nuclear research programs by financial aid or by providing nuclear supplies and facilities. But it also has its own research program.

Euratom has encouraged the construction of a limited number of atomic power stations in the Community on an industrial scale. Some of these were included in the joint power program —part of the 1958 United States-Euratom Agreement—and receive United States loans. Personnel from Euratom and from other atomic projects in the Community are seconded to the projects, and technical reports are submitted to the Commission. Euratom has also encouraged secondary uses of atomic energy.

In general, Euratom has behaved rather differently from what was intended originally. The Community has a large sum of money to spend, and, once this has been granted by the Council of Ministers, the Commission has autonomy on how it is to be spent. Yet instead of a strong supranational body with considerable power to prevent the production of nuclear weapons through its control of the supply of uranium, and ownership of key production plants, Euratom has largely become an organization for sponsoring research into the commercial development of nuclear power and supplementing the nuclear research in the individual countries. This has been due partly to the attitude of France, which has not only insisted on nuclear production for military purposes, but also has prevented Euratom from inspecting its plants, such as the Marcoule nuclear power station, using the argument that they are military installations. In 1961, France refused to reappoint Etienne Hirsch as President of the Commission. Hirsch had urged a greater political role for the Euratom Commission, had favored a plan to spend $32 million for assisting in the construction of reactors of American and European design, and had adopted viewpoints opposed to those of the French Government. He was replaced by Pierre Chatenet. The $32 million program itself was approved by a weighted majority vote which overruled French opposition.

The insistence by France on its own nuclear energy program has reduced the ability of Euratom to coordinate all nuclear development in the Six, altering its role to that of cooperation, to a large degree through bilateral agreements. Moreover, those projects requesting the support of Euratom on the basis of their technical needs have been rare, and most projects have been politically inspired.

For the smaller countries, Euratom represents a substantial part of their research in the nuclear field. France, however, has been inclined to regard Euratom as an auxiliary to its own nuclear program, has continually tried to keep the budget of Euratom low, and has opposed increases due to rises in prices. In 1964 France proposed that Euratom concentrate on the important and large scale, expensive nuclear projects and dispense with other activities that are not fully nuclear, such as the information processing center, computers for translation, and ship propulsion. France, in its proposal, also argued that Euratom should concentrate on gas-graphite reactors, and that the Euratom program must be complementary to those followed by the different countries of the Community. During its existence the Commission has tried to balance the pressure of France for gas-graphite reactors with the desire of technicians for the United States type of enriched uranium reactors.

Research in Euratom

Another reason for the reorientation of Euratom activity has been that the premise of a shortage of available power which would necessitate a large nuclear power program by Euratom has proved to be unfounded. In a Europe with a changing fuel picture —increasing imports of oil, the discovery of natural gas, a severe coal crisis—the strongest emphasis of Euratom has been on research. The Community had $215 million available for research in its first five-year period; in its second period, 1963–1967 this has been increased to $425 million. Of this latter sum, $94 million was made available for research in 1963 after France, which had wanted a smaller sum, had been outvoted for the second time in the Council of Ministers.

The national research programs are communicated to the Commission, which must give a "reasoned opinion" on them and ensure that no unnecessary duplication is taking place. The Commission then draws up its own program, which is examined by both the Scientific and Technical Committee and by the Consultative Committee for Nuclear Research. Euratom sees that work is being done on all important aspects of nuclear research and development, and that gaps are filled in the research programs of the six countries. There are three ways in which the Community aids research on nuclear problems: by joint research, by association contracts, and by individual contracts.

About half of the expenditure on research goes to the four establishments of the Joint Research Center. These four establishments are multinational, and provide the Community with a permanent staff of atomic experts. There are two general-purpose centers at Ispra, Italy, and at Petten, Holland, which are national centers, wholly or partly taken over by the Community. The other two, the Central Bureau of Nuclear Measurements at Geel, Belgium, and the Transuranian Elements Institute at Karlsruhe, Germany, are more specialized. Some of the research is in fields in which the member countries are not active, such as the ORGEL project at Ispra, the most important center of Euratom. Other research provides the Community with a centralized service such as the Scientific Information Processing Center at Ispra, and the standardization research at Geel. A third type, such as the plutonium work at Karlsruhe and the material testing facilities at Petten and Mol (Belgium), is closely linked to research being performed under association contracts.

The association contracts are made between the Commission and national institutes or private organizations which are planning, or have already started, large-scale research programs. The Commission finances up to half of the total cost and forms joint teams with the enterprise; it often works through coordinating committees which bring together staff from the projects. Most of the fusion, ship propulsion, fast reactor, advanced gas reactor, and biological research is performed through these contracts. They were not foreseen by the Treaty, but they have been a successful method of research.

The third way in which Euratom fosters research is by contracts with research institutions, private firms, and universities, the resulting research being the property of the Community. Of the 400 contracts of both types, about 130 are performed jointly for Euratom and the United States Atomic Energy Commission, each side providing the funds and sharing the results. This is one of the results of the Euratom-United States Agreement for a joint power and a joint research and development program.

Euratom research is concerned with a number of areas: the industrial exploitation of atomic power, the study of thermonuclear reactions, the development of nuclear ship propulsion, the study of radioisotopes, health protection, the reprocessing of irradiated fuel, the treatment of radioactive waste. Euratom contributes money and personnel to the study of nuclear ship propulsion. A Nuclear Marine Liaison Committee, consisting of representatives from the projects and from the governments, supervises this work and prevents unnecessary duplications in the research now taking place under four association contracts. The Eurisotop Bureau was set up to provide information to consumers and producers of radioisotopes on their possible uses in industry. It maintains an information service which is at the disposal of all organizations and industries in the Community.

Most research has been focused on the reduction of the cost of producing power from nuclear sources. Euratom has played a significant part in encouraging the construction of full scale power stations which require large investment. Through the United States-Euratom Joint Power Program and through Euratom's own reactor participation program, experience in full scale power reactor construction is being put at the disposal of the Community as a whole. The current policy of Euratom is not to undertake a large scale nuclear power station program, but to help build a limited number of full-size power stations. Under the United States-Euratom Agreement, three reactors of United States design are being built, two of them with American loans. These are the Italian SENN, the German KRB, and the Franco-Belgian SENA plants. Euratom allocates $32 million to these plants and to two other power reactor projects, the Dutch SEP and the Italian SIMEA, and contributes to the cost of the initial fuel charges if these are made in the Community. In return, Euratom benefits by sending personnel to the projects to follow the construction and operation of the reactors, by sending trainees to the projects, and by joint meetings between personnel from the Commission and from the enterprises concerned. For the Community, atomic energy offers a better long-term solution to its energy problem than any other new source of energy, and should stop the increasing dependence on imports. The consumption of electricity in the Community has been rising by an average of 8 percent since 1950, while fuel imports have been rising more dramatically. By 1960 imports accounted for 27 percent of energy consumed, and by 1970 are expected to account for over 47 percent. Large scale nuclear power stations in the Community may become economically feasible in 1968 or 1970 on the basis of a 6,000 hours per year or more load factor, and costs will decrease after then. But by 1975 it is not anticipated that atomic energy will supply more than 3 to 5 percent of the total energy needs of the Six.

The Community has been encouraging the development of three main types of reactors: conventional or "proved," advanced concepts, and fast reactors. The first group includes the natural uranium, gas-cooled systems already operative in Britain and France, and the pressurized or boiling water reactors developed in the United States, which depend on enriched uranium. It is anticipated that by the late 1960s power produced from these reactors can be commercially competitive with conventional power stations. But this type of reactor will absorb only 7 percent of the funds allocated to the second five-year research program. The second type is that of the high temperature gas-cooled, or of the heavy water-moderated and organic liquid-cooled reactors. The most important of these is the ORGEL project at Ispra. Fuel costs are not expected to be higher than those for the first type of reactor, and investment costs should be lower. But it is not expected that they will produce power until after 1970.

The third type, in which Euratom is placing most hope, is the fast breeder reactor, which will be enormously more productive in power since it produces as much or more fissile material than it consumes, and therefore will vastly increase the amount of power from a given quantity of fuel, perhaps making atomic energy a cheap commodity. This type is still in an experimental stage and will probably not be in operation until the late 1970s. In the second research period, from 1963 to 1967, Euratom is spending over one-sixth of its total research expenditure on this type and has signed three association contracts in this area. Under the revised United States-Euratom Agreement, cooperation is extended to the field of fast reactors. The United States, in 1963, removed the 30-ton ceiling on the quantity of enriched uranium for the Community's power and research reactors and also agreed to the delivery of substantial quantities of plutonium.

External Links

The United States enthusiastically supported Euratom from the start, and since 1958 has been cooperating in a joint program for the construction of reactors producing electric power in the Community and in an extensive research and development program to improve the type of reactors being built. The 1958 agreement provided for loans to Euratom of $135 million through the Export-Import Bank. A United States-Euratom working group was set up in the same year. The United States offered to build a number of nuclear power reactors to give Euratom an extra 1,000 megawatts by 1963, later extended to 1965, but the Community objected to the American condition of inspection to ensure that no weapons would be produced by these reactors. The United States-Euratom Agreement provided for a $350 million program for nuclear power stations in the Community, equipped with reactors developed in the United States, as well as for a ten-year joint research program, and the supply of enriched uranium. The Commission itself would see that there was no improper use of the fissile material supplied by the United States.

The program has had only a limited success in stimulating the construction of the American type of atomic power stations in Europe. The original plan called for five or six American reactors with a total generating capacity of 1,000 megawatts to be built. But only three plants are being built, with a total of about 700,000 kilowatts. The original emphasis was on the construction of the power stations, but the long-range importance of the program will come more from the secondary objectives of starting a European nuclear industry and of mutual research links. In May, 1962, the Agreement was amended so that up to 30 tons of United States-supplied fissile materials, which could be either leased or purchased, could be made available to power and research projects in the Community. The two sides agreed to exchange information on the development of fast reactors and to the supply of United States' plutonium and enriched uranium to the Community. In the first five-year period, the emphasis was on using American technology and finance to build a few "first generation" atomic power plants in Europe. In the second period, 1962 to 1967, there will be greater emphasis on research and development of a broader type of atomic reactor, and on the peaceful application of fusion.

The Community also cooperates and has established links with a number of other countries, especially with Canada and Great Britain as a result of agreements signed in 1959. Great Britain supplies Euratom with fissile materials and some of the plutonium needed for the fast reactor program, and the two sides cooperate in exchanges of information, materials, and personnel. The cooperation agreement with Canada is largely concerned with collaboration on heavy water reactors. Euratom also participates in two important projects of the European Nuclear Energy Agency, the Dragon and Halden projects. In the Dragon reactor project at Winfrith, Dorset, Euratom and Great Britain each contributed 43.4 percent of the $28 million cost between 1959 and 1964; under the agreement of 1964 Euratom is contributing 46 percent of the cost of the project which is run by a board of 14, of whom three come from Euratom. In the Halden project, Euratom was represented in the Steering Committee and in the ENEA Council. Among its other links, Euratom has concluded a 20-year association contract with the Mol Center in North Belgium, with which it shares the operation of a high-flux materials-testing reactor, one of the most powerful in the world.

Euratom has not been the political or economic force that its proponents had wanted. It has aided economic growth to some degree, and has been an additional organization fostering pacific relations within the Six. But it has not been able to integrate the national atomic programs nor has it made any substantial contribution to European political fusion. Since Etienne Hirsch was removed from the presidency of the Euratom Commission, no politically significant figure has been a member of it. Community authority has been reduced by French opposition to the idea of communal control of nuclear installations producing plutonium for military purposes, and by the reluctance of states to transfer their bilateral and foreign nuclear agreements to Euratom.

Euratom has not needed to concern itself with the equitable sharing of available supplies of nuclear materials, since no shortage has occurred. To the distaste of France, Euratom has been partially dependent on United States reactors. The founders of Euratom proposed a European university offering scientific training in the nuclear fields, but although the Commission became interested in a European educational project on a broad scale, no agreement has yet been reached by the Six. Euratom is handicapped, to some extent, by the fact that the work of the European Nuclear Energy Agency has seemed to duplicate its own functions in certain areas such as research, safety regulations, and maritime nuclear propulsion. As a supranational organization Euratom has been disappointing, and the six states have been eager to keep their own atomic programs. But it remains an important international organization emphasizing research and the dissemination of scientific knowledge, and enabling the Six to cooperate in atomic matters.

CHAPTER NINE

The Seven Reply to The Six:
The European Free Trade
Association

THE European Free Trade Association, set up after the breakdown of negotiations aimed at establishing a single free trade area for all the OEEC countries, is a more defensive and less ambitious organization than the EEC. Its members, Austria, Denmark, Great Britain, Norway, Portugal, Sweden, and Switzerland, with Finland as an associate, are not physically contiguous. Its population of 95 million is little more than half that of the EEC nations, but its combined national income is about two thirds that of EEC. The nations form a varied group: four are Protestant, two are Catholic, and Switzerland is both. Four are members of NATO, while three are neutral. Five are traditional democracies, Austria struggles to remain democratic, while Portugal is a right-wing dictatorship. The Seven are really Eight since Finland has joined as an associate. There is a wide variety of living standards between the eight nations: the per capita income in Sweden is over six times greater than that of Portugal. But it is a group with a high standard of living, some 10 percent higher than that of the EEC, and comprising a formidable trading bloc accounting for 17 percent of the world's total exports and 20 percent of its imports.

EFTA consists of nations who have refused or been unwilling to join EEC. Austria is obliged to be neutral by its treaty of independence of May, 1955, Switzerland is traditionally neutral, and Sweden insists both on its freedom of action to maintain its neutrality and on safeguards for the supplies of vital products in the case of war. Denmark is closely tied commercially to Britain which buys nearly all Danish butter and bacon. Switzerland and Sweden are low-tariff countries, wanting to import basic materials and semi-manufactures as cheaply as possible. For Britain, EFTA had tactical advantages and represented a second-best solution. It was a device to keep the Seven together, to prevent them from making bilateral agreements with the Common Market as Greece and Turkey were doing, to increase the collective bargaining power with the EEC, and at the same time to be an instrument for accommodation between the two groups. In particular, Britain hoped that forming EFTA would influence Germany which does 30 percent of its trade with them, and which in turn might exert pressure on the Common Market for tariff concessions. But when EFTA was being proposed, the United States opposed it on the ground that politically it would weaken the unity of the Six without providing commercial advantage; at the same time any arrangement between EFTA and the EEC would be economically disadvantageous to the United States.

The Stockholm Convention setting up EFTA is largely confined to technical rules for freeing trade through tariff reductions, elimination of quotas, and origin rules. The stated objectives are to promote and sustain expansion of economic activity and full employment, to ensure that trade will take place in conditions of fair competition, to avoid significant disparities between members in the conditions of supply of raw materials in the area, and to contribute to the expansion of world trade. But essentially EFTA was to help the Seven gain access to new markets to compensate for possible losses in the Six and to be a means of reaching accommodation with the Six, a bargaining weapon in talks for European unity.

Through EFTA tariffs and quotas will be gradually eliminated, but it has no common external tariff as does the EEC. It calls for economic cooperation among the members, but not for economic integration, harmonization or common policies. Each country can pursue its economic policies as it pleases, and retain its own

external tariffs and commercial policies. The Seven did not regard
EFTA as an end in itself nor envisage it as a supranational organization. They therefore set up only the minimum machinery and
written rules necessary to establish a free trade area. There are no
institutions responsible for common policy, and no political objective or intention of attaining political integration. Unlike the
Treaty of Rome in which there is no provision for withdrawal, the
Stockholm Convention allows a member to withdraw after giving
a year's notice.

Membership or association is open to other nations, on terms
and conditions to be approved by the Council. In March, 1961,
the Seven nations and Finland signed a treaty of association which
came into operation in June, 1961. The special position of Finland in relation to the Soviet Union prevented it from applying
for full membership, and a joint Council was set up as the administrative body linking the eight nations. Finland does not participate in the EFTA institutions or in meetings to coordinate
policy, except the Consultative Committee and some of the working parties by invitation. The treaty of association calls for tariff
cuts of 30 percent, although Finland will make reductions of only
20 percent for a number of products and will then be excused from
further cuts until 1965. However, all tariffs are to be eliminated
by 1970. Also, because of trade agreements with the Soviet bloc,
Finland may continue to apply quotas against EFTA members on
several products especially oil, coal, and fertilizers.

The Institutions of EFTA

The only institutional organs of EFTA are the Council of
Ministers, a small secretariat, and committees set up by the
Council.

The Council consists of one representative from each country
interpreting and applying the rules of unanimity. Some decisions,
however, such as those concerning a complaint by one member
against another, are made by majority vote of four. In a few cases
the members have agreed that the will of the majority shall be ac-

cepted unanimously to prevent a deadlock. At ministerial level the Council meets every few months, but it also meets at the level of heads of permanent delegations in Geneva once a week.

The Council has no powers of compulsion and is free to decide on its procedures except that for complaints. It is responsible for reviewing all complaints, publishing a report and recommendations based on majority vote, and for suspending the obligations of other members to the noncomplying member. Disputes between states if they are not settled through bilateral discussion can be referred to the Council.

The Council has set up six permanent committees to assist it. The Customs Committee, composed of national customs officials, is mainly concerned with the daily operation of the rules for tariff reduction and origin, and sees that the rules are applied effectively. It ensures that a uniform mode of practice exists throughout EFTA. The Committee of Trade Experts deals with technical aspects of trade matters. The Consultative Committee, composed of representatives of business and labor and academic personalities who are appointed by their governments, has not so far been a useful mechanism for providing advice. In 1963, the Economic Development Committee was set up to help deal with the problems of the underdeveloped areas of the Seven. There are also the Agricultural Review Committee, created in 1963, to help the Council carry out its analysis of trade in agriculture, and the Budget Committee. The Council has also set up ad hoc groups on a number of specific problems.

The Secretariat of seventy is headed by Mr. Frank Figgures, a British Treasury official who helped set up the European Payments Union and the program for trade liberalization in OEEC, and who took a prominent part in the negotiations leading to the founding of EFTA. The organization had hoped to make Paris its home, but the reported opposition of General de Gaulle to this idea obliged it to settle in Geneva.

There is no provision for a parliamentary assembly, but the representatives from the EFTA countries to the Consultative Assembly of the Council of Europe met informally in Strasbourg in September, 1963, and agreed it would be valuable to meet again from time to time to exchange ideas on EFTA. A second such meeting took place in Strasbourg in April, 1964, after the meeting of the Consultative Assembly.

Tariffs and Quotas

The Stockholm Convention called for gradual elimination of internal tariffs on industrial products by January 1, 1970. On July 1, 1960, two months after EFTA began, tariffs were cut by 20 percent. But to keep pace with the tariff reductions of EEC, the timetable was accelerated, especially after the breakdown of the negotiations in January, 1963. By 1964, the tariffs had been cut by 60 percent, and were to be ended by December 31, 1966, a day ahead of the ending of internal tariffs of EEC, and three years ahead of the original intention. A member can reduce its tariffs on imports from other EFTA counties at an even faster rate.

There are two major exceptions to the tariff cuts. There is no provision for a common agricultural policy, and farm and fishery products are generally excluded from the move to free trade. But if bilateral agreements in farm products lead to tariff cuts, the cuts must be extended to all EFTA members. In fact both multilateral and bilateral trade agreements have been made to facilitate trade in agricultural goods. A range of goods normally regarded as "agricultural," such as melons, have been reclassified for EFTA purposes as "industrial" and therefore qualify for normal EFTA treatment. There is a regular review of agricultural trade in EFTA. The United Kingdom agreed to help Denmark which is not aided by subsidies and protection, as are the other countries. In 1963, the British 5 percent duty on butter imports from Denmark was suspended, putting it on the same footing as the Commonwealth producers. Britain also granted concessions on fresh fish exports from Norway, and agreed to reduce more speedily the import tariffs on Norwegian canned fish.

There are also special provisions for Portugal, Finland, and, to a lesser degree, Norway. Both Portugal and Finland are allowed to introduce the tariff reductions at a slower rate, and Norway is allowed to keep certain industrial items protected, such as man-made fibers and some electrical goods. Also, duties and excise taxes levied for revenue, rather than protection, need not be eliminated within EFTA, and states are free to establish new revenue duties or modify existing ones. But members were expected to end any protective element in duties by the end of 1964.

After the January, 1963, breakdown and the realization that EFTA was not going to be immediately absorbed into the EEC and as tariffs are progressively reduced, the organization has concerned itself to a greater degree with non-tariff barriers to trade and with the problem of fostering fair competition. EFTA has dealt with subsidized agricultural exports, remission of taxes and duties, dual price systems for raw materials used for industry, preferential rates for power, transport or government services, differences in industrial standards and health regulations, and any form of aid, the main purpose and effect of which is to interfere with free trade. But though the Seven are pledged to eliminate discrimination and deal with restrictive business practices, they have made no rules, as in the Common Market, to deal with cartels and monopolies. In the Convention there is no provision for freedom of labor or capital, but freedom of establishment is endorsed to the extent necessary to make free trade work.

Since EFTA has no common external tariff, the members had to devise rules to prevent imports into a low-tariff country from being exported to other EFTA counties at reduced rates. This was done by the "rules of origin" procedure. The Seven agreed that goods became eligible for the reduced tariff rates if they had been wholly produced within the EFTA area, or if they had been produced by certain specified processes within the area, or if at least 50 percent of their value had been added within the area. In addition, a basic materials list was formulated, consisting of a number of primary products and raw materials which were considered to have originated in the Free Trade Area, even if they were imported from outside. Although the technical difficulties of such a procedure seemed formidable, the system has worked surprisingly well and easily.

The Seven agreed to increase quotas on industrial goods imported from each other by at least 20 percent a year until they were ended by 1970. This proposed timetable, too, has been accelerated, and the anticipated ending is now December 31, 1966, except for the Finnish restrictions on most solid and liquid fuels and fertilizers, and the Portuguese restrictions on automobiles for which a slower timetable has been allowed. However, states can reimpose quantitative restrictions if they suffer balance of payments difficulties, or experience unemployment caused by rising imports, or if particular sectors are badly affected, or for non-commercial reasons such as protection of public health or order. Also, quotas on agriculture were kept, but the Agricultural Review Committee set up in 1963 is considering means of expanding agricultural trade.

Unlike the EEC, the Seven have no common commercial policy, but there has been a growing cooperation and consultation in this field. The EFTA nations took a common position on the disparities formula proposed by the Common Market, and supported the United States view of the across-the-board cuts in GATT. Because of their pattern of trade all the Seven are interested not only in internal cooperation, but also in the opening of the European market and the expansion of world trade.

Since the level of economic development in the eight nations differs widely, EFTA allows a slower elimination of tariff protection for those industries in Finland, Norway, and especially in Portugal, needing more time to prepare themselves for international competition. No common financial institutions were set up to provide direct assistance to the less developed regions as in EEC. But in May, 1963, the Seven agreed to create an Economic Development Committee that will promote investment in Norway and in Portugal through cooperation between private enterprises and among governments to promote balanced expansion of the economies, and will facilitate cooperation among the members in financial and technical matters. The Committee has set up working parties to assess methods for promoting Portugal's machine tool industry, and wood pulp and paper production, but has not established any fund or formal obligations. It is largely acting as a clearing house for information, expert knowledge and advice on economic development in the different countries. But those who had hoped for a Committee with stronger powers and concentrating on problems such as a comparison of planning techniques in the members, were disappointed.

As a trading group, EFTA has been a moderate success. In 1958, trade between the seven nations was 16 percent of their total trade; by 1963 it had risen to 20 percent. Between 1959 and 1963, trade grew 31 percent while intra-EFTA trade grew 51 percent. In 1963, the members promised to trade more with each other. Norway agreed to buy more wine from Portugal, Sweden to buy more Danish beet sugar and Norwegian fish. The imports of the Seven represented 20 percent of those of the world, and exports 22 percent, compared with comparable figures for the Common Market of 31 percent and 27 percent. The two groups are oriented differently. EFTA, especially because of Great Britain's interests, is particularly dependent on trade with non-Europeans. By contrast less than half the exports of the Common Market are outside Europe.

Ironically, the EEC is EFTA's main trading partner, taking 24 percent of EFTA's exports and providing 29 percent of its imports. Since the formation of the two groups, EFTA's exports to the Six have grown more quickly than trade in EFTA itself. Between 1959 and 1962, EFTA nations have increased their trade with EEC by 40 percent, but with each other by only 34 percent. In 1963, EFTA had a trading deficit of $1.7 billion with EEC. The fact that Austria sends 50 percent of its exports, and takes 59 percent of its imports from EEC, as compared with 12 percent exports to and 14 percent of imports from EFTA, explains its application for association with EEC and for freedom of action in its trade relations. The relationship between the two groups as such remains unsettled. Although there is little likelihood at present of them merging, they have taken some cooperative action in dealing with specific trade and business problems, while several EFTA countries have asked to participate in the work of EEC on patents and trademarks.

But the EEC policies have adversely affected the trade of the EFTA countries. The Common Market common agricultural policy has hurt Scandinavia, resulting in a sharp reduction in the export of pork and eggs to Germany, and an almost complete elimination of exports of live pigs from Sweden to Germany. One particular result of EFTA has been a rapid increase in trade among the Scandinavian nations which has reinforced their desire for increased cooperation across Scandinavian borders and may lead to Scandinavia becoming a more closely integrated region and to a possible common Nordic agricultural market.

The utility of EFTA is arguable and its future uncertain. The EFTA Council has accepted the fact that there is little prospect in the immediate future of an end to the split in Western Europe, and has turned down a suggestion that a special body be set up to maintain contact between the Six and the Seven. But an agreement on association between the EEC and Austria is likely to lead to some kind of accommodation between the two groups in order to reduce trade discrimination. Yet even without such an accommodation there are many opportunities for members of EFTA and the EEC to cooperate within the framework of existing Western European organizations such as the Council of Europe, WEU, OECD, the European Nuclear Energy Agency, the European Conference of Ministers of Transport, and the European Civil Aviation Conference.

The existence of EFTA and its role largely depends on Great Britain. During the 1962 negotiations between Britain and the EEC, EFTA was unkindly called "Mr. Heath's albatross." In October, 1964, the decision of the new British Labour Government in imposing a 15 percent surcharge on all imports except raw materials and food showed a disregard for its Treaty obligations to EFTA. The British action not only cancelled the effect of all tariff reductions made within EFTA; it was also taken unilaterally without prior consultation with the other EFTA countries. But the other six could do little in protest for any attempt by Britain's partners to suspend tariff concessions to Britain as the offending party would have meant the breakup of EFTA.

As a result of sharp criticism of the British unilateral action, EFTA set up an Economic Committee of senior officials from EFTA capitals. This will hold regular periodic exchanges of views on the economic and financial policies of states and on the effect of those policies on the economies of the other states. The EFTA nations belatedly remembered in November, 1964, that the Stockholm Convention not only lays down detailed rules on tariffs, quotas, and rules of origin, but also explicitly refers to a number of other fields where joint action is possible even if no detailed rules were laid down. The Seven were faced with the sad realization that the creation of a free trade area demands more than a treaty time table for tariff cuts.

CHAPTER TEN

Atlantic Cooperation

THE RAPID STEPS taken towards integration have been the most exciting post-war political development in Europe, but the ultimate objective still remains undefined and institutional arrangements vague and uncertain. Europe is still in the formative stage of constructing a sense of identity in a world of circumstance. And besides the difficult problem of deciding its own internal differences and determining its own structure, there remains the question of its relationship with the United States.

The United States has given constant and eager support to the integration process for political, economic, and military reasons. It sided with the EEC in its opposition to a European Free Trade Area, partly to foster the political objectives of integration as well as to prevent itself from being excluded from trade concessions. In the period from 1945 to 1962, U.S. grants and credits for foreign military and economic assistance totaled over $140 billion, over half of which went to Western Europe. This aid permitted a much faster European recovery than was otherwise possible, and was instrumental in helping the European nations keep up their level of consumption, reduce inflationary pressures, and restore their monetary systems. The United States has been helpful to the new Communities, loaning $100 million to the ECSC in 1954, granting a credit of $135 million to Euratom in 1958, and participating in joint research and development programs with it.

At the end of World War II it seemed that the relationship of Europe to the United States could at best be that of the Greeks to the modern Romans, exercising a civilizing effect on the holders of power. During the last decade this relationship has changed drastically as Western Europe has not only recovered economically but has become the most dynamic and fastest developing economic unit in the world. It no longer has a dollar shortage, but on the contrary has considerable short term claims against the United States while the United States now has a balance of payments deficit caused largely by foreign investments abroad, foreign economic and military aid, and the cost of American forces stationed abroad. From being a recipient of American aid, Europe is now an important disburser of aid to the underdeveloped countries of the world.

The relationship has also been affected by international events. The military situation changed as the Soviet Union reached nuclear parity with the United States and the monopoly of American nuclear power ended. This has led to the direct confrontation of tactical atomic weapons on the continent with its consequent dangers of escalation. Yet one of the results of the Cuba missile crisis in October, 1962, has been a lessening of the fear of immediate hostilities between the Western and Communist camps, which has brought up, in an acute form, the relevance of NATO. The bipolarity of the world, familiar since the end of the War, has ended. The differences between the Soviet Union and China over the tactics and leadership of the international Communist movement have led to a political split, the results of which are incalculable. The rise to nationhood of a large number of states in Africa and Asia has led to an increase in the group of neutral or nonaligned nations, while at the same time their formative stage of economic development has caused the West to realize that liberalization of trade is not enough and that financial aid, technical help, and the maintenance of their export earnings are all necessary for them.

The Atlantic Alliance was forged in the days of a single dominating issue around which the different nations could coalesce. Its inner cohesion is less apparent now with the more complex international climate of the mid-60s, and the "building of bridges" across the chasm that has divided East Europe from the West. Militarily, the new conditions have led the European nations to demand a greater share in the use or control of nuclear weapons. This has meant the United States supplying more military information to the other NATO nations. It might mean providing medium range ballistic missiles to the allied forces in the European area as both Generals Norstad and Lemnitzer have requested, or deploying the MRBMs under the "two key" system which was used for first generation intermediate range ballistic missiles and is still used for shorter range tactical nuclear weapons. This system involves the national ownership of the missiles, but decisions on the release of warheads for them would be made jointly by the individual country and the United States. Some Europeans have asked for control over the U.S. deployment of its nuclear forces. The United States has chosen a third alternative, that of the Multilateral Nuclear Force (MLF). This will not only have military value, but also, it is hoped, could lay the basis for greater unity in the Alliance in other areas, especially that of arms control.

Besides strengthening the Alliance, two other possibilities exist by which to take account of the changing relationship between the United States and Europe: building an Atlantic Community or an Atlantic Partnership. The concept of an Atlantic Community goes beyond the ending of customs barriers and quota restrictions between the two continents, and calls for some institutional framework in which decisions can be made, possibly including a common political authority, common citizenship and law, and a union of North Atlantic states. Under present circumstances the prospect of expanding the European Communities and their system of organized integration on an Atlantic scale appears remote. General de Gaulle has already expressed his opposition to a colossal Atlantic community which would absorb the European community and Walter Hallstein has expressed doubts about the value of a central Atlantic body and questioned its precise role. On the other hand, others, including Lord Franks, have argued the need to go beyond mere cooperation and to create a new Atlantic institution like the Common Market Commission to formulate proposals to deal with common problems. Since 1956, there has been some support for a single consultative Atlantic assembly to replace, or supplement, the existing European assemblies; there is considerable likelihood that such an Assembly will emerge out of OECD.

There has been more speculation about the possibility and desirability of an Atlantic partnership, built on the two equal pillars of America and a united Europe, operating in the economic, political and military fields, and sharing responsibility for the principal tasks devolving on the free world. Militarily, this could lead to a coordinated defense policy in which Europe would share in the control of nuclear weapons. Economically, it could result in freer trade by abolishing discriminatory barriers and collaborating in aid to underdeveloped programs.

The idea of an Atlantic partnership was most eloquently expounded by President Kennedy in his July 4, 1962, speech when he proposed interdependence between the two continents, the sharing of responsibilities, and an equitable distribution of financial burdens. The twin elements in the American approach to partnership were to be the MLF in defense and a closer trade relationship.

The closer relationship had been suggested by a 1962 report of a bipartisan committee headed by Will Clayton and Christian Herter who had urged the United States take a "giant step" in its trade behavior. The traditional trade policy of the United States had been outdated by a number of developments: the growth of the Common Market, the pressure on the U.S. balance of payments, the need to accelerate U.S. economic expansion, the trade offensive and development aid programs of the Communist countries, the need to open up new markets for Japan and for developing countries. The difficulty of negotiating reciprocal tariff reductions on a slow, item-by-item basis, was especially clear and the need for broader powers evident. The handicaps for U.S. trade would be even greater if Great Britain became a member of the Common Market as was anticipated in 1962.

The authority of the President to enter into trade agreements expired in June, 1962, but it was reinforced by the Trade Expansion Act passed in the same year. The Act, valid for a five-year period, authorizes the gradual elimination of tariffs by the U.S. in return for concessions by the EEC on those products in which the United States and the EEC together supply 80 percent of world trade. On other products, tariff reductions of 50 percent can be made, and these reductions can also be made reciprocally with nations outside the EEC. This can be done on entire categories of products instead of an item-by-item basis. The President can decide what rates are to be reduced and by what percentage in order to reach a given over-all percentage reduction. Tariff reductions negotiated with the chief U.S. trading partners will be extended to other nations on a Most Favored Nation basis. The President can also reduce or eliminate duties on products of tropical agricultural and forestry, subject to the condition that the Common Market take similar and nondiscriminatory action. In this way markets would be opened to the tropical products of Latin America, Asia, and Africa. As usual, certain safeguards are allowed by the statute so that retaliatory tariffs can be raised if there are unreasonable import restrictions against American products, and the President can impose tariff measures against articles detrimental to national security. Unfortunately, one of the main provisions of the Act became meaningless with the veto on British entry into the Common Market since the EEC and the United States supply 80 percent of world trade in only a few goods.

There are significant differences between the trade effects of the Trade Expansion Act and the Common Market. In the Common Market all trade barriers will be eliminated by the end of the transition period. The Trade Expansion Act does not include products for which purely internal arrangements allow escape clauses to be applied. In the Common Market the temporary reintroduction of protection is subject to the approval of the Community organs while the Trade Expansion Act provides for the maintenance and establishment of duties as a safety measure. The Treaty of Rome allows the abolition of all quotas and of all customs tariffs; in the Trade Expansion Act the general rule is that tariffs may not be cut by more than half of their original level. For the Common Market the Common External Tariff is applicable to relations with the rest of the world; by the Trade Expansion Act tariff reductions apply to all countries.

For the American Administration, the Trade Expansion Act does not make trade liberalization an end in itself, but rather a means to greater expansion, improved productivity, and a higher standard of living. Both the United States and Western Europe recognize the interrelationship between liberalization of trade and the coordination of economic policies. Trade competition must not lead to a balance of payments crisis. The threat to full employment that might result from the liberalization of trade needs a concerted trade policy. Both continents share a mutual interest in economic growth, and in the efforts of OECD to achieve this. Agricultural trade necessarily demands intercontinental, if not global solutions. Trade policies based on the Most Favored Nation concept mean they must be applied to underdeveloped as well as to industrial countries, and therefore imply a common policy towards the underdeveloped areas.

The United States and Western Europe have recognized their mutual interest in dealing with problems such as agriculture, the international monetary mechanism, supplying aid to underdeveloped countries as well as increasing trade, and in developing common policies and rules.

Both are currently preoccupied with helping the underdeveloped countries whose plight has worsened in recent years for a number of reasons. The share of the producers of primary products in world trade has been reduced from 47 percent in 1945 to 36 percent in 1963. In the last decade the prices of primary products have fallen while those of manufactures have risen. With the development of the chemical industry, the West has been using an increasing number of synthetic materials, and plastics. The consumption of food and beverages produced by the least developed areas has risen much more slowly than the increase in incomes of industrial countries. The 1964 United Nations Conference on Trade and Development made clear the dissatisfaction of the underdeveloped countries with the trade policies of the Western nations, not all of whom were prepared to grant trade preferences, or make commodity stabilization schemes or compensatory financial arrangements in their favor.

Since the early postwar schemes to deal with the problem, it has been clear that the international mechanism is inadequate and that it does not provide enough liquidity to allow time for countries to make adjustments. This has hampered economic expansion which is controlled, to a certain extent, by the lack of foreign exchange. The total amount of reserves is increasingly dependent on international cooperation since the expansion of world liquidity has depended to a large degree on accumulation by other countries of dollar balances which they hold as international reserves, but this in turn may lead to a lack of confidence in the dollar and to international financial instability. The European Payments Union was successful in removing any financial reasons for intra-European discrimination, and in providing international reserves which helped the removal of quantitative restrictions on imports. But the dollar problem has remained even under the European Monetary Agreement which allows market convertibility and the exchange of certain currencies for dollars. By 1962 the gold and foreign exchange holdings of continental countries were over $25 billion, while in the same year the United States' balance of payment deficit was $2.3 billion and the U.S. reserves had decreased from $24 billion in 1949 to $15 billion in 1963.

The reinforcing of the international monetary mechanism is linked with the provisions made for the underdeveloped countries and with the abolition of the barriers to international trade since a shortage of liquidity can lead to a reduction of trade and a slowing down of economic development while a surplus can produce inflationary distortions. These problems are partly dealt with by OECD, which with NATO now forms an essential pillar of a future Atlantic partnership. But the trade problems are largely under discussion in GATT on a global basis.

Bilateral trade agreements have severe limitations in that they are time consuming, they have rarely dealt with import quotas, and most important trading countries undertook similar obligations on a reciprocal basis. After the war a multilateral approach to trade was thought more desirable. The idea of an International Trade Organization was dropped for lack of support, but in October, 1947, the General Agreement on Tariffs and Trade was signed by 23 nations in Geneva. GATT is essentially a multilateral trade agreement, to which there are now 62 parties and 11 associates. Of the Communist countries, Czechoslovakia is a member, whereas Poland and Yugoslavia have special status. It does not have a permanent governing body, but consists of a number of working groups set up for specified purposes which report on their work and recommend action, a committee which maintains continuity and organizes the agenda of meetings, and a complaints panel, the membership of which excludes the disputing nations. It was loaned rather than given a secretariat; since 1952 its secretariat has been technically on loan from the United Nations. Negotiating sessions are conducted by a steering committee of representative nations.

GATT has three essential features. It comprises a series of tariff schedules, covering some 60,000 items, which have resulted from a number of multilateral tariff negotiations. These schedules provide the maximum level of tariffs which the countries apply to each other. It contains provisions governing the conduct of trade among its members: these include the principle of nondiscrimination in the application of trade regulations by its members and the prohibition of quotas on imports or exports as a means of trade restriction or protection, and certain rules on subsidies, dumping and customs administration. It has granted waivers from its provisions for regional groupings. These include rules concerning customs unions and free trade areas to ensure that such regional arrangements lead to the reduction and elimination of barriers within the area without raising new barriers to trade with the outside world. The EEC satisfied the GATT conditions that a customs union must come into existence within a reasonable length of time, and that the common external tariff shall not be greater than the individual tariffs it replaces. GATT is the chief existing link between the European economic groups and world trade arrangements.

The third and most public function of GATT is to hold periodical meetings which constitute the major international forum for the settlement of current trade problems. In its first decade GATT largely concentrated on the reduction of tariffs by multilateral item-by-item negotiations at conferences in 1947, 1949, 1950, 1956, and 1960–1961. But valuable though these have been, the method used has yielded diminishing returns until by the end of the 1950s it had almost exhausted its possibilities. The countries with low tariffs found their margin for bargaining was gradually narrowed; obstacles to trade other than tariffs became increasingly important. In 1963 GATT agreed on a new set of principles for trade negotiations. The most important of these are that negotiations should cover all classes of products, agricultural and primary products, as well as industrial; tariff reductions should be based on equal, across the board reductions with a minimum of exceptions; nontariff barriers would be included; reciprocity should not be expected of the underdeveloped countries which, on the contrary, might be given preferential treatment. The 1964 Kennedy round of tariff negotiations is based on these principles.

Both the United States and the Six had looked forward to the Kennedy round as the most comprehensive trade negotiations in history. But a number of significant differences were soon revealed. The United States has been eager to include agriculture in the negotiations; the Common Market, and France in particular, has objected that agricultural trade cannot be discussed until the EEC has fully developed its own agricultural policy. A second problem has been the nontariff obstacles to trade such as anti-dumping, customs evaluation procedures, and taxation. But while in the United States most of these obstacles are made known, in Europe a number of them are concealed, such as special taxes against U.S. automobiles in the form of road taxes, or against grain liquor.

The most complicated issue has been the nature and extent of tariff cuts to be made. The United States favored across the board cuts of 50 percent in almost all tariffs, with as small a reserve list as possible. The Common Market Commission agreed on this as a working hypothesis but argued that it was more meaningful to reduce the unusually high tariffs, most of which are American, in order to achieve a moderate level on industrial goods of around 10 percent on both sides. For the Commission this is more equitable since the U.S. tariffs include a large number of very low duties and a large number of very high ones, but the Common Market tariff is bunched in the range of 10 to 25 percent. The Commission therefore has insisted that where significant disparities exist in the tariff levels of the United States and the EEC, they be excepted from the general rule of linear reductions and different rules made. The United States has replied that the tariff disparities must be meaningful in trade terms and be an obstacle to greater trade if exceptions are to be made, and that the whole value of the negotiations will be lost if too many exceptions are made to the general 50 percent rule. This dispute on tariff disparities is complicated by the fact that for many items on which the Common Market would claim special treatment because of disparities in the United States or in Great Britain, other countries are the chief suppliers and therefore would suffer most from cuts.

A fourth major problem is that the principle of nondiscrimination is suitable only for developed countries, and the underdeveloped countries have asked for preferential treatment. The latter group of countries have tended to see GATT as a rich nations' club, while they have little with which to bargain. The Western nations have agreed that there must be some relaxation of the Most Favored Nation rule, which often tends to restrict rather than enlarge trade, in the interest of the less advanced nations.

But difficult as these issues are in themselves, the progress of the Kennedy round has also been slowed by the differences between France and Germany on the policy to be followed by the EEC. At the end of 1964 France cooperated with the other five nations in compiling a short common exceptions list—a list of items whose tariffs the nations would cut by less than 50 percent in the GATT negotiations—in return for German cooperation in accepting a single system of grain prices. The mutual assistance agreement between France and Germany means that the success of the Kennedy round is linked with the implementation of a common agricultural policy by the EEC.

Although initial fears that the split between the Six and the Seven would result in major changes in the traditional channels of European trade have not materialized, the Kennedy round provides a unique opportunity to lessen the undesirable effects of the Western European division and thus to contribute to an Atlantic arrangement as well as to stimulate world trade. An

Atlantic partnership implies a close relationship between two separate but equal powers, the United States and Western Europe. This in turn is based on the achievement of some kind of European unity.

A highly complicated pattern of relationships now exists in Western Europe with overlapping circles of members. New habits of cooperation have developed and nations have not only accepted the idea of submitting their policies to a critical examination by friendly partners and by groups of international experts, but also have taken account of the impact of those policies on other countries. But Europe is still far from being a political entity. An Atlantic partnership between two centers of power welding the North Atlantic nations with basically similar political systems more closely together is a noble idea. But it will remain little more than rhetoric unless Western Europe goes further along the road to political integration and unless a common Atlantic solution is found to the problem of the control of nuclear weapons.

BIBLIOGRAPHICAL NOTE

THE LITERATURE on the European integration movement is now voluminous and the official documentation is enormous.

Some of the better general works in English on recent developments in Western Europe are:

Beloff, Nora. *The General Says No.* Baltimore, 1963.

Beloff, Max. *The United States and the Unity of Europe.* Washington, 1963.

Camps, Miriam. *Britain and the European Community, 1955–1963.* London, 1964.

Kitzinger, U. W. *The Politics and Economics of European Integration.* New York, 1963.

Lichtheim, George. *The New Europe.* New York, 1963.

Mayne, Richard. *The Community of Europe.* New York, 1962.

Shanks, Michael, and John Lambert. *The Common Market, Today and Tomorrow.* New York, 1962.

Some books dealing primarily with European economic problems are:

Dell, Sidney. *Trade Blocs and Common Markets.* New York, 1963.

Lamfalussy, A. *The United Kingdom and the Six.* Homewood, Ill., 1963.

Meade, James et al. *Case Studies in European Economic Union.* New York, 1962.

Sannwald, Rolf, and J. Stohler. *Economic Integration.* Princeton, 1959.

Scitovsky, Tibor. *Economic Theory and Western European Integration.* Stanford, 1958.

Triffin, Robert. *Europe and the Money Muddle.* New Haven, 1957.

Uri, Pierre. *Partnership for Progress.* New York, 1963.

Useful books on the European historical background include:

Beloff, Max. *Europe and the Europeans.* London, 1957.

Coudenhove-Kalergi, Richard. *An Idea Conquers the World.* London, 1953.

Dehio, Ludwig. *The Precarious Balance.* New York, 1962.

Halecki, Oscar. *The Limits and Divisions of European History.* London, 1950.

Some valuable specialized works include:

Diebold, William. *The Schuman Plan.* New York, 1959.

Haas, Ernst. *The Uniting of Europe.* Stanford, 1958.

Lindberg, Leon. *The Political Dynamics of European Economic Integration.* Stanford, 1963.

Polach, Jaroslav. *Euratom.* Dobbs Ferry, 1964.

Pryce, Roy. *The Political Future of the European Community*. London, 1962.

Among the better books dealing with military affairs are:

Buchan, Alastair. *NATO in the 1960s*. New York, 1960.

Kissinger, Henry. *The Necessity for Choice*. New York, 1961.

Mulley, Frederick. *The Politics of Western Defense*. London, 1962.

Osgood, Robert. *NATO: The Entangling Alliance*. Chicago, 1962.

Strausz-Hupé, Robert et al. *Building the Atlantic World*. New York, 1963.

INDEX